Christine Jorgensen

A PERSONAL AUTOBIOGRAPHY

INTRODUCTION BY SUSAN STRYKER

CLEIS

Published in the United States by Cleis Press Inc., P.O. Box 14684, San Francisco, CA 94114.
Printed in the United States.
Cover design: Scott Idleman   Text design: Karen Quigg   Logo art: Juana Alicia
First Edition.
10 9 8 7 6 5 4 3 2 1

Library of Congress Cataloging-in-Publication Data

Jorgensen, Christine, 1926-1989
Cristine Jorgensen : a personal autobiography / Christine Jorgensen ; introduction by Susan Stryker.
p. cm.   ISBN 1-57344-100-7 (alk. paper)
1. Jorgensen, Christine, 1926-1989. 2. Transsexuals—United States—Biography.
3. Sex change—Denmark. I. Title.
HQ77.8.J67 J67 2000
305.9'066—dc21
00-063904

Grateful acknowledgment is made to the following for permission to reprint: *American Journal of Psychotherapy* (Vol. 8, No. 2), April, 1954, an article by Bob Sherwin; Copyright © 1954 *by American Journal of Psychotherapy.* Harry Benjamin, M.D., excerpt of the pamphlet of the Harry Benjamin Foundation, Inc., New York, 1966, and two excerpts of articles from journals: Copyright © 1954, *American Journal of Psychotherapy;* Copyright © 1964, *Western Journal of Surgery, Obstetrics and Gynecology.* Curtis Brown, Ltd., New York, to excerpt from *Rebecca* by Daphne du Maurier, Doubleday & Company, Inc., Copyright © 1938 by Daphne du Maurier Browning. *Editor and Publisher,* for permission to quote from an article in the March 28, 1953, issue; Copyright © 1953 by Editor and Publisher, Inc. Dr. Christian Hamburger, for permission to reprint from his letters and an article appearing in the Danish medical journal, *ACTA Endocrinologica,* Copyright © 1953 by *ACTA Endocrinologica.* Dr. Hamburger consented to read the manuscript and shared his valuable suggestions for definition and clarification of the medical aspects, for which I am most grateful. Harcourt, Brace and World, Inc., New York, and to Paul de Kruif, for permission to quote from *The Male Hormone* by Paul de Kruif, Copyright © 1945 by Paul de Kruif. The Hollywood Reporter Corporation, for permission to quote part of a review from an issue of May, 1953. The Julian Press, for permission to quote several portions of text from *The Transsexual Phenomenon,* by Harry Benjamin, M.D. Copyright © 1966 by Harry Benjamin, M.D., reprinted by permission of Julian Press, Inc., New York. The Macmillan Company, New York, and Lurton Blassingame, agent, for permission to reprint an excerpt from *The Press in the Jury Box* by Howard Felsher and Michael Rosen; The Macmillan Company, New York, Copyright © 1966 by Howard Felsher and Michael Rosen. The *New York Times,* for the article concerning the Johns Hopkins program in Gender Orientation, appearing in the issue of November 21, 1966, © 1966 by The New York Times Company, reprinted by permission. News Syndicate Company, for permission to use a portion of their news article released in March 1953; Copyright © 1953 by Robert Dwyer and Neal Patterson. Dr. George Stürup, for permission to quote him directly; and my thanks to him for reading a portion of the manuscript and for his suggestions to clarify. *Time Magazine,* for permission to quote a paragraph from the issue of December 15, 1952, reprinted by permission. Copyright © 1952 by Time Inc. *Variety,* for permission to quote a part of a review from a May, 1953 issue; Copyright © 1953 by Variety, Inc. Viking Press, Inc., New York, for permission to quote from "Inventory" from *The Portable Dorothy Parker,* Copyright © 1926, 1954 by Dorothy Parker. *World Journal Tribune* for permission to quote from an article by Walter Alvarez, M.D. which appeared in the *New York Herald Tribune* August 1, 1957.

PUBLISHER'S NOTE

The Publishers wish to acknowledge Brenda Lana Smith for sharing her memories, as well as many of the photographs and documents that appear in this book.

We also wish to thank Susan Stryker for the intelligence and the passion she brings to her work as an historian of the transsexual movement, and for travelling to the Christine Jorgensen archives in Copenhagen and bringing back some of the wonderful photographs included here.

Thank you, Donald Segretti for executing Christine's will so that the rights to and proceeds from this book be transferred to The Woodlands Hills Home of the Motion Picture and Television Fund.

Thank you Sherri Conrad, lawyer extraordinaire, for making it all fall into place.

And to Christine, who lives in all of us, and who doesn't need anyone's opinion because she has her own.

ACKNOWLEDGMENTS

Special gratitude is due many people who contributed to my life their friendship, understanding and support. Among these are my parents and members of my family. My thanks to my Danish doctors; also Professor Dahl-Iversen. They never wavered in their belief. The late Dr. Joseph Angelo and his wife, Gen, are due the greatest regard and appreciation for saving me anguish. I am especially indebted to them for having saved my letters written during the extended period in Denmark which has given me the opportunity to readily recall those years.

My thanks to William Hunt, the producer-director, who gave me his wonderful support and shared with me his talents for the development of my career in the theatre.

My gratitude to Mrs. Charles Yates and Mr. Steve Yates, for permission to use letters by the late Charles V. Yates, my first agent, and friend, who guided my controversial career with deftness and tender concern.

To Creative Management Associates, Ltd., and particularly Warren Bayless and Ernest Dobbs of CMA's literary division, who contributed more than a client may expect from her agents.

Special thanks freely goes to Lois Kibbee who, finding herself involved in the task of assembling and preparing the manuscript, became truly co-author. With her sensitive, diligent probing and her gracious, intelligent manner, she, more than anyone, brought forth the buried facts and forgotten emotions from my memory, causing this autobiography to be as honest and truthful a document as can be written at this time. The identity and names of a few individuals have been altered for obvious reasons. The responsibility for the content is mine.

INTRODUCTION

Christine Jorgensen was arguably the most famous person in the world for a few short years nearly half a century ago, though her name is not widely remembered today. The journalism trade publication *Editor and Publisher* announced in the spring of 1954 that more newsprint had been generated about Jorgensen during the previous year than about any other individual—over a million and a half words, the rough equivalent of fifteen full-length books. That Jorgensen now requires any introduction at all underscores the truth of that old adage about how fleeting fame can be. At the dawn of the 21st century, it seems almost quaint that Jorgensen should have provoked such widespread attention simply by having the shape of her genitals surgically altered one late-November morning in Copenhagen in 1952. But she did, and as a consequence of doing so she helped introduce the word "transsexual" into the American vocabulary.

As Jorgensen herself recounts in the pages that follow, her celebrity began December 1, 1952, when a banner headline screaming "EX-GI BECOMES BLONDE BEAUTY: OPERATIONS TRANSFORM BRONX YOUTH" greeted readers of the *New York Daily News*. Hearst Publications' popular Sunday newspaper supplement, *American Weekly*, subsequently paid twenty thousand dollars for an exclusive interview with Jorgensen that brought her story into millions of American homes, and whetted the appetite of the world press. When she returned to the United States in 1953, an unprecedented three hundred reporters were on hand to meet her plane at New York

International Airport. She was inundated with offers to appear in nightclubs, strip joints, wrestling arenas, and other sensationalistic settings. Such mundane activities as walking her dog were reported in obsessive detail to an avid worldwide readership. If reporters couldn't find a legitimate story, however trivial, they simply made one up. Jorgensen received letters by the thousands, many reaching her addressed only "Christine Jorgensen, USA." Some were from other transsexuals who wanted to do what she had done; most of her correspondents sought nothing other than an autograph or photo; only a few sent pieces of hate mail, and the vast majority simply wished her well. Still others, however, spoke of Jorgensen's physical transformation as an event with profound religious significance. Her "sex-change" was viewed by many as a miracle of God in which not Christ, but Christine—Man reborn as Woman—heralded a new dispensation of human history.

In spite of beginning life as the son of a carpenter, Christine Jorgensen hardly seemed destined to become anyone's messiah. Born in 1926 to Danish-American parents and raised in unremarkable working-class circumstances, she had been a delicate, painfully shy child who always felt more feminine than masculine. By adolescence she was attracted to boys and terrified at the thought she might be "homosexual," a word she'd learned by furtively reading books in the locked "medical" case at the public library where she worked after school. Upon graduation from high school she studied commercial photography, held a low-level job in the film-stock archives at RKO Studios, and reported for military service when drafted in 1945, months after World War II had ended. Jorgensen served a brief enlistment as a file clerk at Fort Dix, New Jersey, processing demobilization paperwork for the combat troops streaming home from overseas. Later, after failing miserably to find work in the Hollywood film industry, she returned to school in New York and resumed her photographic studies.

Jorgensen was desperately unhappy with her lot in life as the 1940s drew to a close. One ray of hope, however, were the stray accounts she'd read in the popular press of hormone experiments carried out on animals, which had reportedly changed their secondary sex characteristics. After a handful of humiliating visits to clinical endocrinologists to see if such treatments were available for humans, followed by a few research trips to a medical library, Jorgensen decided to take matters into her own hands. She prevailed upon an unsuspecting pharmacy clerk to sell her a bottle of estradiol, a recently synthesized version of estrogen. She began to self-administer the drug, which promoted breast development and a general softening of her appearance. A few months later, Jorgensen set sail for Europe—and the history books—in search of doctors who would provide the sex-change procedures she sought. She found them in her ancestral Denmark, and soon became for all the world the woman she had long considered herself to be.

Jorgensen's subsequent celebrity is especially remarkable given that she was not the first person to undergo surgical and hormonal sex-reassignment—that had been going on for more than twenty years before her story hit the headlines. The procedures employed on her behalf, as well as the rationale for using them, had been championed by the eminent German sexologist Magnus Hirschfeld, at his Institute for Sexual Science in Berlin, in the years between the World Wars. Jorgensen herself notes that her doctors were familiar with dozens of prior cases similar to her own, some of which had even been widely reported in popular media in Europe and the United States. None of that seemed to matter—Jorgensen was christened the atomic age sex marvel the second her story leaked out.

Historical context helps explains why Jorgensen became an emblem of her era, an icon representing some fundamental shift in human affairs to an audience of millions. First and foremost, it is crucial to recognize the extent to which massive population mobilization of World War II refigured conventional notions of men's and women's proper social spheres, and helped unsettle familiar concepts of sexuality. Women left the home and entered the paid workforce in unprecedented numbers to meet the demands of the burgeoning wartime economy, while members of the armed services could scarcely help but notice the homosexual activity that flourished as never before in sex-segregated military settings. American society hasn't been quite the same ever since. Jorgensen's story became a lightning rod for many post-World War II anxieties about gender and sexuality, and called dramatic attention to issues that would drive the feminist and gay-rights movements in the decades ahead. Years later, in the twilight of her career, Jorgensen herself commented that while she couldn't personally take credit for launching gay liberation, the women's movement, or the sexual revolution, her notoriety had given each a "kick in the pants" by drawing unprecedented scrutiny in the mainstream media to questions of personal identity, sexual orientation, and gender roles. Many formerly taboo topics were publicly discussed in the post-war era with specific reference to Christine Jorgensen.

Jorgensen's fame was undoubtedly structured to a certain degree by the paranoid logic of Cold War cultural fantasy. At the height of the United States global military dominance, "traditional" American masculinity seemed from some reactionary perspectives to be paradoxically on the defensive: subverted from within by an increasingly visible homosexuality, challenged from without by an economically empowered womanhood, and menaced from abroad by the specter of communist totalitarianism bent on subjecting it to unmanly servitude. In an era when atomic bombs could now rip open the fabric of the physical universe, the sudden spectacle of male-to-female transsexual re-embodiment offered further giddy proof that science had indeed triumphed over nature. Jorgensen's notoriety in the 1950s was undoubtedly fueled by the pervasive unease felt in some quarters that American manhood, already under siege, could quite literally be undone and refashioned into its seeming opposite through the power of modern science.

All this cultural baggage—everything from the mind-numbing implications of the atom bomb to tectonic shifts in gender roles—added up to a rather heavy cross for a twenty-six-year-old American to bear as she lay convalescing in a Copenhagen hospital in December, 1952. At first, Jorgensen seemed utterly bewildered by the storm of publicity that surrounded the revelation of her intensely private quest for personal happiness, though rumors persist that she herself leaked her story to the press. Whether she intended it or not, the sheer magnitude of her celebrity quickly precluded any prospect of returning to a low-profile career in photography. From the moment she hit the headlines, Christine Jorgensen was a star— destined to stand before, rather than behind, the camera.

If a perceived crisis of American masculinity fed some of the hysterical attention to Christine Jorgensen, her stardom definitely played itself out in terms of American womanhood. She was presented in the media as a blonde bombshell—fashionable, desirable, slightly aloof, blending Doris Day's wholesome propriety with Marlene Dietrich's sly wisdom in the ways of the world. Jorgensen rose admirably to the occasion. Fate placed her in the limelight, but her own talent and charisma kept her there. Other transsexuals made news in the immediate aftermath of Jorgensen's story, but they all sank quickly into obscurity.

Fortunately, the formerly introverted Jorgensen blossomed into her new role. Following the advice of seasoned theatrical agent Charlie Yates, who later became her manager, Jorgensen pulled together a surprisingly polished nightclub act in the summer of 1953. She sang a little, danced a little, told some jokes, and made quick costume changes, but mostly she simply performed her own identity on stage for paying customers. Though her audiences initially seemed interested in gawking at a freak show—harboring the same expectations they might bring to a female impersonator act or a burlesque show—Jorgensen generally left them feeling enlightened as well as entertained. She managed to keep her name in marquee lights well into the 1960s, often earning more than five thousand dollars a week in top venues around the world.

Christine Jorgensen's long-awaited autobiography—reissued here by Cleis Press—first appeared in hard-cover in 1967, just as her life on stage was coming to a close, and it helped launch the next phase of her career. The Bantam paperback edition issued the next year sold over four hundred thousand copies, yet it remains hard to find in second-hand book shops due to its continued popularity with the many transgendered people who consider Jorgensen a pioneering role model. An exploitative film version of Jorgensen's life story based on the autobiography appeared in 1970, starring cross-dressed Olympic swimmer John Hanson in his acting debut.

The film quickly disappeared into well-deserved oblivion. Jorgensen, however, rode the new wave of attention created by her book and movie to establish herself as a highly sought-after speaker on the college lecture circuit, where she regularly drew audiences of thousands into the mid-1970s. By the time she slid more or less gracefully into a modest retirement in the 1980s, she had been in the public eye for more than a quarter-century. Even in her final years she remained a feisty presence in the social circles in which she moved. With her health and fortune failing fast by the late 1980s, she would still pry herself out of her favorite armchair where she spent much of the day reading newspapers and working crossword puzzles, put on a carefully chosen outfit, fix her face in a flattering style, and announce "It's show time!" to whomever was listening as she dashed headlong from her apartment and into the night. Bravado notwithstanding, bladder cancer eventually brought down the curtain on Jorgensen's life in 1989, at age sixty-two.

In her autobiography, Christine Jorgensen does an admirable job recounting the inner turmoil of her youth, as well as the triumphs and tribulations of her glory years. She does so with a steadfast determination to present her story in a dignified and understated manner—so understated, in fact, that the book sometimes makes for admittedly dull reading. So intent is she on proving her respectability and countering the many untrue and unkind things said of her in the press, that parts of her story seem little more than lists of which famous and important people she lunched with during any given week, which fabulous and exclusive clubs she performed in, and which tasteful ensembles she wore while doing so. This is a pity, for Jorgensen's life was anything but dull. It's a shame the prejudices of others persuaded her to tone down a vibrant, often bawdy personality for the sake of posterity's opinion.

The photographs included in this new edition of her autobiography offer tantalizing glimpses of the woman behind the veil of propriety she draped around herself: Christine at the racetrack with two handsome male escorts, Christine surrounded by hungry eyes at a Havana resort, Christine belting out tunes in a Philippine nightclub. To see Jorgensen in her prime in old newsreel footage is to be struck by the ironic distance between the staid persona presented in the pages of her autobiography and the vivacious starlet who exudes sexuality for the camera like a young Marilyn Monroe. To read her own descriptions of her nightclub act one would think she recited Shakespeare in a high-necked gown; to read her actual stage material is to appreciate her keen assessment of the roots of her popular appeal. "It's a Change," one of Jorgensen's trademark numbers, was full of double entendres that played on the public's titillation with her shift in gender presentation, and with the ambiguous desires that eddied in its wake:

> Every hour every day we encounter something new
> Electric this, Atomic that—a modern point of view.
> Now anything can happen and we shouldn't think it strange,
> If oysters smoke cigars
> Or lobsters drive imported cars,
> For we live in a time of change.
>
> When baby starts to cry
> And the volume's like hi-fi,
> It's not because he's dry—he wants a change.
>
> Wagner, Beethoven, and Tchaikovsky wrote symphonies
> complete
> But they never heard rock and roll and they never had
> a beat.
> In '56 we reek with chic, but those boys would think
> we're deranged
> That a man called Elvis
> Can wave his pelvis
> For a handsome piece of change.
>
> When the Dodgers sign up girls,
> When Liberace cuts his curls,
> When Cartier's sells battleships
> And marijuana has filter tips,

When a stripper bumps and grinds
And you're impressed with her brilliant mind
Instead of her behind—it's a change.

When the First Lady is a he—and the President is me
It's a switch—it's a twist—it's a change.
Still these things would shock most people
But I really don't know why,
For the world is full of changes—who knows this more
than I!

Understandably, Jorgensen's autobiography also skimps on the details of her many behind-the-scenes struggles and personal shortcomings. She smoked and drank excessively, and had a tongue sharp enough to drive away the most dedicated and long-suffering supporters. She was more than a little star-struck, perpetually impressed with herself for having hobnobbed with show business glitterati. She was litigious, constantly embroiled in petty lawsuits and legal actions. She peddled an endless stream of improbable projects that never went anywhere: Danish cookbooks, wretched screenplays for movies in which she played the female lead, a guide to the graves of movie greats. Towards the end of her life she even contemplated a new no-holds-barred, tell-all autobiography, complete with nude photos of herself. It, like all the other projects, ultimately failed to pan out.

But what of it? Christine Jorgensen's human failings do little to tarnish the zest with which she tackled the role that history handed her. She threw herself heart and soul into playing the part of the world's first famous transsexual: educating and entertaining, being gracious and glamorous, striving for the respect that every individual should be given as a birthright, but which is all too often denied those—like Jorgensen—who express their gender identity in an atypical fashion. Even now, straying too far from rigidly enforced gender norms makes one vulnerable to employment discrimination, familial abandonment, emotional violence, vicious hate crimes, and other potentially life-threatening difficulties. Jorgensen faced those challenges in far less tolerant times, and transcended them. Given a very narrow path to walk through life, she found a way to walk it with style. This act of simple dignity is her enduring achievement and greatest legacy.

For the personal courage she showed in her public life, Christine Jorgensen remains a heroine for many transgendered people today, though she has largely faded from our general culture's collective consciousness. It is a pleasure to introduce her story to a new generation of readers, and to celebrate her life once more with those for whom her memory is still very much alive.

Susan Stryker
San Francisco
May 2000

PREFACE

Three seemingly unrelated incidents—one medical, one professional, one personal—can be cited as representative of my life since my return from Denmark, in the culminating series of events that was to make me, unwillingly and unwittingly, an international controversy.

The most significant of these incidents consisted of a few words in a letter written to me in April, 1965, by Dr. Harry Benjamin, the distinguished medical scientist.

"Indeed, Christine," he wrote, "without you, probably none of this would have happened; the grant, my publications, lectures, etc. You will find me giving you credit in the book."

The book to which he referred was *The Transsexual Phenomenon,* his scientific report on transsexualism and sex conversion in the human male and female, published by Julian Press in 1966. I knew Dr. Benjamin had been engaged for many years in the study of the psychological, endocrinological, surgical, and sociological aspects of transsexualism. At the time I received his letter, I gave it no further thought until I received a copy of his book and read the glowing tribute to my trials and tribulations.

If Dr. Benjamin felt that I had donated something to his studies and findings, it seemed to me that I was more prominently in his debt than he in mine, and to be acknowledged was to be overpaid. If, indeed, I had made any contribution, it must be admitted that at the time of my transition it was purely an unconscious one. To me, it was a matter of survival. As the object of one of Nature's caprices, I was merely searching for my own personal expression of human dignity, with no thought of what the consequences might turn out to be.

Although many times in the past I had been the recipient of great kindness and support from the medical fraternity, I had also been the subject of much controversy and attack, particularly in the United States, and I hoped *The Transsexual Phenomenon* would help to dispel some of the enigmas of my case for the medical profession.

The curious unpredictability of the second aspect of my life, the professional, is seen in the following somewhat startling and disturbing news release:

CHRISTINE JORGENSEN RULED OFF LIMITS

FRANKFURT, GERMANY, SEPT 11 — THE U.S. ARMY'S 3D ARMORED DIVISION HAS REFUSED TO ALLOW A FORMER GI TO ENTERTAIN AT ITS ENLISTED MEN'S AND NONCOMMISSIONED OFFICER'S CLUBS.

THE ENTERTAINER IS FORMER PVT. GEORGE JORGENSEN, JR., 39, WHO HAS TAKEN THE NAME CHRISTINE SINCE UNDERGOING MUCH-PUBLICIZED SEX-CHANGE OPERATIONS IN DENMARK.

A DIVISION SPOKESMAN SAID YESTERDAY THAT "WHILE THE DIVISION BELIEVES THAT MISS JORGENSEN IS PERFECTLY FREE TO PURSUE A STAGE CAREER, IT WAS FELT NOT IN THE BEST INTERESTS OF THE DIVISION TO PERMIT HER TO PERFORM IN OUR CLUBS."

The incident was not unprecedented in my life as a performer. My adventures had been many and varied in the entertainment world over a period of the previous thirteen years, most of them extremely pleasant and rewarding, some of them highly amusing, a few painful. I had already had the distinction of having been banned in Boston, refused permission to entertain troops in the Philippines, criticized for an inept performance in Los Angeles, and badgered by a nervous Las Vegas club owner who wanted to cancel a contract.

However, the spokesman for the U.S. Third Army Division, though magnanimously believing me free to "pursue a stage career," seemed to imply that I was surrounded by an aura of ungodliness or immorality, by which my presence would corrupt, in some mysterious way, the United States military forces in Germany.

The third incident, trivial perhaps, though significant to me, involves the personal meaning: my life simply as a woman, and as a human being.

It occurred quite accidentally, a few months after the newspaper item appeared, in another community where I had been performing professionally. I happened to find myself in the unavoidable position of eavesdropping on two attractive young matrons who had witnessed one of my nightclub performances a half hour earlier. Always a dangerous pursuit, it is one which I admit finding irresistible, particularly when I am the subject of discussion.

"Christine Jorgensen is a shock!"

"What do you mean?"

"Well, I mean she is. I thought she was going to look—well, you know, different. But she's as feminine as we are. Wears clothes like a fashion model. I read someplace she was engaged or married, or something. I mean do you think it's possible?"

"Anything's possible, but I wonder what she's really like, personally?"

What is she really like—personally? It was a question that echoed in my mind. That, coupled with the medical contribution of my "case," and the stir my professional aspirations continued to cause everywhere, led me to review the events and people who had contributed so heavily, both positively and negatively, to my whole existence. For the first time in many years, I labored through the thousands of words printed about me in the newspapers, periodicals, journals, and scandal magazines. I tried to regard it all as objectively as possible, and was made aware again that much of the information about the "Christine Jorgensen case" was confusing, often biased, or made sensational and bizarre by the press. I thought it small wonder that I have been regarded, occasionally, with suspicion and mystery over the years, although there had been perhaps thirty cases of sex conversion on record before mine.

At one time or another, I had been called a male homosexual, a female homosexual, a transvestite, an hermaphrodite, a woman since birth who had devised a sensational method of notoriety for financial gain, a true male masquerading as a female, or a totally sexless creature—the last category placing me in the same neutral corner as a table or chair.

Another surprising fact was brought to my attention during this critical survey, one that hadn't occurred to me before. Never once, in all those acres of newsprint, had I been asked about my faiths and beliefs, both of which had played important roles in my life. What I slept in, apparently, was considered more important than what I believed in.

Whatever the value of this judgment of myself as seen through the eyes of others, it helped to open a route through which I can now examine my life from the vantage point of time, to weigh its realities, successes, and failures in light of my own interpretation, and to bury once and for all the rumors, speculations, untruths, and misconceptions by which I have been surrounded for almost a decade and a half.

There is also the hope that a clear and honest delineation of my life may help lead to a greater understanding of boys and girls who grow up knowing they will not fit into the pattern of life that is expected of them; of the men and women who struggle to adjust to sex roles unsuited to them; and the intrepid ones who, like myself, must take drastic steps to remedy what they find intolerable.

A statement written in 1952 has remained indelibly in my memory: "Only time will tell how Miss Jorgensen will adjust to the world and the world to her." Time, indeed, has told...

All religion, all life, all art, all expression comes down to this: to the effort of the human soul to break through its barrier of loneliness, of intolerable loneliness, and make some contacts with another seeking soul, or with what all souls seek, which is (by any name) God.

—DON MARQUIS

Christine Jorgensen
A PERSONAL AUTOBIOGRAPHY

CHAPTER 1

As is the case in the history of most American families, the Jorgensens immigrated to the United States from a foreign land. It is possible that my attachment to the world of make believe was influenced even before I was born, for my paternal grandfather, Charles Gustav Jorgensen, came to this country from Odense, Denmark, the birthplace of Hans Christian Andersen. The great Danish novelist and spell weaver was still living when Grandfather left Denmark for the United States in 1870 and settled in New York City.

Charles Gustav was in the building trade, and as an immigrant to America he brought with him little but his skills and a determination to prosper. With the construction activity that prevailed in the post-Civil War decade, he was soon thriving in an expanding world and became a citizen of his new country.

Twenty years after his arrival, he returned to Denmark for a brief visit and met Anna Maria Magdalena Petersen, who came from the city of Aarhus. Anna Maria followed him to America two years later and they were married the day after she landed. Therefore, Grandma became a citizen one day after she arrived in the United States.

Their first child, my Aunt Esther, was born in 1893; my father, George Jorgensen, the following year. Seven more children followed in rapid succession, making a total of nine.

With the growing responsibilities of an increasing brood, Grandpa sent to Denmark for a teenage girl named Augusta, who was believed to be his younger sister. She was affectionately welcomed into the household and helped Grandma with the care and upbringing of the younger Jorgensen children. Augusta was to play an influential role in my life and, in addition, to reveal a heavily guarded family secret many years later.

My grandparents, Charles and Anna Jorgensen, quickly assimilated into the Danish-American community in New York City, retaining many of the traditions and customs of the Old Country. They helped establish the Danish Beach Club, which was a young people's social organization, at a place known as Askov Hall, named for a famous gymnasium school in Denmark. A standard joke at the time was that when the Jorgensen family got together, there were enough members to start a club of their own.

It was at a social gathering at Askov Hall that my father, George, met the attractive young lady who was to become my mother, Florence Davis Hansen. Her father, John Kreogh Hansen, was born in the small Danish town of Horsens and immigrated to the United States as a young boy, accompanied by his parents. He was an accomplished artist, who occasionally worked at house painting during the leaner periods. One of his major assignments during the 1890s was painting the original ceiling of Grand Central Station, an enormous expanse of blue sky and countless silver stars. He also painted a sizable number of draped nudes in oils and a faithful copy of Rosa Bonheur's *The Horse Fair*. In 1892, he met and married Caroline Rohre, who was born in Baden-Baden, Germany, near the Black Forest. They had two children: Otto and my mother, Florence. Soon after, John and Caroline Hansen were divorced. Mother and Uncle Otto went to live with their paternal grandmother and were never again to know the influence of their own parents.

One day, my Grandfather Hansen accidentally kneeled on an exposed nail and developed blood poisoning. His physical resistance at low ebb when the flu epidemic struck in 1918, he was unable to withstand the onslaught of the disease and died in November of that year. His wife, Caroline, whom we called "Nana" Hansen, lived until 1956.

As a young man, one of my Dad's earliest hobbies centered around his fascination for radio communication, when it was still in its infancy. In 1910, when he was sixteen, he earned an Operator's Certificate of Skill in Radio Communication from the United States Department of Commerce. On his home sending and receiving set, he heard the distress signals from the ocean liner *Titanic* when it sank on April 15, 1912, taking with it 1,517 people.

Dad entered the Coast Guard in August of 1917 and while in service, he suffered a serious fall in which his hip and lower leg were fractured in several places, which necessitated eighteen months of hospitalization. In later years, he loved showing off the x-rays of his injury, because they clearly showed the silver plate in his leg. The result of the accident left him with a slight limp which became habitual, though it in no way hindered him from doing manual labor. He was retired from the Coast Guard in 1920.

After Dad retired from the Coast Guard, he formed the Jorgensen Realty and Construction Company, along with his brother, William, and his father. With the end of World War I hostilities in 1918, the country was enjoying a construction boom and the Jorgensens erected many houses in the New York area, as their company successfully expanded.

My father and mother, George and Florence Jorgensen, began their happy married life together in 1922, on a wave of expectant prosperity.

The first introduction to parenthood for Mom and Dad came in 1923 when my sister, Dorothy Florence Jorgensen, was born. A vivacious little blonde girl, Dolly was three years old when on a warm, sunny day in the late spring, Dad hurriedly bundled Mom into a taxi and started out on a mission of extreme urgency. There were, no doubt, some traffic laws broken that day, as the taxi careened wildly through the streets of the Bronx, headed south. After what must have seemed to them an interminable trip, the cab came to a grinding halt in front of a large hospital, but one look at the building and Mom gasped, "It's the wrong one!" They continued their desperate journey and finally arrived at their correct destination, the Community Hospital in Manhattan. Within the hour, Mom gave birth to the Jorgensens' second child, a normal baby boy. It was on Memorial Day, May 30, 1926 that I was born, while lines of marchers paraded down the streets to the lively accompaniment of numberless brass bands.

Some years were to pass before I realized that the parades and flag waving had nothing to do with celebrating my birthday, but later I enjoyed the fact that, at least, it always meant a holiday from school.

There seemed to be nothing unusual about me at birth, except that I was slightly tongue-tied and a snip of the surgical scissors quickly rectified the minor defect.

A few weeks later, I was christened George William Jorgensen, Jr., in a small neighborhood Danish Lutheran church.

From the very beginning of our young lives, Mom took over the reins of our care and discipline. When Dolly and I were ordered to take a nap we did, with no exceptions. Mom never let anyone pick us up unless it seemed to her the proper time, and there was no careful tiptoeing around the house while we slept. As a matter of fact, my crib was placed right next to the radio and I learned early to sleep through the sound of voices and any other noise. No doubt this conditioning is the reason why Dolly and I are such great sleepers today, an ability for which I've always been grateful and without which I couldn't have survived some of the crucial moments of my life.

When one of the childhood diseases took turns, Mom worked on the theory that if one of us was attacked, the best thing to do was to stick the other one in the same room and get it over with all at once. That seemed a sensible arrangement as mumps, measles, and chicken pox came and went in pairs at our house.

A few years before I was born, Dad had taken advantage of his trade as a contractor and carpenter and built a two-family house on Dudley Avenue in the Throgs Neck section of the Bronx. We lived in one unit and Dad rented out the other. It was there that I was to live the first twenty-six years of my life with my parents and my sister Dolly. I remember that the house had a small square of lawn in front and a backyard garden, where I probably first developed a lifelong love of growing things and a frustrated desire to be an expert gardener.

I still retain fond memories of that pleasant residential area in the Bronx. The favorite hangout of the local small-fry was the neighborhood grocery and candy store where we bought licorice hats for a penny and were loudly reprimanded by an irate proprietor if we left dirty fingerprints on the glass showcases. Those were the "good old days," when grocery staples were bought in bulk and milk was sold by the dipper from big shiny cans. Later, when I learned to smoke at sixteen, we bought cigarettes singly at one cent apiece, a price that seems extremely modest today.

In those days, Dolly and I were both victims of cereal-box advertising, a childhood blandishment that seems to have changed very little. I saved oatmeal box-tops to send away for a pair of cowboy chaps made of imitation leather and tired fur, and Dolly and I must have consumed a ton of oatmeal for that prized dividend.

We had the standard older-sister-younger-brother relationship as children, with the usual number of juvenile altercations. Dolly, three years older than I, generally had the advantage of her seniority, and the roughhouse that ensued frequently left me with a few well-planted "lumps." Today, Mom vehemently insists that we were model children, but I'm afraid that maternal love has clouded her vision.

I recall that Mom frequently made Dolly take little brother, or "Brud," as I was affectionately called, with her on after-school outings. Dolly wasn't filled with enthusiasm, a reaction that was perfectly understandable, but in spite of her protests, I usually ended up by tagging along. Jumping rope, playing jacks, hide-and-go-seek, and potsie (hop scotch) were our favorite games. How much these girlish activities were to contribute to my future problems and the inability to identify myself with the masculine sex, I don't think I will ever know.

Dolly and I were surrounded by a closely knit, affectionate family of the sort that gives a child a warm feeling of belonging. Happily, we had the advantage of being in a family that enjoyed activities as a unit, and that still applies today. Mom and Dad had a faithful Model A Ford that often got a good workout in the summertime. On vacations, we four Jorgensens rode through the New England states and Canada, stopping at night in what were then called "roadside cabins." They were flimsy structures, made of little more than two-by-four beams and clapboard, and I can remember inspecting the thick cobwebs in the corners, wide-eyed with fear that I'd find a spider in residence. A dollar a night for the whole family was the going rate and we set up our own cots and cooked on a portable stove. We could never have imagined then that these crude, unkempt little cabins would grow in the next thirty years into the slick and luxurious motels of today.

As with most everyone, some of the cherished memories of my childhood revolved around the Christmas holidays. To me, the Scandinavian Christmas was and is the grandest of celebrations. Starting December 1, we children were allowed to select one small parcel from a pile of twenty-four (usually ten-cent store items), before we went to bed. It wasn't surprising that Mom didn't have to employ any of her usual disciplinary measures to get us to go to bed on each of the twenty-four evenings before Christmas. A few days before Christmas Eve, Dad brought in the tree and Dolly and I helped decorate it. Some of the decorations were brought from Denmark and I still have a few in my possession today.

The family festivities were always centered at Grandma Jorgensen's house and it was deluged with children, grandchildren and, ultimately, great-grandchildren. The entire clan congregated there on Christmas Eve, laden with packages which soon formed an enormous ring around Grandma's tree.

Dinner gave rise to the single disharmony of the evening. Although the largest available turkey was prepared for the dinner table, it wasn't possible for each of six grandchildren to have a drumstick, when even the noblest of birds had only two. To preserve the peace, the thighs and wings of the turkey were immediately referred to by the grownups as "drumsticks," and I can remember that we children accepted that gentle deception for years.

One of the charming Danish customs was serving the traditional rice pudding, which contained a single almond. Whoever found the almond in his dish of pudding, kept it tucked into his cheek, watching gleefully as everyone else searched each spoonful for the elusive prize. The beneficiary received a gift, usually a little pig made of marzipan.

After Christmas dinner, we sang traditional carols and marched hand in hand around the tree. At this point, our patience was strained to the breaking point, for we awaited the appearance of The Yule Man, the Danish equivalent of Santa Claus. When finally the bells rang, announcing his arrival and the time for distributing presents, I recall once I froze in terror and ran for Mom's protection, for indeed, he was a frightening apparition, dressed in a red bathrobe and a distorted starched mask. His disguise had been stuffed in an attic when not in use at Christmas and the years had taken their toll of both the shape and color of his costume and mask. I often wonder how I could have believed in The Yule Man as long as I did.

Some of the strongest and most enduring of childhood memories are inevitably linked with my paternal grandmother, who exerted a great influence on my early life. There were twenty-six aunts, uncles, and cousins in our Bronx neighborhood, but the matriarch and focal point of the clan was Grandma Jorgensen. She was a generous, commonsense woman who enriched the lives of our family, friends, and neighbors, enveloping us all in a warm glow of love.

In stature, Grandma was short and pleasantly plump. She chose mostly gray and lavender shades for her clothes, which complemented her white hair. In my mind's eye, even now, I can picture her silvery hair brushed high on her head and topped by a shining knot. Another outstanding thing about her was an aristocratic, "Indian-type" nose, which was a genetic feature in the Petersen family. Dad and Dolly inherited it, while I was endowed with the prominent Petersen ears.

Grandma had small, plump hands that seemed to have a life of their own as they worked incessantly at some form of handiwork: needlepoint, knitting, or crocheting. As the years passed, she met the rudeness of time gracefully, and her hands, particularly, seemed never to age. I remember the scent of lavender that surrounded her. She was always a person of grace and dignity.

As a child, I used to pick violets for her. They were her favorite flower, and she had a green thumb for raising the African variety, an ability which I've tried to match, unsuccessfully, for years.

I developed into a frail, tow-headed, introverted child, but I learned early that society laid down firm ground rules concerning my behavior. A little boy wore trousers and had his hair cut short. He had to learn to use his fists aggressively, participate in athletics and, most important of all, little boys didn't cry. Contrary to those accepted patterns, sometimes I did feel like crying and I must have felt that Grandma understood and didn't disapprove when I ran away from a fistfight or refused to play rough and tumble games. Once, when I ran to her in flight from some childish altercation, she said, "Fighting is the ugliest part of life. To live without fighting is much more important, and much more satisfying."

After Grandpa Jorgensen died in 1927, Grandma lived comfortingly close to our house in the Bronx with her son-in-law and daughter, Helga, Dad's sister. As soon as I was permitted to travel the few blocks to Grandma's house alone, I began to spend many hours with her. I loved listening to the stories about Denmark, told in her soft voice and Danish accent; the customs and traditions of the Old Country and the charming, funny things she did as a child. Always, as we talked, her small hands were busy crocheting doilies or antimacassers and our conversation was accompanied in the background by the ticking of a beautifully carved wall clock which was given to Grandpa in 1868, and is still in my possession today. Occasionally, I was allowed to admire her collection of fine porcelain, at reasonably close range.

I suppose I knew instinctively that I didn't have to tell Grandma when someone had hurt my feelings or when I had been cruelly disappointed. Had I told her of my childish prayer one Christmas when I was five, asking God for a pretty doll with long, golden hair, Grandma might have helped answer that prayer. At least, she would have eased my disappointment when my present turned out to be a bright red railway train.

It must have been about this stage that I became aware of the differences between my sister, Dolly, and me. Those differences, to me, lay in the order of "masculine" and "feminine" things. Dolly had long blonde hair and wore dresses, both of which I admired but which were not allowed to me, and I was upset and puzzled by this.

"Mom," I asked, "why didn't God make us alike?" My mother gently explained that the world needed both men and women and that there was no way of knowing before a baby was born whether it would be a boy or a girl.

"You see, Brud," she said, "it's one of God's surprises."

"Well," I replied, "I don't like the kind of surprise God made me!"

I believe the spirit of rebellion must have been taking a foothold in me, even though I was a shy and introverted child. Though I don't remember the incident, I've been told that my childish revolt manifested itself one day when I was about four or five, and I went to visit my maternal grandmother, "Nana" Hansen. During the course of a shopping trip, I planted myself stolidly in front of a neighborhood store and demanded some candy.

"No," Nana replied, "you're going to eat shortly."

"Then I'll go home," I answered, and started on my way. Nana followed, block after block, but at a distance. Reaching another candy store, I stopped, turned to see Nana regarding me, and said, "Candy now?"

"No," came the prompt and firm reply. True to my word, I plodded my determined way home. Evidently, I was a willful one even at that age.

CHAPTER 2

In 1928, the nation was riding at a prosperous high tide and reflecting that spirit was one of the popular song hits of the time, "Happy Days Are Here Again." Newly elected President Herbert Hoover was proclaiming "a chicken in every pot and a car in every garage." Wall Street's ticker tape machines clattered away at a great rate and stocks rose to new heights. The Jorgensen Realty and Construction Company expanded its credit and continued to build more houses. Even the death, in 1927, of Grandpa Jorgensen, one of the company's founders, didn't stop its meteoric rise.

But The Roaring Twenties were about to quiet down to a whimper. October 29, 1929, was the beginning of one of the darkest periods in American financial history, for it ushered in the Great Depression. With the sudden, swift market crash on Black Thursday, everything lost value, the economic stability of the country was destroyed, and the Jorgensen Construction Company was swept along with the wreckage of countless others. Fifteen houses, built by the company on bank credit and mortgages, stood in lonely vacancy in the New York area. A few of them sold for a tenth of their original cost; others the family couldn't give away. Even our home on Dudley Avenue was in jeopardy for a while. Dad and his brother Bill had all their resources in those buildings, even including Grandma Jorgensen's money. The stock certificates were worthless and, as Dad said, "Good for nothing but papering a wall." As I was only three years old at the time, I don't recall that financial catastrophe, but many years later, I took Dad's pronouncement literally and papered a wall behind the bar in my home with those colorful, worthless certificates.

In the wake of the depression, Mom and Dad managed to survive and keep a car, a house, and a family intact. Dad had cashed in his government insurance and funds were low, but he worked at various jobs in the building trade in order to keep going.

After the crash, when her children contributed to her support, Grandma had an efficient, if unusual system of bookkeeping. She had a sheaf of envelopes, each marked and set aside for a specific purpose: "Birthdays," "Christmas," "Funeral" (her own), "Crocheting cotton," etc. When one of the envelopes was empty, Grandma was "broke" in that department and she would never think of taking from one to satisfy the needs of another. After noting Grandma's unique accounting system, I tried to set up one of my own. Of course, my weekly allowance never seemed to find its way into the envelopes, but the feeble attempt was probably the first to make me aware of the principles of thrift.

A couple of years after the demise of Dad's company and totally unaware of the drastic changes in the lives and fortunes of the Jorgensens, I began to prepare for the great adventure of going to school. I remember that I anticipated school with a great deal of excitement, for my one great ambition at that period was to learn to read. Dolly could already decipher meaning from the printed pages and I imagine I didn't want to be outdone. The daily arrival of newspapers and the large library of books at home were a constant frustration, and attempts to get others to read to me were futile more often than not. Dad, who was an avid reader, always seemed to me to know so much. He'd point to the newspaper and heatedly discuss an item and, later, when I tried to get some meaning from the printed symbols, I met with no success. School was the place where I could learn to read and I looked forward to it eagerly. When I was five-and-a-half, the day finally arrived, and I went to Public School 71, within walking distance of our home.

During my first week in kindergarten, I met a little boy named Carl, the first new friend with whom I wasn't shy. Carl came from Swedish parents and as we were both Scandinavians, we had common family backgrounds. Diabetic children were relatively unknown at that time, and I can remember watching with fascination one day when his Mother gave him an insulin shot. We became fast friends and all through our school life together, Carl was my one uncritical ally.

We often appeared in school plays and that was one of the activities I loved best of all. "Play-acting" was fun and I could hide my shyness behind the facade of someone else, in a shining world of fantasy. I remember my first role was as an organ-grinder's monkey, and by the time I was in the third grade, I'd graduated to the most cherished of all character parts, Mickey Mouse. The long rubber tail and suffocating mask were a mark of distinction and I wore them proudly.

At some time during that period, I acquired a set of marionettes. I never seemed to tire of manipulating the tiny figures in their fanciful world.

Outwardly, I was a very submissive child, but the sense of rebellion must have been growing rapidly within me and established itself more openly the following summer, when Mom and Dad sent me to a boys' summer camp, located at Dover Furnace, New Jersey.

Camp Sharparoon was a typical vacation camp, operated in what seemed to me then a far too militant manner. The day's schedule was posted each morning on a bulletin board and, although I was too young to read the notice in detail, I was sure in advance that I wasn't going to like the "orders of the day." The first day's regimen confirmed my fears when we flew from one activity to another, commanded by the shrill, piercing sound of a whistle.

High on the mountainside above the camp was a large rock with a gigantic letter "S" painted on it, and the penalty for an infraction of the rules was the job of painting the "S." A fearful, whispered rumor told of the many boys who had fallen to instant death from that dizzying height, while painting the camp symbol. The story held me in terror for several days, until I finally realized that it was, of course, false.

I fell a victim to other tricks played on the newcomers, when I was told that a "Sky Hook" and a "Jericho Pass" were absolutely essential to every camp member. I don't remember why the Sky Hook was necessary, but a Jericho Pass had no little importance, as I was informed that it was the only thing that would permit use of the latrines. Finally, in dire circumstance, I rushed around the camp looking for someone to give me the vital Jericho Pass until a sympathetic senior counselor put a stop to my frantic search. My relief—in several aspects—was so great that it is, even now, memorable.

I can still remember that a desire for seclusion grew more positive with each passing day, and my plans never included others. There was more freedom in carrying out those plans alone and, therefore, less chance of being made to feel ridiculous, strange or different.

"Hey, George, c'mere!" I was often ordered to join the other boys in a game. It seemed to me then it was always like that, just when I was having fun on my own. I resented these intrusions so much that I began devising ways of disappearing for a whole day, but when I returned, I knew I'd have to face the discipline of the counselors.

After a few miserable days of inadequately trying to fight against the regimentation, I made a tearful but determined request to be taken home. "I want to come home," was all I wrote on the penny postcard that I sent to Mom and Dad.

No one could understand why I was so unhappy or why I delighted in visiting Dolly when Mom and Dad took me on a trip to the girls' camp, some distance away. Somehow, I felt more at ease, more comfortable there. The girls didn't call me "sissy" or ask me if I was really a girl dressed in boy's clothes, like the boys at Camp Sharparoon did.

Fortunately, neither of my parents saw any reason for forcing me to continue something I disliked so violently, so each summer after that I was shipped off, with a blanket roll and a few dollars in pocket money, to relatives who owned a farm in northern New York State.

Many of the leisure hours on the farm were spent at an old, familiar "swimmin' hole" in the area. Like the children at the summer camp, the neighboring farm boys couldn't understand me either. To them I was "that strange little kid from the city."

"C'mon, George," they challenged. "Why don't you swim in your birthday suit like we do?"

I remember that I wanted so much to have them admire me and to be included as a member of the gang, but I shrank back in confusion and fear. "I get too cold in the water," I lied. Though I liked to swim and was a good swimmer, I couldn't break the habit of wearing a complete swimsuit with both top and bottom. I have no doubt that my embarrassment stemmed from shyness and a natural modesty which I had learned at home.

There were other ways in which I didn't measure up to the acceptable standards of a budding young male, as one of my school teachers was to point out so graphically and cruelly.

Most youngsters are acquisitive and prone to annoy adults with the oddities they collect and hoard. To a childish mind, anything from tattered comic books to a chipped marble are considered rare and valuable treasures to be admired, cherished, and sometimes even traded. In that respect, at least, I wasn't any different from other children.

I can't recall how, but when I was eight, I had in some way acquired one of those rich treasures: a small piece of needlepoint which I kept hidden in my school desk. Occasionally, I would reach in my desk and touch it, or if no one was watching, I'd take it out and admire it secretly. I didn't display it openly, probably sensing the derision that might result.

After recess one day, I was astonished to find that the lovely piece of handiwork had disappeared from my desk. Even now, I remember that I was heartbroken, for one of the small pleasures of my life had been lost or misplaced. Or had it been stolen?

Our teacher called the class to order and stood beside her desk, apparently waiting for the last echoes of childish freedom to die. She must have sensed her triumph as she paused significantly for complete attention. "George Jorgensen, come here," she said finally and a steely look in her eye reinforced the command. "I'd like you to come up, too, Mrs. Jorgensen, so you can hear what this boy has to say."

I turned to see Mom, quietly making her way from the back of the classroom. In distress over my loss, I hadn't noticed her sitting there before. In growing panic, I wondered what Mom was doing in class. She hadn't told me that she was coming to school. The teacher must have asked her, but why? Mothers were asked to school only when the kids did something wrong and I wondered what I had done.

In the silence that followed, the teacher took an object from her desk. "Is this yours?" she asked, with a prim little smile, holding the precious needlepoint just beyond my reach.

"Yes," I answered. I felt the quick sting of tears, the blood rushing to my face and heard a hot little breath sucked in behind me in excitement. I reached out to take the needlepoint from her hand, but she withdrew it sharply and faced my mother.

"Mrs. Jorgensen, do you think that this is anything for a red-blooded boy to have in his desk as a keepsake? The next thing we know, George will be bringing his knitting to school!"

There were titters from the class which she didn't try to silence. I glanced at Mom. Her lips were quivering and her face was flushed. "I'll take care of it," she said quietly, and guided me ahead of her out of the classroom. We walked home in silence. From time to time she brushed tears from her eyes and even now I recall my feeling of humiliation and confusion. In some way I had hurt her. I wasn't sure just how, but I think I knew that the teacher had hurt her even more. For the first time in my life, I felt the most destructive of all emotions, hate. That woman had cheapened something I loved and, in some way, had injured my mother. I was no doubt too young to realize that a love for beauty was not the sole property of either a male or female, but the teacher's attempt to form that link seemed wrong to me, even then.

Mom never mentioned the incident after that, but to me it has remained a vivid memory. From then on, except for answers to direct questions, I never spoke to the teacher again and I know now how much I must have resented her. I didn't realize that her own tragedy lay in ignorance and a lack of understanding. In her callousness, she couldn't comprehend the fact that in order to follow the normal pattern of development, I needed help, not ridicule.

As I often did when I was troubled, I went to visit my beloved Grandma Jorgensen and told her what had happened. She went to one of her great wooden chests and lovingly unwrapped many samples of her own superb needlework. She handed me a small, exquisitely crocheted doily and explained to me something of the joy and satisfaction she had known in making an object that was both useful and beautiful.

"You mustn't mind if other people can't see or feel a sense of beauty, too, George," she told me gently.

Grandma's explanation seemed more real to me than the teacher's ridicule. I thought that I knew what beauty was in my own way and that it was a mistake to categorize it as either masculine or feminine.

But Grandma was always my champion when others laughed at my "sissified" ways. I've been told that once, at the age of four, I had insisted on carrying a miniature cane and wearing a beret wherever I went. "Never mind," she said, "it's his way of expressing the yearning for dignity in his life."

I remember I was about eleven or twelve years old when my sister Dolly began to notice my outstanding feminine mannerisms. One day when we were walking home from school, Dolly said, "Why do you carry your books that way? It looks silly for a boy!" I was carrying my books up in my arms, just as she carried hers. It was something I'd never been aware of before.

I thought a great deal about those books during the following few days. "Does the way in which one carried books have to be 'boyish' or 'girlish'?" I wondered. I tried carrying them at my side, but it was awkward and I kept dropping them, so I simply went back to the old, more comfortable method.

A few years later, when Dolly was in college, she devoted a thesis to the effects of environment on the development of a child. I never read the thesis, but was told I was the subject of it and that she had won considerable acclaim for her work, in analyzing my feminine ways and attributing them partially to the fact that I played with girls so much as a child.

At the time, I was angry, though I never mentioned it. I felt that a very personal thing had been explored and exposed and I didn't like being used as the subject for such a disclosure.

Undoubtedly, my distress stemmed from fear and the total self-absorption of my thirteen years and, therefore, blinded me to her motives. Today, I know that she was deeply concerned and was trying to help me by searching for more understanding within herself. In a way, she was shouldering the problem and facing it squarely; a giant step for the average college girl in 1939, when such subjects as the "feminine" boy were not openly discussed.

How many of my emotions could be attributed to this early environment I couldn't determine then, of course, but deep within myself, even at that early age, I felt that all these basic feelings were an integral part of me and not highly influenced by outside conditions.

CHAPTER 3

Newspapers were filled with earthshaking events in 1939, but I
viewed the war in Europe as something very far away and not
affecting me greatly.

The closest thing to viewing a tragedy in my life was two years
before, when Dolly and I saw the German zeppelin, the *Hindenburg*,
pass over our house on its way to landing at Lakehurst, New Jersey. It
was a night in May of 1937 and the *Hindenburg* exploded and burned
at its moorings with a terrible cost of life. I remember thinking how
curious it was that I had seen the powerful ship in all its blazing,
lighted glory just a short hour before its total destruction.

The circumstances of the Jorgensens had improved slightly
since the financial holocaust of Wall Street in 1929. Dad had worked
at various jobs in the building trade until 1936 when, under the
newly formed WPA (Works Progress Administration), he got a job in
the mud flats of Flushing Meadows in Queens, helping to build
LaGuardia Airport.

They were no doubt hard years for Mom and Dad. I
remember waking in the dark to hear my parents' voices, whispering
in the kitchen over their breakfast. Dad left home before daylight
each morning and didn't return until after dark at night. I can still
see him bundled up in "long Johns," thick woolen socks, a heavy
sweater and jacket, and carrying a large thermos of coffee, as he
climbed into the trusty Model A Ford.

By 1939, LaGuardia Airport was completed and Dad took the
Civil Service examination and joined the ranks of New York City

employees in the Parks Department.

The World's Fair of 1939 was an exciting period in my childhood. Dolly and I would walk from our home to the Bronx end of the yet unopened span of the Whitestone Bridge and look out toward the fairgrounds, located in Queens on the same site as the 1965 World's Fair. The Exposition symbols of the Trylon and Perisphere loomed in the distance and our excitement mounted as the exhibition buildings grew.

Shortly before the Fair opened, we had received special "invitations" to welcome King George VI and Queen Elizabeth of Great Britain, who were arriving in the United States to join President Roosevelt in the opening ceremonies of the Fair. I remember that it was a bright, sunny day in April of 1939, when we found places on the West Side highway in Manhattan and watched the beautiful new liner, Queen Elizabeth, move slowly up the Hudson River. The large engraved invitations, displaying the British and American flags in color, were clutched in our hands and as the crowds grew, we soon realized that they were not exclusive with us, but that everyone else had one, too.

Sometime later, we saw the royal motorcade pass slowly by our viewing spot. King George sat quietly in the rear of an open limousine and next to him sat the Queen, waving and smiling graciously to the crowd. I can even recall her pale blue, off-the-face hat. The memory of this sight was to return to me many years later, when I saw the Queen Mother in 1953 at the coronation of her daughter, the young Queen Elizabeth.

I had a season pass to the World's Fair and I used it every weekend and on holidays until school closed, and almost daily from then on. The world of knowledge was unfolding and the foreign exhibitions brought faraway places closer to me.

On the evening of September 3, 1939, after an exhausting day at the fairgrounds, I was heading toward the gates on my way home, when I began to hear the first startling rumors of the declaration of war. I remember turning to see the lights in the British Pavilion go out.

To me, "the war" had been the one Dad had told us about when I had so often looked at his personal collection of World

War I photos as a child. Mom huddled by the radio when I arrived home that night and by their expressions, I knew that the war talk was something serious. The German occupation of Denmark on April 9, 1940, brought the war a little closer, and I felt, to a degree, something of Grandma's concern for our relatives in her native country.

I can remember a clear, bright Sunday afternoon in winter when I was fifteen, and we took a leisurely drive through the beautiful hilly countryside of Westchester. When we arrived home, Dad turned on the radio and the first few minutes of the broadcast were like the famous Orson Welles program a few years earlier, when he panicked the country with his dramatized reports of a Martian landing. Except this time, the reports were true. It was December 7, 1941, and we heard the first reports of the Japanese attack and destruction at Pearl Harbor.

I must have been about sixteen when the acute feelings of loneliness which had been accumulating began to possess me even more. Instead of assimilating into a group as most teenagers did, I felt like an outsider. I didn't like sports and I wasn't interested in dating girls, which had become the chief topic of conversation among the boys of my acquaintance. I tried to find some solace in books and they became my closest companions.

There was a vacancy at the Westchester Square Branch of the New York Public Library, and since I was devoting so much time to reading books, I thought I'd like to work around them. My job application was accepted and for the next year, books were a substitute for the friends I seemed unable to find in my school life.

I devoted more effort to the library job than I did to my school work. I was never a great scholar, but I think I had an inquisitive mind and the travel section, with its fascinating trips to far places, particularly intrigued me. My travels thus far had been limited to the yearly trip to the farm, but as I read, I began to plan.

I collected travel folders. Yellowstone Park, the Grand Canyon, the Blue Ridge Mountains, and Washington, D.C. were a few of the places I wanted to visit. Though my dreams were unlimited, my funds were not. I had managed to save a hundred dollars from my earnings at the library, which considerably narrowed down the distance for my first solo trip. Thus, Washington, D.C. became the logical choice and on a day in July of 1943, I boarded a plane at LaGuardia Airport, disregarding Mom's fearful protestations.

I stayed in a tourist home and all of my meals were eaten frugally in a nearby cafeteria. I visited the Mellon Art Gallery, went to the top of the Washington Monument, took a limousine tour of Arlington, and visited the Library of Congress. The week passed all too quickly, but most important to me at the time was the fact that I had accomplished something by myself, independently. I had looked at a slice of a world beyond my own and, for a time at least, satisfied my restlessness.

Around the age of seventeen, I recall that I was even more keenly aware that I was different from other boys. Once I overheard one of them say, "George is such a strange guy." At other times, they didn't have to say it; I could read the thought in their attitudes.

In spite of that (aside from my childhood friend, Carl, who was almost like a brother to me), I formed another friendship during those mid-teen years. Tom Chaney lived in a small town near the farm in upper New York State where I spent my summer vacations. Our friendship grew during my annual trips to the farm and also through correspondence following those visits, when I returned to New York. Tom was four years older than I and one reason that I liked him was that he didn't engage in embarrassing conversation about kissing and petting parties, accompanied by worldly-wise comments on sex. Friendship was the only feeling I had for him until he demonstrated that he was like all the other boys. He wrote me a letter that was devoted almost entirely to the irresistible attractions of a girl he had met, with little or no mention of the elaborate plans I'd made to visit the Hayden Planetarium on our next meeting in New York City.

I read the letter over with misgivings and disappointment. It was then, for the first time, that I experienced the abrasive feelings of jealousy—emotions which fed what must have been an already mounting inferiority complex. It was a puzzling ambivalence. I didn't like or understand these feelings for Tom, they were new and foreign. At the same time, though I liked him, I resented him for being the object of these strange emotions.

During this period of disillusionment, I tried to involve myself in fumbling attempts at self-analysis. Quite accidentally, I came across a book in the library that revealed to me new and incomprehensible facts about human relations. Dealing with the subject of homosexuality, the book was concealed from the general reading public in what was known as the "closed shelves." Between its covers, I found many perplexing statements about sex deviation. I scanned paragraphs and pages of case histories, all of which left me even more bewildered than before.

Question after question raced through my mind. Was this the same thing I felt? Was I one of these people? Was I living half in shadow? Was my feeling for Tom one of love, like the love described in the book?

I didn't think I was "in love" with Tom, I only knew that I didn't want him to be in love with some girl. But wasn't that the same thing? Why did I want to keep him from the accepted ways of men toward women? Wasn't it inevitable that he would meet a girl sometime and marry and have children? Then why did I want to hold on to him if he was only a comrade and our friendship a platonic one?

All of these questions continued to flood my mind. Increasingly tortured and confused by them, I could only grope blindly for the answers.

CHAPTER 4

Askov Hall was the Danish-American Beach Club, located at Throgs Neck on Long Island Sound, where the young people of our community congregated for social activities and companionship.

Grandpa Jorgensen had been one of the club's founders and when funds were finally raised for the building, Dad was one of the principal architects and was later to serve as president. The club had been organized through the Danish Trinity Church and the actual construction was donated by its members. Dad also contributed a good deal of spare time and effort to the building. I tried to assist with the project at one point, but as Dad said, I had no real aptitude for the work and had to be directed specifically to everything pertaining to the job.

Once, I remember, Dad asked me to help him build a boat, an enterprise that would have delighted most boys. I did try, just in order to please him, but my interest soon flagged. My relief was probably no greater than his when I shortly withdrew my services.

Around 1943, at the height of the war years, I seldom missed attending the Saturday night socials at Askov Hall, yet I subconsciously feared them. In a party atmosphere, my failure to conform to the patterns expected of a young man of seventeen was even more noticeable, not only to me, but I was sure to other people, too. I didn't like to dance, but I was envious when I saw girls in the arms of their escorts, skillfully employing the standard devices of flirtation. Being surrounded by these lighthearted young people only served to heighten my sense of isolation.

As a result, there were times when the aching loneliness became unbearable and I left the bright lights and youthful gaiety of the beach club for a solitary walk along the edge of the bay. Pinpoints of light winked on the opposite shore and the quiet darkness, broken only by the gentle lapping of waves on the sand, seemed more friendly and inviting. I believe it was during one of these lonely walks that I must have decided my only salvation lay in some sort of absorbing activity—one which would involve me so wholeheartedly that I wouldn't have time to think about myself or my problems. I hadn't graduated from high school as yet, but I felt the time had come for me to start thinking of a profession.

Photography had always been a fascinating hobby to me, since the days when Dad would improvise a darkroom by putting blankets over the kitchen windows. He, Dolly, and I would closet ourselves there for hours, developing negatives and making prints on his elderly World War I printing box.

"I have the largest private collection of World War I pictures in the world," Dad would say confidently. His boast was no doubt true. During the First World War when he was in the Coast Guard and had been hospitalized for injuries incurred by a serious fall, he had set up a darkroom in the hospital and printed pictures for all his mates in the navy. Dad always made an extra copy of each photo for himself. Years later, throughout our childhood, Dolly and I regarded those boxes of photographs as old playmates. Looking through them was a wonderful escape on rainy afternoons or a welcome distraction when we were bundled into bed to cure a cold, reeking of Vicks VapoRub and fretting under hot, itching mustard plasters. (Mom was always adamant about those.)

Dad had given me my first camera and I was taking pictures with abandon, if not precision, as far back as I could remember. Sometime during my last year of high school in 1944, I spoke to Mom and Dad about the possibility of taking an evening course at the New York Institute of Photography. I wasn't surprised that they both welcomed the idea, because they were always anxious to encourage Dolly and me in any educational advancement.

I didn't know it at the time, but Dad took out a loan on his government life-insurance policy to pay my tuition. Armed with my parents' encouragement and the money they had given me at a sacrifice, I enrolled at the Institute and started evening sessions in commercial, portrait, motion picture, and color photography. Whatever artistic inclinations I may have had seemed for a time to be satisfied, and light and camera became my brush and palette.

Immersed in my studies at the Photography Institute, I was daydreaming of the time when I would have an important place behind the cameras of Hollywood, the gilded Wonderland of make-believe. I think I was fairly sure that I would know exactly how to photograph Greta Garbo, Barbara Stanwyck, and Bette Davis. My preoccupation with the motion picture industry was so great at the time, I can even now recall the Academy Award winners for that year: Ingrid Bergman in *Gaslight* and Bing Crosby in *Going My* Way.

Involved with these new interests and my high-school work, I was able to push the perplexing thoughts of Tom Chaney into the background and the confusion about my place in the world seemed to be resolving itself slightly. My euphoria was short-lived, however.

I received a letter from Tom telling me that he had joined the navy and, after his boot training, would be sent to the South Pacific. Reading that letter, I remember being overwhelmed by the revelation that, despite earlier denials, I was in love with him. I was also filled with a consuming fear that he would be facing unknown danger, maybe even death. Here was something—a forbidden emotion—of which I had to feel ashamed, and it was abhorrent to me. I couldn't discuss it with anyone, not even my beloved Grandma Jorgensen and, certainly, I knew I would never mention it to Tom. With an accompanying stab of guilt, I added this sorrowful secret to the already large burden of my inability to cope with life.

Throughout Tom's boot training, however, I wrote to him regularly, never expressing any feelings other than friendship. When he was finally sent to the South Pacific, I admitted an ugly thought and one which undoubtedly served to increase my feeling of guilt. If he never returned, I would be free from a bond that could never know fulfillment, only sorrow. If he were to die, there would be no conflict, and I could continue to live in a world of fantasy, in which our love was not only perfect, but possible.

I remembered a passage from Daphne du Maurier's novel, *Rebecca,* which had so impressed me that I jotted it down in a small, ruled notebook that is still in my possession. "If only there were an invention that bottled up a memory, like scent. And it never faded and it never got stale. And then, when one wanted it, the bottle could be uncorked, and it would be like living the moment all over again."

Accepting the existence of this new and terrifying love had left me emotionally drained and, again, it seemed that any salvation life had for me must come through my work. Having graduated from high school, I knew the time was approaching when I would have to look for a suitable place to begin.

By then, however, filled with an unreasonable sense of fear and insecurity, I looked for excuses to postpone the inevitable business of hunting for a job. Helping Mom with work around the house filled in some of the time before I had to go out and face the world.

During that period of indecision, I can recall standing on a table, scrubbing the kitchen walls, a radio playing music in the background. Suddenly the music was silenced and an announcer's voice said, "This is a bulletin. The White House has just announced that President Roosevelt is dead. The President died in Warm Springs, Georgia..." The following words were lost as I stood staring in disbelief. President Roosevelt was the only president I had ever remembered in the White House. When he came to office, I was seven years old and it was inconceivable to me that anyone else could occupy the presidency. His voice was almost as familiar to me as my Dad's. It was my first encounter with death and I can remember the shocking impact of that April 12, 1945.

Within two months, I was to know the death of someone much closer to me. On May 30, 1945, my nineteenth birthday, my Aunt Esther, Dad's oldest sister, suffered a cerebral hemorrhage and died. I remember that Dad and I threw coats over our pajamas and drove quickly to Grandma's home. She was sitting in the living room and for the first and last time, I saw her hands lying inactive in her lap. "I know," she said quietly. "Esther is gone," and she went to her room and closed the door. Even though she had just lost her oldest daughter, Grandma had found it impossible to cry. Years before, she had told me, "Crying can be a wonderful outlet, but somehow when I am deeply hurt, I can't cry. I wish I could." Because I didn't know how to go about consoling her, I felt strangely inadequate, especially as Grandma had always been such a great comfort to me.

On May 7, 1945, less than a month after the death of President Roosevelt, the war in Europe ended. V-E Day was one of wild excitement. I remember taking the subway to Times Square, where thousands of people milled around in a mad kind of revelry and it was like five New Year's Eves wrapped into one.

The jubilation didn't put an end to my personal problems, however, for I was still faced with the need to find a job. Once again, Mom came to the rescue with the suggestion that I approach Larry and June Jensen, both of whom were members of the Danish-American Beach Club and longtime friends of the Jorgensens. I remember them as a happy couple, envied for their seemingly perfect marital relationship. They enjoyed a common interest in sailing and both held responsible positions at RKO. Larry, as an engineer, maintained the film-developing machines and June was a film editor. The interview that the Jensens arranged netted me a job in the library cutting department at RKO-Pathé News in Manhattan.

I set out to take my place in the business world with the ever-increasing knowledge that I had been a miserable misfit for the previous eighteen years, and though a ray of happiness was present in the fact that I had a job in the field I'd chosen, I had little hope that the future would resolve my, by then, serious emotional problems.

CHAPTER 5

When I went to work for Pathé News in the spring of 1945, I tried to accept the bewildering responsibilities of a grown person that were then thrust upon me.

I wondered if my new associates would notice what I had long since known: that I was one who deviated, emotionally, from what had been termed "normal." But I was determined to behave like a man, even if I didn't feel like one, and try to hide the pretense behind a brave exterior. When someone in the cutting room questioned me about my successes on dates with girls, I learned to hand out an acceptable line, though I'd never had a date with a girl.

Undoubtedly, at the time, I must have had an exaggerated idea of other people's concepts of masculine and feminine behavior. Most people aren't aware of the inner turmoils of others, and unless the feminine male is totally without self-control, it isn't difficult for him to put on an acceptable front in public. But my own conception of the difference in behavior was definite and total and I was too immature to see the shades of gray that lie in between.

Within the protective framework of my job, however, I felt fairly secure, almost happy. Every film company has a library which contains all of their films and each scene has to be catalogued for possible future use. If, for example, a filmmaker needed footage of a horse coming over a hill, an erupting volcano, or a herd of stampeding cattle, we could produce those scenes from the vault, through a system of cross-indexed files. These were called "stock shots." In addition to my work in the stock library, I spliced the title film of the Pathé Rooster on to the beginning of the newsreels. I remember that the famous Pathé News trademark was affectionately called "The Chicken."

I can only wonder how my life would have progressed if, one October morning in 1945, I had not received the special "Greetings from the President." I had already been rejected by the army twice during the active fighting years because I was underweight. I didn't tell Mom and Dad about the third call, because I didn't want another rejection to make them feel that their son, something of a nineteen-year-old social recluse, was also a physical misfit. Dad and I had joined the Army Air Force Command as volunteer observers with the Aircraft Warning Service. I'd also tried to join the Red Cross as an ambulance driver, but had dropped the idea when I found that uniforms and other expenses were too heavy for my budget.

Once having reported, I thought I'd be back at Pathé News the next day.

It was a gray morning when I joined hundreds of other draftees for my physical examination at Grand Central Palace in Manhattan. I was rushed shivering through the routine of being weighed, measured, thumped, and stethescoped, in rapid succession. My eyes, ears, nose, and throat were examined, and after answering a few cursory questions, my papers were thrust back at me with the word ACCEPTED stamped across them in bold letters.

Many thoughts stuttered through my mind as I stood confused and more than a little shocked. I was "in"!

Parenthetically, some members of the press, who at one time or another were skeptical or unwilling to accept the truth, were to make much of the fact that I passed all of the pre-induction tests without the examiners questioning my maleness. The fact that I weighed less than a hundred pounds and was physically and sexually underdeveloped might have seemed significant, were it not for the fact that late development is not an uncommon occurrence. The army medical men had no doubt become accustomed to examining many such cases, with the apt thought: "The army will make men out of them." In most of these cases, the results justified the prognosis.

The war had ended and the great need of the armed forces, at that time, was for clerical help to go about the enormous job of disbanding those numberless forces. Many men were inducted during that period who were not perfect physical specimens. Besides, there was a popular cliché of the time, that if you could see lightning and hear thunder, they'd take you, regardless. On the third try, I managed both.

When the examining psychiatrist asked me, "Do you like girls?" I knew, as did every other draftee, that the question was designed to weed out the men with homosexual proclivities. Therefore, I answered simply, "Yes."

I wanted to be accepted by the army for two reasons. Foremost was my great desire to belong, to be needed, and to join the stream of activities around me like the other young people of my acquaintance who were contributing to the times. Second, I wanted my parents to be proud of me and to be able to say, "My son is also in the service." Although they never mentioned it, I was poignantly aware that Mom and Dad must have felt their child was "different" and, therefore, unwanted.

At any rate, I was proud of my acceptance papers. When I returned to Pathé News the next morning, it was to announce that I was no longer a civilian but was now a piece of government property with a number, 42259077. I had become a GI.

Two weeks later, along with many other inductees, I was at Fort Hamilton, New Jersey, anxiously wondering where I would be sent from there. I wore an ill-fitting uniform and was subjected to the multiple shots with which the army was presenting each new draftee. I had always had a great curiosity about medical procedures and I didn't expect to mind the experience much. A two hundred ten pound man in front of me fell fainting to the floor after a triple-typhoid injection, while ninety-eight pound Jorgensen moved on, apparently unaffected by the shots. I thought it was pretty funny, but my humor was short-lived when I found myself in the hospital the following morning, alternating between chills and fever, a delayed, though purely physical, reaction to the shots.

Though my contribution became a necessary and possibly important one, I've always felt that my army service was nothing to boast about. I didn't fire a single shot in combat or pilot a fighter plane or parachute down behind enemy lines. My job in the army was strictly a clerical one, and it began after a brief journey to the Separation Center at Fort Dix, New Jersey.

When the fighting in Europe ended in June of 1945, there loomed the great task of separating veterans from the services and returning them to civilian life. I was one of the many who were assigned to the job of helping discharge four thousand of these men a day. My specific duties involved sifting thousands of manila envelopes, sorting the records they contained, and checking the myriad details in connection with each discharge.

On November 2, 1945, less than a month after my induction, I received my one and only promotion and became Private First Class.

As the numbers of returning troops mounted, it seemed to me that the working days approximated twenty-four hours each, hours in which I had no opportunity to retire into my own private world. For the first time in my life, I was forced to live and work continually in close association with young men and women of my own age.

I couldn't help comparing myself with the boys in my group and I was aware that the differences were very great indeed, both mental and physical. My body was not only slight, but it lacked other development usual in a male. I had no hair on my chest, arms, or legs. My walk could scarcely be called a masculine stride, the gestures of my hands were effeminate and my voice also had a feminine quality. The sex organs that determined my classification as "male" were underdeveloped.

It was, of course, quite possible that some men having the same physical build would feel completely masculine, but my mental and emotional chemistry matched all the physical characteristics which in me seemed so feminine. "What is masculine and what is feminine?" I thought. The question plagued me because I couldn't find a clearly established dividing line.

After the first hectic months of discharging shiploads of battle-weary GIs had slowed down to a normal routine, we received passes to leave the base on weekends and every evening after work. Most of my fellow workers were men with average hopes and desires, several of them married and with families. The greatest number of my acquaintances simply did their job, went home for weekends when distance permitted, and waited for the eventual discharge from the service. A few GIs in my barracks, however, left the base at every opportunity, to "girl-chase," returning with lurid tales of their sexual prowess in these adventures. I tried to keep out of the way during these discussions because I felt embarrassed by them and could in no way share their enthusiasms.

During the week, I spent much of my free time in the library or at a movie and usually ended up at the USO Center, which had an extensive collection of classical recordings. It was the beginning of a lifelong friendship with music.

On weekends, however, I went quietly home to my photography or a good book—close enough to my family in the Bronx, fortunately, to make the trip possible. Of course, there were letters I wrote to Tom, but they were part of a secret dream world.

However, during the busy weekdays at Fort Dix, I had little time to indulge in that dream world. When Topic A: "women," was not the subject of discussion, I found that each of these men, whom I'd expected to be average and untroubled, had his own adjustments to make. These had to do, mainly, with separation from friends and family and, surprisingly to me, they were willing to bring their numerous problems out into the open and discuss them freely. It was a new experience for me. The idea that other people had problems was a revelation, for within my private world, I thought I was the only troubled one.

In order to preoccupy myself even more, I took an after-hours job in the post library and, once again, books became the center of my small, detached universe.

One day, on a weekend pass, I remember I was poring over a book in the living room at home, when I was brought back to reality by the sharp, insistent ring of the telephone. It was Tom Chaney's voice. "Hello, I'm back," he said casually.

Somehow, I managed to stammer, "Where are you?"

"I'm in New York at the Commodore Hotel," he said. "Come on down and have dinner and then we'll spend the evening on the town."

"Wonderful," I said, but wonderful was an inadequate word when applied to the excitement I felt at the prospect of seeing my special friend after two years of separation and the exchange of many letters—letters in which no word of my emotions had been expressed.

I remember that the hours of the afternoon seemed to creep by while I waited for the reunion with Tom. I'd already taken a stand in my own mind, by then. I knew, conclusively, that I could never give myself totally to love and affection for another man.

During the months in service, I had seen a few practicing homosexuals, those whom the other men called "queer." I couldn't condemn them, but I also knew that I certainly couldn't become like them. It was a thing deeply alien to my religious attitudes and the highly magnified and immature moralistic views that I entertained at the time. Furthermore, I had seen enough to know that homosexuality brought with it a social segregation and ostracism that I couldn't add to my own deep feeling of not belonging.

Late that afternoon, I entered the lobby of the hotel and stopped at one of the house phones to announce myself. The elevator ride seemed endless, but finally I stepped out at the designated floor and saw Tom waiting in the doorway. The memory of that meeting is still fresh and vivid. He was taller than I had remembered and with some extra weight he looked vigorous and healthy. He extended his hand and said, "How are you, George?" For a split second, I thought he was going to embrace me, but the moment passed and I realized that it was only my own desire that had led to the delusion.

When we were settled, I sat still, looking at him. It seemed inconceivable that there were only four years' difference between us. He had a muscular, rugged physique and a strong, tanned face, while I was slim and pale with a hairless, peaches-and-cream complexion. As I sat there watching him, I remember trying to call the things I was feeling toward him by other names: friendship, affection, fondness. But I knew it was none of these, or perhaps a combination of them all and beyond that, I knew it was love. The truth of that fact could not be rejected or denied.

Tom's voice interrupted these thoughts. "Hey, are you in a daze or something? Come on, this is my first evening back in New York!"

"I was just thinking how long it had been since we sat and talked together," I answered, in an attempt to be lighthearted. The moment of awkwardness was over and we talked easily of other things, punctuated by "whatever-happened-to?" and "do-you-remember-when?"

However, fearful of betraying myself, I began to wind down at dinner. I sat silently toying with my food, painfully aware of my untenable situation. As long as Tom had been gone, I was free to fantasize and believe that when he returned, he'd be returning to me. But I had dreamed the impossible and I knew it could never come true.

The evening limped closer to an end and I knew that I would have to destroy the thing that I had allowed to develop within me, that I must be strong enough to let the desire slip into the past. Plans for an extended night on the town having faded by mutual consent, we walked slowly back to the hotel and I turned to him in a gesture of farewell. "It was great seeing you again," I said.

"It was fun, wasn't it? Come on up to the country, George, and visit us sometime soon."

"Yes, I will, soon," I said lightly, trying to keep conviction in my voice.

When I reached home that night, I took a small gray strong box from a drawer in my room and went down to the basement. I opened the furnace door, sat down in front of it, and unlocked the box. Most of the happy moments of the past few years, all there ever was and all there ever could be of my relationship with Tom, were contained in that small chest. I read each letter, looked at each picture and matchbook cover, recreating the times when I had acquired the mementos that had built that small, wretched collection of memories. One by one, I threw them into the fire.

Sitting there, in the light of the diminishing flames, I knew that I was running—running from a situation that could have destroyed me.

To me at the time, it was another example of the strange, infernal limbo in which I was living. Emotionally, the strings were stretched taut and I awaited a miracle to release me from the growing horror of myself.

I didn't see Tom Chaney again until ten years later, in 1956, after I had been the subject of an inordinate amount of newspaper print. At his invitation, I visited his home. He had married and was the father of two children. He met me at the door and said, "Hello, Chris, welcome to our home," as he leaned forward and kissed me on the cheek. My thoughts went back to our last reunion and the moment, ten years before, when I thought, or hoped, he was going to embrace me. Then, it would have been the culmination of a dream, but this time it was merely the greeting of an old friend.

"Hello, Tom, you don't seem to have changed very much," I said, though gray had begun to creep into his hair and a few lines that I didn't remember had formed around his eyes.

"You've changed a great deal," he said with a smile, "but I think I understand you, now. I didn't understand you before, you know."

I knew then that he had never been aware of my emotional attachment to him and though that attachment had long since ceased to exist, I still held him in warm regard. I don't believe that I could stop loving someone without retaining some sort of fondness for him. He was, by then, a part of my past, but I know he will always own that small part of me which I gave to him and which he did not know existed.

It is fortunate that the weeks following Tom Chaney's return from the navy were busy ones for me, and I was plunged again into my work at Fort Dix. After spending almost a year there, I learned that a discharge from the army wasn't possible without going through basic training, something I hadn't been required to experience up to that time.

Along with a group of men from my unit, I was sent to Camp Polk, Louisiana, in August of 1946. As one of the clerical personnel at Fort Dix, I not only had never shot a gun, I hadn't even seen one. That's when a whole new world of experience opened up before me.

It was at Camp Polk, located a few miles from Shreveport, Louisiana, under the pressure of endurance tests such as marching, drilling, and other more rigorous activities, that I again realized my physical insufficiencies in the world of men. My comrades took the strenuous daily routine in stride, but each night I fell into bed half sick with exhaustion, already dreading the moment when the bugle would blow and I'd be forced to drag myself to attention again.

Target practice with a carbine ceased to be a problem of accuracy—for me, it became a challenge in weight lifting.

The oppressive heat, humidity, and ever-attentive mosquitoes made life increasingly unbearable. My "fatigues," drenched in sweat, weighed almost as much as I did as my weight continued to go down to an alarming ninety-three pounds.

By sheer force of will, I progressed satisfactorily enough, until a dummy in human form was placed on the shooting range as a target. I rebelled and couldn't bring myself to shoot at it. I was faced with the stark reality that it wasn't just a game and that some day I might be called upon to use a human being as a target. One of my friends shot my rounds of ammunition, for which I got credit. His favor didn't net me a marksman's medal, but at least I passed the tests.

Fortunately, in the final weeks at Camp Polk there was more opportunity to escape the rigors of training because of over-crowded conditions. I was grateful for that.

Rumors spread that we were to be sent to Japan as occupation troops. The chance for travel was certainly inviting, but I knew that being so completely separated from home ties would only serve to increase my loneliness.

One day, along with several others, I heard my name bawled out over the loudspeaker that sometimes summoned lowly privates into the presence of the Commanding Officer. The C.O. told us that a telegram from the War Department had ordered our immediate return to our former clerical jobs at Fort Dix, and a few days later, I was back in New Jersey. The chill November weather was a shock after the hot, sultry climate in the South and I developed bronchitis, and then pneumonia. My tour of duty was transferred to the Tilden General Hospital at Fort Dix.

During my recuperative period, the doctors admitted the possibility that I might have TB, but after weeks of x-rays and examinations, the suspicion was dismissed. Perhaps some added weight and a tougher constitution would have given me more resistance to the illness and hastened my recuperation.

Rumors again began to filter through the base that the postwar drafted clerical workers would soon be discharged, and I began to contemplate some plans for that happy eventuality.

In the meantime, I continued my analysis of the differences between me and the army friends I had come to know and like. They spoke with excited anticipation of marriage and raising a family and I, so emotionally converse, wondered if it wasn't time to creep even further into my protective shell. At the same time, I knew such action was impossible and unrealistic.

At least, I thought, I had progressed far enough to want to face my problems honestly and in a constructive way. But just what were those problems? I restated them squarely to myself. I was underdeveloped physically and sexually. I was extremely effeminate. My emotions were either those of a woman or a homosexual. I believed my thoughts and responses were more often womanly than manly. But at that point, I was completely unaware of the many variations and combinations of masculinity and femininity, aside from homosexuality, that exist side by side in the world.

I was honorably discharged from the United States Army on December 5, 1946, after fourteen months of service. The final official statement on the discharge papers read, "Recommended for further military training." My immediate response to that was one which may not have been original but it was certainly sincere: "They'll have to catch me first!"

CHAPTER 6

I returned home from my army service in 1946 with some trepidation, for I knew that I would soon have to face the realities and adjustments of civilian life, including the problem of finding a regular job.

My wallet was bulging with mustering-out pay, but my confidence was somewhat slimmer than my bankroll. I felt I was suffocating under the same old dilemmas. By then, these confusions had been reduced to a few vital and recurring questions in my mind. "I am twenty years old, but what am I?' "Why am I this way?" "What can I do about it?"

On the day that I finally got up enough courage to head for RKO-Pathé News, I remember trying to pump myself full of assurances. I was on my way to ask for my old job back in the cutting library, and as I walked down Madison Avenue in Manhattan, I kept telling myself that it was as simple as opening my own front door and saying, "Hi, Mom."

My appointment was with one of the vice-presidents, and I squared my shoulders in a gesture of confidence, as I gave my name to the receptionist. A few minutes later, the executive was kind but firm, when he told me that my employment at RKO had been only temporary; the job was no longer available and he wished me success elsewhere.

A wave of humiliation swept over me and I wondered if he had seen what I felt about myself, that I was plainly a misfit. There seemed to be a kind of dread finality in the click of the door as it closed behind me. I went home, too discouraged to think clearly, and shut myself in my room. I knew it was no use, convinced that I just didn't have what it took. Worst of all, I felt Mom and Dad were ashamed of me and that made me feel even more desolate and properly sorry for myself.

A knock at the door interrupted that little moment of self-indulgence. It was Mom and, as always, she gave me encouragement and some good advice, suggesting that I approach Larry Jensen again. He and June had helped me before, and although they were by then divorced and June was in Hollywood, Mom was sure that Larry would do everything he could in New York.

As usual, Mom was right. Through Larry's intercession, I was given a job as a chauffeur for the RKO Studios in New York City.

Days, weeks, and months passed in a humdrum fashion, as I drove producers, actors, and other VIPs to their various destinations.

I must admit the feeling of envy on that job. I now realize that I envied not the wealth or prestige of my passengers, but their ability to advance in their chosen fields while I did nothing more than sit behind the wheel of a limousine because I lacked the courage to do anything else.

One afternoon, an inner urge must have sparked my nerve and I spoke to the film executive who was my sole passenger, with what I hoped was the proper amount of deference.

"I've studied professional photography and I believe that I have some talent for it. What chance do you suppose I'd have of getting a job in Hollywood?"

"Too many stragglers out there now!"

I gulped and felt my ears grow red at the thought of my own temerity. "Oh, I'd be willing to start as an apprentice," I said.

"Yeah? That's what they all say!"

I knew the subject was closed. The incident may have been insignificant to my dour passenger, but to me it seemed like a major catastrophe. That night, I chain-smoked until dawn and struggled with the problem of what to do next. I knew I couldn't be a chauffeur all my life and other steps had to be taken if I wasn't going to remain one.

Larry Jensen had helped me thus far, but June was in Hollywood editing films, and that shining wonderland was still the object of my hopes. One day, on impulse, I wrote June a brief inquiry, knowing that she would be honest with me. "What are my chances of getting into the photographic end of the film industry?" I asked. At last I had taken a positive step on my own initiative.

Each morning after that, I looked nonchalantly in the mailbox, pretending to myself that I wasn't at all anxious for a reply, but on the day June's letter finally arrived, I was excited and apprehensive when I tore at the stubborn envelope.

"Hollywood is big enough for both of us," she wrote, "come on out and give it a try."

I was elated but I had to keep on with the tedious driving job for a time, until I could build my small savings to the goal I had set of five hundred dollars, a sum that was a small fortune to me.

I remember the chill autumn day in 1947 when I took my bags and photography portfolios and, accompanied by Mom, arrived at the Greyhound station in Manhattan. I'd said goodbye to Dad and Dolly earlier, and I knew that Mom was equally unhappy to see me leave. Although she never tried to discourage my move to Hollywood, she kept hinting that "work was the same wherever you go." I realize now some of the things she must have felt: that while I was home in New York, possibly she could soften the blows that life would deal in my direction. But she also knew that if I didn't try my wings then, I might never make the attempt, so, regretfully, she pushed me out of the nest and headed me toward the new world of Hollywood.

When the bus departed, I had mixed feelings of elation and despair. I was grateful that the little old lady who occupied the seat beside me was more inclined to doze than talk, for I had before me what I hoped would be five uninterrupted days in which to think and make plans for a new life. It was only a temporary lull, however, for she proved to be an extremely voluble companion. Her running commentary on the scenery was followed by detailed accounts of the folks she was going to visit on the West Coast and how much she looked forward to the cross-country trip. As I recall, I think there was even a cake recipe thrown in. Finally, I managed to sneak in an observation. "You must have a lot of stamina to make a long trip like this," I said. "I expect to be pretty weary myself when we get there, but you're just a frail little lady."

"Well," she replied brightly, "you look real frail yourself, what with your pale, girlish looks and all. If you're weary, I guess it'll be because you're so delicate."

That comment, made in the kindliest way, brought back all the old doubts and fears. If she spotted my feminine appearance so easily, I was sure the other passengers had, too. I shrank within myself, hoping that no one would notice me. Slowly, I remember becoming aware of the hum of the bus tires on the highway pavement. They seemed to repeat an endless refrain, and I found I couldn't shut it out of my consciousness. "You can escape...you can escape...from everything...but not yourself!"

I recall the grueling miles passing one after the other, and in spite of a certain self-imposed detachment, I looked forward to our arrival at the Grand Canyon. Other passengers formed in groups as they alighted from the bus, but I stood alone on the edge of the cliffs, looking into the bottomless chasms below. The image of that first overpowering sight is still with me.

Without warning, the scene blurred and I felt a strange dizziness, then almost immediately, a friendly touch on my arm. It was one of the park guards who had, apparently, been watching me.

"I'm sorry," I said. "For some reason, I suddenly felt dizzy."

"Well, now, that's not uncommon," he said. "The Canyon has a hypnotic effect on some people. That's why I'm here, to see that nobody falls over the edge."

I turned to look more closely at the man beside me. He was elderly, with steel-gray hair and moustache and wise, kindly eyes.

"It's so..." I said, unable to finish.

"Powerful," the old man added. "Yep, it gets under your skin. I've been here thirty years and I've never got used to the feeling yet."

For a moment, he seemed almost like a harbinger of something yet to come. I wanted to articulate my thoughts, for I could feel his empathy, but all I could do was nod in mute agreement.

I looked into the vastness again and watched the colors change with the movement of the sun: red, then coral, and finally, slowly undulating into a thousand variated shades of lavender and purple.

Slowly, one thought separated itself from the others in my mind, at first ephemeral and then a consciously formed idea. "I am looking at the work of God," I thought, "but am I not a work of God, too?" Suddenly, I wanted to stay longer, to savor more of that sublime spectacle and to give myself time to understand the new horizon in my mind that had shown itself, however vaguely.

The bus departed without me and I stayed on for several days at the nearby Bright Angel Lodge, a name that might have seemed prophetic. I visited the Canyon again and again and the breathless enormity of it seemed to open the way for me to a new concept—the awareness and imprint of a greater power. I seemed so small, so frighteningly infinitesimal by comparison to the great expanse of God and Nature. My problems, for a time, seemed to recede and I was becoming aware that I was no longer the center of the universe. Undoubtedly, a change of view was taking place and I regard it, even now, as a turning point in my life.

I would like to return sometime and see if the Canyon would have the same effect on me. I'm certain that it would inspire me as it did then, but since I have come such a long way from that frightening, insecure period in my life, I think I would probably have a greater sense of unity with, rather than of contrast to, so gigantic a spectacle. Then, my feelings of inferiority made me relegate myself to the borders of nothingness but today I believe I would stand erect in the knowledge that I am one with a creative force.

I remember that though I was overwhelmed at the time by these new thoughts and ideas, I also felt a kind of tranquillity I hadn't felt before. Refreshed and somehow renewed, I continued my journey to Hollywood.

I had sent a card to June telling her of the delay, so I wasn't surprised to see her standing in the crowd at the Hollywood bus depot. There she was, my oasis on the West Coast, straining to catch a glimpse of me. We greeted each other excitedly and then drove through brilliant sunshine and palm-lined streets studded with small stucco houses. The sunshine, the palm trees, and the knowledge that I was at last in the very center of the photographer's dream world, made me feel that I had finally reached Mecca.

We arrived at a squat, Spanish-type house, located a short distance from the Paramount Studios in the heart of Hollywood. It was June's home, where she occupied a furnished room with kitchen privileges, and at her urging, the elderly owners showed me another room they were willing to rent.

It was a small room that looked as though it might have been an afterthought, but two of the walls were composed of windows that looked out on a small and untidily overgrown patio. The sunlight streamed through the windows and the room was warm and cozy— almost too cozy, for the bed took up most of the floor space. Happily, I delved into my wallet to pay the first month's rent and asked that I be permitted the use of the patio, a luxury to an old New Yorker. The owners agreed, with startled expressions. The patio had certainly been neglected and I'm sure they were thinking, "Who would want it?" but already I had made plans in my mind for a lush loafing spot where I could spend my leisure hours in semitropical splendor.

Finally settled over a cup of tea, June and I talked endlessly of home, my aspirations, and of her own struggles in Hollywood. Tom Chaney and the world I had left were far behind me. "I think I've found the place where I belong," I thought, contentedly.

When June left for her studio job early the next morning, I was out buying soap, paint, and cleaning agents, determined to transform the patio into the haven I had imagined. When she returned from work that afternoon and had admired my labors, she disappeared into the kitchen for sandwiches and beer, and I dropped wearily into a chair to survey my handiwork.

"Thanks," I said, accepting a plate. "Now, this afternoon we'll start on the furniture and the flower boxes, and then in the morning, I'll…"

"George!" From her serious look, I knew it was no time to discuss my plans for further improvements. "You came out here to look for a job as a motion-picture photographer, not a landscape artist! You're afraid to start looking for a job. You're like the writer who sits around sharpening pencils because he dreads facing the first blank page. Well, I won't let you do that, so forget it!"

"Okay," I agreed quietly. "Tomorrow, I'll start on the rounds of the studios," but the cold chill that had always accompanied the thought of asking anyone for a job returned. We discussed two or three possibilities, prospects which I knew I'd have to face the next day. Only then, did June allow me to return to my ideas for renovating the patio.

My first attempts at job hunting in Hollywood were painfully unsuccessful ones. It seemed to me that I was merely repeating the same pattern of failure that I had known at home. The only difference was three thousand miles of American geography.

When the patio was finished a week later, June and I celebrated with a cocktail party. Our only guest, uninvited, was a large black cat named "Babette," who came seeking sanctuary from an aggressive neighborhood hound. Though we were comfortable in each other's company, it seemed a rather limited party, and we decided that we should meet some new people and try to have a more active social life.

With that in mind, I looked for the name and address which had been given to me by an acquaintance from RKO in New York. "Tony Romano," as I'll call him, was a man in the Hollywood film colony. The day after our patio celebration, I telephoned Romano, who immediately invited me to his apartment for a drink, with a considerable show of enthusiastic welcome. I arrived at the appointed time to find him in a modern, "arty" apartment. My host was smooth and handsome and I thought his manner insinuating when he handed me a skillfully blended martini.

"Why didn't you call me sooner?" he asked. "Where are you living? Maybe we can arrange something here."

"Oh, I'm—I'm very comfortable," I stammered.

"There are a lot of us out here," he continued. "You've got to meet the crowd." He seemed unaware of my discomfort and embarrassment and suggested another drink, while I floundered in small talk. He mixed a second drink, offered it to me and let one hand rest provocatively on my shoulder. "You know, George, you and I are going to get along just fine together!"

Though I was startled by that sudden intimacy, I knew immediately that I was being confronted by a homosexual and, even more startling, that he considered me one, too. For the first time to my knowledge, I had been classified openly.

I stifled an impulse to throw the drink in his face. Instead, I raised my glass and using the Danish salute, I politely said, *"Skoal."* As soon as I could, I made my excuses and left.

Even now, I can remember that I was appalled and disgusted at his behavior, and I may even have known a moment of fear—a fear of homosexual contact that was probably based on the hidden belief that I, too, deviated from what was termed "normal."

I vowed never to allow myself to be placed in that position again and slowly I made my way home to June. I had hoped to tell her that I'd made at least one new friend in Hollywood, but I couldn't bring myself to say anything about the unpleasant encounter.

After dredging up sufficient courage a few days later, I presented myself at the awesome offices of RKO Studios. "I recently worked for Frederick Ullman in New York," I told the receptionist, "and I'd like to see Dore Schary." By her answering smile, she seemed to assume that Mr. Ullman, the President of Pathé News, and I were old friends. Actually, he had nodded to me in the hall a few times, but I was sure he didn't even know my name. Much to my surprise, a few minutes later, I was ushered into the inner sanctum. "What will I say?" I thought, in momentary panic.

Smiling, Mr. Schary rose from his desk as I entered the elegant office and held out his hand. "Hello," he said. "I understand you're a friend of Fred Ullman's. I'm glad to see you. How's Fred?" Friendliness seemed to fill the room and my nervousness abated somewhat as I took a deep breath.

"Well, to be honest," I said, "I don't really know Mr. Ullman, personally. I worked for RKO-Pathé News in New York, then I was drafted and when I got back my job was gone. Now that I'm in California, I thought perhaps you'd have something for me." The truth poured out like an overflowing well.

Mr. Schary's smile faded and he replied, "Well, we're pretty well fixed on the staff right now, but if you'd leave your name and address with the secretary..." The phrase had a familiar ring.

I bitterly wished I hadn't started talking like a fool, that I'd said Mr. Ullman was just fine and of course I knew him well. I told the truth, but did I have to tell all of it, I wondered?

I left the office with my large photo portfolio under my arm, unopened.

Today, I realize that Mr. Schary must have been bombarded many times over the years by aspiring young actors, starlets, photographers, and any number of other people, all wanting something. I certainly had not been singled out for rejection. I simply must have been one of many who sought favors, and though it was terribly important to me at the time, it was no doubt a passing moment to him.

Depressed at what I felt was another failure, I went home to my small, comfortable room and took out a ruled pocket notebook in which I had frequently jotted down quotations as well as my own thoughts and ideas. Thoughtfully, I began to write what hardly could be called immortal poetry, but what pretty well reflected my state of mind at the time:

I think as I look at the foamy white clouds
How wonderful it would be to live among them
And to have their protecting films as shelter
To float along through eternity,
Never to have the stress and turmoil of the earth disrupt my life.

Always to be detached from the earth's pulling forces
Just to be alone with the elements.
The elements—the one thing human minds can't control
Always moving as they like.

I was running low on money and had no job because I didn't know how to look for one, and the old fears jumped to the front when I thought of asking a stranger. To me, the importance of money was survival, not wealth. The idea of my present survival and thoughts of Tom and the past seemed to envelop me. "I'm a loser at everything," I thought, in a flood of self-pity, and I turned to a fresh page in the small notebook.

The lost soul whose heart reaches out to grasp love
While his arms were forced through precedent to hang lifeless
Whose very soul cries out to a love that cannot be returned
Where can a substitute, a partial relief be found?
How can a futureless life go on? Yet, it does.
Year after year, the body lives, while the soul dies.

Once more, necessity prodded me into action. I went to the unemployment insurance office and joined the line of ex-servicemen in the "52-20 Club," a vernacular term for the government unemployment rehabilitation program, by which veterans received twenty dollars a week for fifty-two weeks. For me, at that time, it was a humiliating procedure.

The day of my insurance application, I returned home, put away the photo samples in a closet, firmly closed the door on them and decided to have a brief vacation from the ceaseless office-to-office search.

I felt listless and tired and probably very sorry for myself, when June bounded into the house in irrepressible spirits. We had become more like two sisters, threatened with spinsterhood, than a young man and woman starved for outside companionship.

"I've made a decision," she announced grandly. "We just can't sit here like two sticks, out on the patio every evening. I'm tired of having you cry on my shoulder and I'm sure you're equally tired of me. What we now have to do is meet some other people, have more social life. We're going to join the Hollywood Athletic Club!"

Since I felt anything but athletic at that moment, I laughed. "That's a great idea," I said, "but how do we get through the front door?"

"Don't be a kill-joy, George. A friend at work belongs to the club and he said I could contact his father who lives there, Colonel

H. T. James. The club has a smörgåsbord every week, and we're going tomorrow night!"

"Well, a couple of Danish square-heads like us should fit nicely at a smörgåsbord!" Rapidly, I fell in with her spirit of excitement and I knew that she was trying to pull me out of my emotional doldrums.

When June and I arrived at the Athletic Club the following evening, Colonel James invited us to join him. I remember him as a charming, dapper old gentleman, jauntily sporting a cane and spats who, without waiting for the amenities, immediately confessed his age as ninety-eight. He was an amusing companion and shared with us many fascinating stories from his adventurous life. I recall one in particular that impressed me at the time.

"Lost my first fortune in the San Francisco earthquake in nineteen-ought-six," he announced, with a casual air that stunned me. "I was in Oakland at the time it hit and my wife was in San Francisco, so I hired a rowboat and somehow made it across the bay. The house was destroyed, but my wife got out all right. I owned a paint factory and that went up in flames, too." He smiled wickedly. "Well, there was nothing much left, so I picked up stakes and came down to Hollywood. That was still the silent days in movies, of course, and the 'flickers' did pretty well for the next few years, but then they hit a bad slump." The Colonel laughed and leaned back in his chair. "Warner Brothers' Studio was on the verge of bankruptcy and they offered me a quarter interest for twenty-five thousand dollars. Well, naturally, I figured that to be a pretty bad investment at the time, so I refused. A couple of months later, they released *The Jazz Singer* with Al Jolson, the first talking picture, and you know what happened after that!" The old man laughed and slapped his thigh. "I sure missed the boat that time!"

I listened to these stories of defeat and failure taken so lightly and with such good humor, and was struck by a new attitude. "Why should I accept defeat any more than the Colonel did?" I thought. When tragedy destroyed his home and business, he didn't settle down in the ashes and moan about it, he sought a solution. It slowly registered in my mind as an object-lesson and I would not soon forget it.

In my own case, I knew my tragedies were emotional and physical, and though I had earnestly tried to understand these conditions, I had never done anything positive about them. I had tried to compensate for my insufficiencies by withdrawing into a protective world of unreality. I had never asked aid from my friends, because the idea of discussing the problems openly had always been unthinkable. Beyond that, I had never sought professional help. Not even knowing if there was one or not, I had never sought a cure. I knew I must contemplate that as an eventual step and no matter how painful, I meant to take it.

CHAPTER 7

Sometime during that period in Hollywood, Helen Johnson, a school friend of June's, arrived in California from Denmark for a visit. She was a petite young woman with reddish hair and a lively, professional interest in dancing, for she operated a dancing school in Copenhagen. Helen was an enviably accomplished person who spoke and wrote five languages fluently, played the piano well, and was knowledgeable in the subjects of art and literature. I admired these abilities and immediately responded to her outgoing nature.

In the atmosphere of openness and warmth that June and Helen generated together, I began to wonder vaguely if I could discuss my uncertainties with them. They both had been brought up in Europe, where ordinarily censored subjects of conversation were more apt to be discussed free of personal inhibition.

At length, they discussed their marital problems in front of me, freely and objectively. June had divorced Larry Jensen. It was a hasty mistake, she felt, but it had grown into a full-blown explosion and by then divorce seemed to her the only solution. June had regretted her decision but it was too late to pick up the pieces of a broken marriage.

Helen, on the other hand, had made a marriage of convenience when she discovered that her father was about to lose his farm through a generous act of his own. He had signed a note for a friend who had failed to pay off the loan, and the bank had threatened to foreclose on Helen's father as the co-signer. Marriage to a prosperous man in the fabric business had saved the farm, and

Helen went to work for her husband. During the war and German occupation of Denmark, Helen's husband, Olaf, was afraid to carry home the day's receipts from his shop, so Helen put the money under her hat and blithely rode past the marauding Germans each day, on her bicycle.

My unemployed state was of great concern to both Helen and June, and the fact that I had been so unsuccessful was placed out in the open and examined thoroughly, though I always held back my deepest and most troublesome thoughts. As the weeks passed, our discussions broadened in scope and I slowly began to realize that whatever I might tell them in confidence would be accepted and handled in the same objective manner as any of the other delicate subjects we had covered.

Fortified by determination and the desire to take some step, no matter how small, I approached the girls one day on my "luxurious" patio. I uttered a brief and silent prayer that they would understand and made a faltering start. "I'd...like to...talk to you girls about something," I said. "It's—something terribly personal and I don't even know how to begin." I looked from one to the other and tried to stifle my embarrassment, but encouraged by their quiet receptiveness, I continued.

"Maybe you'll think I'm insane, but did either of you ever look at me and think that I might not be a man at all, but a...woman?"

The two girls were silent for a moment, then Helen made the first response. "But George, you're made like a man, aren't you?"

I nodded dumbly. June looked at me suspiciously and said, "Is that why you always try to hide your body? You never sunbathe here and you never go swimming."

"Yes," I admitted, hopelessly. "I have the physical characteristics of a very immature male, but as far back as I can remember, I've always had the feelings...the emotions of a girl."

"How do you mean?"

"Well, there are certain symbols the world has adopted that differentiate between the sexes almost from birth. You know, blue for boys and pink for girls, toy trains for boys and dolls for girls, and so on. I always wanted the things girls wanted, because somehow I felt they just naturally belonged to me. Gradually, of course, I had to accept the things that were forced on me."

"In other words," June interrupted, "you only did the things you had to do because they were expected."

"Yes, but my adolescent years were so mixed up…confused, and those confusions have continued; I just didn't know how to handle any of it." I felt that perhaps I wasn't making sense and maybe I was explaining it all badly, but once having taken the plunge, it didn't seem quite so painful to discuss it as I had thought.

"Well," Helen said, "there are a lot of effeminate men in the world, George. Maybe you're one of them."

"You mean a homosexual." I remember it came out as a statement, not a question, even though I flinched at using the word.

"Yes," June said. "I have to admit, George, that I've wondered about it myself. But all this time you've been in California, I've never seen you with another man. You've never brought any of your friends here and you were never away from the house long enough to be visiting elsewhere."

It must have been at that point that I related my experience with Tony Romano and confessed my shock and fear at being openly classified by an admitted homosexual. "I can't even think of a relationship like that with another man," I said. "Yet I have to admit I'm drawn to some men. I know I notice them, not as a man, but as a woman might. I just don't know what category to put myself in."

"Why put yourself in any category," Helen replied, "until you've seen a good doctor?" June agreed, at once.

The question struck me with considerable force. I knew my friends were talking sense and without any signs of shock or aversion. Some years later, I would know that Helen had reflected the attitudes of her homeland, Denmark, where sexual problems were accepted as a normal way of life for some people and not subject to legal or social persecution.

Not only had my growing desire to seek medical help been reinforced, but I had broken through a heretofore impregnable barrier. I was able, at last, to discuss my burdensome problems openly and release the terrifying frustrations of a lifetime. However, I did not at that time consult a doctor.

Within that period, except for membership in the "52-20 Club," which allowed me only a bare subsistence, I was totally without funds. As far as my photographic career in Hollywood was concerned, I had been refused with predictable regularity. I had studied all phases of the photographic field—portrait, commercial, motion picture, and color—and it was the latter that I found the most exciting. My portfolio fairly bulged with all kinds of pictures, including many landscapes and dramatic shots of New York City's famous landmarks. After some years spent in trying to perfect my techniques, I had yet to make a sale of my photos, or of myself as a photographer. However, I had developed, along the way, an acute eye for photographic subjects wherever they happened to be and I continued to take pictures for my own pleasure, if nobody else's.

I had no wish to rely on government aid for the remainder of the year, so I took a job in a chain grocery store, and spent day after day methodically stacking canned goods on display shelves. It was tedious work and my dreams of success behind a camera faded into a montage of Campbell's Soup labels.

One bright moment did occur during my Hollywood sojourn, however, when I received a hurried telephone call from Mom in New York. "We won the Irish Sweepstakes!" she blurted out, a trifle prematurely. "Our horse was chosen and if it wins the final big race, we'll get a hundred thousand dollars! I put your name, Dolly's, and mine on the ticket, so if it wins, we'll split it three ways."

Immediately, I began to build my own photographic business. Days of anxiety passed while I waited for the results. Finally, the breathless news arrived. Our horse not only didn't win, he hadn't even run, for some inexplicable reason known only to him. However, we'd won a consolation prize of $750. I immediately invested my share of $250 in a complete dental repair job, which included an upper plate. Now, it seems a most unglamorous use for sweepstake winnings, but it was extremely important to me at the time. I often think of the many times that people have graciously complimented me on my smile, for the teeth behind it were purchased by Mom's bet on the Irish Sweepstakes.

Still plodding away at a dull job in the grocery store, my spirits were in no way improved when June married a man she had met at the Hollywood Athletic Club and Helen returned to her home in Denmark. More alone and dejected, I thought, "To hell with it, I might as well give up and go home." Home meant going back to New York and again admitting that I had failed, but there seemed to be no recourse. I couldn't stack grocery shelves for the rest of my life.

Regretfully, I packed my photo samples and other belongings and boarded a Greyhound bus for the long trip to the East Coast, via San Francisco. After a disappointing year in Hollywood, I was heading home without having advanced my career by even a scant measure, and with no concrete idea of how I was to proceed from there. As the bus wound north along the beautiful California coastline, I closed my eyes and gave myself up completely to depression and fatigue. "I'm tired," I thought, "I'm tired way into the future!"

Bright sunlight streamed through the window but for some reason I felt uncomfortably chill. Suddenly, my body began to shake with cold, then the trembling subsided in burning fever, and by the time the bus arrived in San Francisco, I had to admit to myself that I was really sick. I sat in the bus terminal, alternately shivering and burning and feeling waves of nausea and dizziness. Through a kaleidoscope of vague impressions, I remember that my last rational thought was, "I have to get home!"

From the time of my bout with bronchial pneumonia while I was in the army, I'd been left with a lung weakness and susceptibility to respiratory infections, which often developed into a raging fever and bronchial cold. It was some years before that weakness faded. It's possible that my illness on the trip home was symptomatic of my emotional state at the time, but be that as it may, I felt miserable.

I opened my eyes and saw a snow-covered landscape slipping swiftly past the window and, slowly, I realized that I was sitting in a railway coach. I asked an approaching conductor where I was and would have been no less surprised had his answer been, "Siberia."

"Just pulling into Minneapolis," he replied. "That must have been some farewell party! The night you came aboard in San Francisco, you were loaded! It's a good thing you had a ticket in your hand."

Minneapolis? A ticket in my hand? And a railway ticket, at that! It was all very bewildering and I recall that my pride was hurt at his accusation of drunkenness. I remembered some vague plan of stopping in Minneapolis to visit Dad's aunt, my Great Aunt Augusta, but I had no memory whatsoever of putting the idea into action.

I began to look around for my luggage but found only one small overnight case and my precious portfolio of photos, though I knew I had left Hollywood with three additional bags. I questioned the conductor, who suggested that I may have checked them through to Minneapolis, but an inventory of my pockets disclosed no baggage checks and the luggage was never found.

I must have looked a wreck and maybe, after all, the conductor had good reason to think I'd been drinking. My clothes were disheveled and my hair tousled and matted as I faced myself in the washroom mirror and prepared for the meeting with Aunt Augusta. I didn't know her very well, for she seldom came to New York, but each birthday and Christmas, we always received a card and a present from her. Having always been very family conscious, I must have thought it was wrong to pass so close and not stop to see her. I looked forward to the fun of surprising her when I rang her doorbell, unannounced, and the anticipation may have made me feel somewhat better.

The December air was cold and bracing when I stepped off the train and made my way into the station. I was startled to see the figure of Aunt Augusta behind the gate, searching for me in the crowd. I thought she must be clairvoyant and wondered how she knew I'd be on the train.

"Augusta!" I called.

"George," she said, "you look dreadful! What's happened to you? Your wire frightened me half to death!"

"Wire? What wire?"

"Why, the one you sent me from San Francisco!" She delved into a spacious, old-fashioned pocketbook and handed me the yellow

square of paper: ARRIVING MINNEAPOLIS THURSDAY MORNING 10:30. I'M
SICK. GEORGE. I had no memory whatever of sending the telegram.

Augusta took me to her home and put me to bed, gave me a
cup of hot chocolate and threatened me with a bottle of citrate of
magnesia, which she placed firmly in full view on the night table, and
I ended up by drinking that, too. I watched her small, vigorous figure
as she bustled about the room, plumping pillows and offering
cheerful bits of gossip and advice. I thought of the sweet simplicity of
her quiet, uneventful life and wondered what it would be like to have
no serious problems, like Augusta.

She was, I knew then, my Grandfather Jorgensen's youngest
sister and she had come to America from Denmark as a motherless,
teenage girl. Grandma Jorgensen, with her customary generosity,
had brought Augusta to live with her, Grandpa, and their nine
children.

As a young adult, she had joined a Lutheran deaconess order,
became "Sister Augusta," and chose a nursing profession. One of her
patients was an elderly woman who invited her to move to
Minneapolis as a nurse-companion. Augusta found contentment in
that service and when her employer died, she was rewarded with a
considerable sum of money and a rambling old house—the same
house to which she brought me after my amnesiac journey from the
West Coast.

Due to her affectionate care, I began to feel better just a few
days after my arrival, and I suggested that I show her some of my color
slides of the family back home. Greatly enthused at the idea, she
invited an elderly church friend to join us in the viewing, and hurried
out to rent a projector. I improvised a screen by using a bed sheet and
began showing my slides to a rapt audience of two old ladies.

Augusta was ecstatic, as one picture followed another. From
time to time, she rushed up to the screen, eagerly identifying the
familiar faces. "There's my sister, Helga!" she pointed, in excitement.
"And that's my brother, George!" she said, indicating my own father.
Momentarily, I remember being startled at the statement. My father
was her nephew, not her brother! But I dismissed the thought,
knowing that she was excited and, therefore, her mistake was

justified. However, the confusing thought stayed with me and later I felt the need to clarify it.

When the last slide had been shown and our guest had left, I asked, "Why did you call Dad and Aunt Helga your brother and sister, Aunt Augusta?"

"Because they are," she smiled quietly. "Didn't you know that, George? You see, I'm Papa's—that is, your grandfather's—daughter, though your Grandma isn't my mother."

"You mean Grandpa was married before?"

"No," she replied simply. "Papa wasn't married to my mother when I was born. When my mother died, your Grandma arranged for me to come over from Denmark and took me into her home." She paused, then replied to my unspoken question. "Of course, she knew the whole story."

I thought of my wonderful Grandma Jorgensen. Yes, it would be like her to open her home to anyone in need, including her husband's illegitimate child.

"She treated me like one of her own," Augusta continued. "But still, I felt somehow different from the others. So, when I was older, I went away and made a life of my own. When I left the family, I naturally wanted to keep in touch with them all, but always at a distance."

I thought of the years she must have spent blaming herself for a tragedy that was not of her making. She had been born with what was, then, a social stigma, and had taken its solution into her own hands by removing herself from the family she loved. I realized that the choice had been hers and that I was probably one of the few family members who knew her secret.

As I look back on the following days with Augusta, I realize how important they were to me, for I was learning that others had some burden or problem that weighed on their life, too, and that their solutions lay solely within.

As the days passed in Minneapolis, I found that I could occasionally break through my habitual reserve and share with Augusta something of my hopes for a career. I told her of my job failures and the fears I felt for the future.

"What about the GI Bill of Rights?" she asked. "If you got a good college education, you wouldn't have to feel afraid of the world."

I dismissed the idea of college for the moment and, as the time approached when I would have to continue my way home again, I knew it wouldn't be long before I would be looking for a job.

In addition to our conversations probing for answers to my professional failure, one of the most vivid moments of my first visit to Augusta came in the small hours of the morning on a cold, wintry day of that year, 1947. Wrapped in blankets and sipping coffee, we huddled close to her ancient radio and listened to the BBC short-wave broadcast from England of the marriage of Princess Elizabeth to Prince Phillip. To us, at the time, it was an exciting moment and the warmth of sharing it returns to me each time I think of Aunt Augusta.

I didn't know it then, but her role in my life was far from being over. Several times in the future we were to meet again and one occasion, in particular, was to be a highly important time in my life.

The time arrived when I had to start for home and New York again. We said goodbye on the railroad platform and I remember thinking that at that moment she looked like Grandma to me, yet Grandma wasn't her mother. She had the same strong, Indian-type nose and the same Danish inflection in her voice.

In those few days of my visit to her, I had come to know Augusta better and to develop a lasting affection for her. During the previous years, she had been merely someone far away, a shadowy relative who sent gifts on birthdays, Christmas, and confirmations. Now, to find that she was really my aunt and had solved, or at least learned to live with, a difficult personal problem, brought her closer to me and made her even more endearing.

I will always be grateful to her for sharing with me at the time some of her enormous and enviable personal courage.

CHAPTER 8

I remember feeling ambivalent about my return to New York that winter. I'd been cruelly disappointed in my attempt to establish a career in Hollywood and hadn't really wanted to leave there before I'd accomplished something. But once more within the comfortable security of my home and family, I felt almost confident of myself. It was the only home I had ever known and, surrounded by its familiar objects and the people I loved, I felt safe and less afraid.

A few days after my return home, I scanned the classified ads in the morning newspaper, full of confidence, but the day I actually started making the rounds of those job opportunities, the familiar haunting fears returned. In order to postpone the moment of decision, I made for the nearest movie theater and sat for several hours in its cool protective darkness, vicariously living the lives that flashed across the screen. Even then, I knew it was only a temporary escape measure and I went home through the darkening streets, determined to put an end to my senseless wandering.

Reviewing the possibilities before me, I remembered Aunt Augusta's suggestion that I go to college and the idea began to appeal to me more and more. After all, I was twenty-two years old and the only things I was trained in were photography and library work. At the time, opportunities in photography were nonexistent and the libraries held no interest for me as a career. That seemed to leave me with a very limited scope. I thought perhaps college, after all, would help to broaden those horizons. With the help of the GI Bill of Rights, I enrolled at midterm in January of 1948 at Mohawk

College in Utica, New York, a temporary school set up to augment the overflow of students from various other universities. Many former servicemen and women were taking advantage of their educational opportunities and most of the recognized schools were severely overtaxed by large enrollments.

The years between the completion of high school and my entrance into college had left me ill-equipped for the disciplined routine of study and concentration. As a result, my liberal arts course, which consisted of science, history, and languages, posed a tremendous challenge at the time. I was continually distracted by my ever-present personal problems, and I found it extremely difficult to concentrate on my subjects.

For me, campus life at Mohawk College was reduced to a minimum, not only due to the amount of classwork, but also greatly influenced by the GI Bill allotment of sixty-five dollars per month, which was my total income at the time. Though social activities were, therefore, somewhat limited, I found myself in close association with my four roommates. We lived in a barrack-type dormitory that reminded me of the army days, and we ate, studied, and sometimes played a few mild pranks together. I remember we rode around in an old Model A Ford that boasted a rumble-seat and that we affectionately called "The Beast." Today, I can recall my roommates only vaguely, perhaps because I was then so involved in my own distractions, but if they were conscious of the wall I had built around myself, they never mentioned it. In order to protect myself the wall was becoming even more impenetrable.

Yet within that isolation, another desire was slowly emerging: an urge for spiritual enlightenment. Until then, I had regarded the mystique of religion as somewhat ritualistic. Although I considered my attitudes as Christian ones, I never felt sure that religion was an integral or personal part of me. My religious influences and training had been strong in childhood, yet I thought of it as a distant abstraction, simply to be accepted without thought or question. Then, years later in a small upstate college town, my mind began to turn toward the investigation of my beliefs and to seek a more positive understanding of religion. Somehow, I felt that I could find the answer to my problems through faith. Perhaps I was groping to pull myself away from the fears of the future, but I think that I was compelled by a force that, even today, I cannot explain.

Now, I feel that faith and the acceptance of God is the most moving and creative force in the universe, but at that time I had not yet grown to understand the complete oneness of God and man. I was confused, frightened, and unhappy and I couldn't understand why I felt my life as an affliction, rather than a great gift. I wondered why I was born, if not to have some part of life in the world, to be able to function without feeling isolated or different. But how to begin? And where to look?

It seemed to me then, that the logical place to find the answers was in church. I'd been baptized in the Lutheran faith, but had attended Sunday school at a Presbyterian church because it was more conveniently located to my home.

The strong and compelling inclinations that I'd been feeling led me to the First Presbyterian Church in Utica on a Sunday morning in the spring of 1948.

I remember the minister as a vigorous young man who spoke earnestly and with conviction, though his voice was strangely soft. His words issued in a continuous flow; Bible quotations, many of which I had heard before, seemed to take on a new significance that morning. Each idea began to relate itself to my own life and aspirations, fusing in a kind of slow crystallization.

"And I heard a great voice out of heaven saying, Behold, the tabernacle of God is with men, and he will dwell with them and they shall be his people, and God himself shall be with them, and be their God. And God shall wipe away all tears from their eyes; and there shall be no more death, neither sorrow, nor crying, neither shall there be any more pain; for the former things are passed away."

Suddenly, I realized that God was not the stern patriarch I had envisioned in my childhood, nor the jealous, vengeful God of Michelangelo's paintings, but an all-loving, all-knowing presence.

After twenty-two years of Sundays, I left the church that day in a state of elation and happiness, and my emotional burdens seemed lighter to me than they ever had before. After that, I looked forward to church services with a new eagerness.

As the weeks passed, I realized that my burgeoning spiritual faith was not a temporary thing but had persistently sustained itself. I wonder now if it was merely because I was emotionally and spiritually ready to accept these truths. Then, I didn't know. I only knew that I felt a serenity that was unknown to me before and, for the time being, that was enough.

Previously, I had prayed often but always timorously, as though prayers were a Christmas list to be only partially filled. But if it were "God's good pleasure to give us the kingdom," then that would have to be accepted totally, without reservation.

On a particular Sunday—one I would never forget—I sat listening to the sermon, the subject of which was taken from the Book of Matthew: "And Jesus came and spake unto them saying, All power is given unto me in heaven and in earth. Go ye therefore, and teach all nations, baptizing them in the name of the Father, and of the Son, and of the Holy Ghost; teaching them to observe all things whatsoever I have commanded you."

Daylight through the stained-glass windows had been dull during the service, but suddenly the sun broke from the cloudy overcast and threw a streaming column of light in front of me. Idly, I watched the particles of dust drifting in slowly, turning the shaft of light into an opaque cylinder. Through my detachment, as though it came from a great distance, I heard the minister's voice: "...and, lo, I am with you always, even unto the end of the world." I knew I was no longer alone.

What to me was extraordinary providence that I had experienced that morning in the Presbyterian church, was still too new and wondrous to think of discussing, but I remember that my acquaintances at college began to notice that I no longer sought a private corner in which to brood secretly. I suddenly seemed to be so cheerful and spirited that they wondered what had happened to me, but how could I tell them of the spiritual revelations that had suddenly entered my life? Sunlight through a stained-glass window, a few meaningful words, an offering of hope? I couldn't expect them to understand it or to believe me.

An unfamiliar energy seemed to burst from me. My newfound faith helped me to improve my general outlook immeasurably, and I was further determined not to sit back and await a miracle. If there was to be an answer to my problems, I must go and find it. I had never forgotten the conversation with my friends, June and Helen, or their sound advice to consult a doctor.

Spurred by my new enthusiasm, I decided to give up my studies at college and return to my first love, photography. I visited the Veteran's Administration, asking permission to transfer to a school where I could continue my photographic studies. With the government's continued assistance, I enrolled at the Progressive School of Photography in New Haven, Connecticut, in September of 1948. By that time, natural color photography had become my primary interest and I wanted to perfect further my techniques in that area.

Settled once again in a school routine, my thoughts returned to the possibility of medical help. Sensing that my femininity might in some way be related to glandular disturbances, I had acquired some small knowledge along the way in the field of endocrinology, the study of the body's glands. However, it was only fragmentary information that I had gleaned from a few articles and books.

Early in October of 1948, I read a newspaper article in New Haven about the work of a prominent endocrinologist, Dr. Harold Grayson, who was working then on some interesting hormone experiments. I was fascinated as I read of the various experiments he had been performing on animals: the masculinization of a female chicken and the return to vigor of a castrated rooster by means of hormone stimulation. I was further surprised to learn that Dr. Grayson was located right in New Haven, where I was attending photography school.

Up to that point, I'd been terribly afraid that I wouldn't find a doctor who would be able to understand the problems that confronted me and afraid, too, that if I did find him, I would be incapable of explaining emotions which even I did not yet understand. The fear of revealing myself made me hesitate.

However, it seemed that the timing of the published article was a miraculous coincidence. Another door had been opened to me and I was determined to walk through it, regardless of the terrifying fear that was a constant presence.

The closeness I felt with God had given me strength to search, but it did not give me the answers—those I must find myself. The newspaper article had generated a surge of excitement in me and finally I found the courage to make an appointment to see Dr. Grayson.

On the day of my appointment, I sat in the waiting room of his office for what seemed like hours, listening to my thumping heart and trying to figure out the best way to present my case to a stranger whose attitude I could in no way foresee. I felt like pacing the floor but sat quietly instead, trying to look as inconspicuous as possible.

I wondered what Dr. Grayson would think when I told him honestly why I was there. Would his answer be a flat statement, such as: "I think you're crazy?" Should I risk it? How would I acquit myself? I wanted to run and in spite of my earlier confidence, I began to feel chills of apprehension and panic.

Once more, I cautioned myself, for I didn't intend to flee from this moment of revealing confession as I had fled so many other moments in my life. My eyes were riveted on the door that led to the consultation rooms and, after what seemed an eternity, a nurse finally appeared.

"Mr. Jorgensen? The doctor will see you now," she said, crisply. Her tone seemed so impersonal, I thought, but then how could she know that this moment was such an important one for me?

I walked past her into the doctor's office, the door closed, and I stood looking at the man behind the desk. Dr. Grayson was a tired-looking, middle-aged man with graying temples and large horn-rimmed glasses. "Won't you sit down?" he asked. "You're a student at the photographic school, I understand."

"Yes, sir."

"Well, now, what's the trouble?"

"Oh, God," I thought, "here it is! How can I tell him or expect him to understand?" It seemed like such a simple question and one I'd been asking myself for so long.

"I...I didn't come here to consult you about anything as simple as a cold, Dr. Grayson. I, uh..."

Apparently aware of my nervousness, the doctor removed his glasses as if to see me better. He cleared his throat, reached for a cigarette box, took one himself, and offered one to me. My fingers trembled, but I managed to light the cigarette and inhaled it gratefully.

"Dr. Grayson," I said, finally, "what do I look like to you? I mean, do I look to you like a man or a...woman?"

Contemplating the end of his cigarette, he gave no sign that he had heard my question and allowed me to flounder on, unassisted.

"I-I've tried for more than twenty years to conform to the traditions of society. I've tried to fit myself into a world that's divided into men and women...to live and feel like a man, but I've been a total failure at it. I've only succeeded in living the life of a near recluse, completely unable to adjust." I hesitated again, feeling like a wind-up doll that was slowly running down.

"Go on."

"Even—even as a child, I was 'girlish,' and I've grown up with what I think are the emotions and desires of a woman. Physically, I'm an underdeveloped male, but—isn't it just possible that the organs that classify me as a male are one of nature's mistakes?"

Still, the doctor didn't respond, but put out his cigarette and nodded for me to continue.

"I came here to ask you what I can do about my feelings of being a sexual mix-up. Is it at all possible that the trouble lies in a glandular or chemical imbalance of some kind? There must be something...someplace I can go for help."

I searched his face, waiting in anguish for some reaction to what I had been saying. Surely, now, the questions would come racing. No doubt he would suggest an examination.

Dr. Grayson sat quietly for a moment, then pulled a writing pad toward him and began to write. "I want you to see this man," he said when he had finished. "Dr. Reznick. He's a well-known psychiatrist."

The interview was over.

I rose, feeling that I had been in his office for the better part of a year, rather than a few minutes. I walked slowly out to the street, barely aware of the slip of paper in my hand. "He thinks I'm insane," I thought. "A hopeless neurotic, to be simply rushed out of his office into someone else's jurisdiction. No examination. No questions. No answers. Nothing."

Although psychosomatic medicine, which treats the body and mind as a whole, was a well-established principle long before 1948, in the mind of Dr. Grayson, evidently, my problem was purely a psychiatric disturbance. I know now what I must have known then, instinctively: that the reason he seemed anxious to dismiss me was that he may not have known what to do. Headaches or heart ailments were perhaps the more familiar enemies.

Despite my discouragement, I made an appointment to see Dr. Reznick, the psychiatrist, a few days later.

Once again, I opened my heart and painfully tried to explain my feelings of the past twenty years. When the bitter monologue was ended, the psychiatrist regarded me impersonally, leaned forward on his desk and folded his hands.

"I can't guarantee you anything," he said, "but I'd like you to start a series of psychoanalytic treatments. About thirty, I would imagine." He then explained to me that through these treatments, he would try to guide me away from these "feminine inclinations." He seemed to give no thought to what would or could be done with my effeminate face and body and laid great emphasis again on the fact that he could guarantee nothing.

I left the interview, convinced that Dr. Reznick was not the man who could help me, quite certain that I would never make a second appointment. A few days later, when I received a bill for thirty-five dollars for the fifteen-minute consultation, I was positive of it. I would have borrowed the money somehow and paid it willingly, however, if I thought I could have been helped or, at least, received a credible answer to the eternal question of what was wrong and why.

As I look back on those two interviews, I know that perhaps, after all, I was looking for a miracle. With growing anxieties, I was groping for a hand to guide me to some place where understanding would destroy the fear and confusion that was tearing me in half.

At the time, I resented the two medical men for not understanding my great anxiety, and I think I resented myself even more for my inability to communicate the importance of those fears to them. My questions remained unanswered and I returned to school, trying to convince myself for what must have been the hundredth time that my photographic work would be fulfilling enough.

CHAPTER 9

It was early in 1948, when I was still attending the Progressive School of Photography in New Haven, that I became a conspirator in what seemed to me then a dramatic kidnapping case.

Five or six of us students had rented a large rambling old house in Woodmont, Connecticut, a suburb of New Haven. By pooling our limited resources, we were able to live in what we described at the time as "comfortable poverty." One of my roommates in this communal living system was a young man unhappily separated from his wife who, shortly after their separation, had abandoned their three-year-old son to a temporary foster home. One night, several of us, accompanied the young father, took the child from the foster home and drove to my home in the Bronx. We stayed overnight with Mom and Dad, and the little boy, unaware of the excitement going on around him, slept peacefully on a mattress on the floor of our living room. The next morning, his father put him on a plane bound for Seattle and the care of his paternal grandparents. To my knowledge, there were never any repercussions from the incident, so I've never had cause to regret my part in the conspiracy as an accessory.

Sometime during this period, after my unproductive attempts to find professional medical aid, I met Jim Frankfort, a friend from high school. When we were in school in New York, four or five years earlier, Jim and I had pondered over homework together and I think we attended a few movies, but our relationship had not developed beyond the casual state.

One day, we met by chance in a lunchroom near the school of photography. The reunion seemed mutually pleasant and I remember that we sat over coffee, chatting amiably, reviewing our school days and exchanging the events of the intervening years.

I remembered him as a quiet, contemplative boy with the ability to close himself off, even when surrounded by a great many people, and recede into some private world of his own. He had a rather laconic philosophy about life—a totally relaxed quality that hid a somewhat stubborn character which he revealed only in defense of what was, to him, an important issue. My own mounting tensions of the period seemed to me in great contrast to Jim's quiet acceptance of life and the world around him.

Again, I couldn't help comparing myself to him and his sturdy virility as I regarded him across the table the day of our meeting. Though we were both twenty-two years old, he was a grown young man and I seemed a pale, fragile boy by comparison. Though his light brown hair and frank, blue eyes were the same as I'd remembered them, the bone-structure of his face seemed more sharply defined and displayed a kind of craggy strength that emphasized the deep cleft in his chin. He'd always been tall, over six feet, but his body had broadened considerably.

He was in New Haven on a business trip and, indicating that his stay would be a brief one, suggested that we have dinner that evening. I remember that dinner was pleasant and companionable and I managed to glean a few facts about the events of his life since I'd last seen him. He was still unmarried and had a good job with a soft-drink company in New York City.

When we parted after dinner, Jim suggested that we get together for a social evening when I returned to New York. I readily agreed and we said goodbye.

Until that time, I hadn't thought of Jim Frankfort or any of my other high-school friends for years and Tom Chaney had, by then, been buried in my consciousness as a painful incident in the past.

However, it was at some moment during the brief encounter with Jim that I became aware of a small, gnawing doubt. The warm pleasure and enjoyment that I felt at our meeting became magnified beyond the proportions of a casual event. That feeling, in turn, began to grow into a nameless dread, a fear that with further contact with him, I might lead myself into another emotional vortex.

In the following weeks, thoughts of Jim recurred with growing frequency and I tried desperately to bury my feelings, trying not to admit them even to myself.

My sense of guilt was no doubt propelling me toward a new and frightening feeling of urgency and, once again, I returned to the possibilities of help for myself by reviewing in my mind the two medical episodes a few weeks earlier. I wondered if I should try psychoanalysis, after all, and if my dismissal of aid from Dr. Reznick had been a hasty blunder. But the recurring questions of what to do about my effeminate appearance continued to plague me. Even if it were possible to adjust my mind and attitudes to a more male outlook, I wondered what could be done about a "masculine" mind in a feminine body.

Again, I immersed myself in my studies, merely marking time, and, suspended in air, I waited for an inspiration. It came in the form of a slim volume.

While browsing through the endless rows of books in the local library one day, a title suddenly caught my attention. *The Male Hormone* by Paul de Kruif. I had remembered reading the same author's *Microbe Hunters* with complete absorption a few years before. I slipped the narrow volume from its place on the shelves, flipped open the cover, and on the title page, I read a quotation that was to stay with me for all time. "Remember, Paul, people are very open-minded about new things—so long as they are exactly like the old ones."

I walked to the nearest library table, sat down, and slowly began to read. For a time on that wintry afternoon, there was no other world but the fascinating, incredible one created by Paul de Kruif. Unfamiliar words and new ideas exploded in my mind from almost every page. "Manhood is chemical, manhood is testosterone. Over and beyond testosterone, manhood seems to be partly a state of mind." Also, I struggled with the term "clinical endocrinology," which dealt with the various glands of the body and their relationship to health and mental outlook. As I read on, my mind raced with this new knowledge, for throughout the narrative, there was woven a tiny thread of recognition pulled from my own private theories.

The book stated that at the time the author was doing his research in preparation for writing it, matters pertaining to glands were considered dangerous and somewhat unsavory, and the men who dared reach into this field had risked their scientific reputations. I read on eagerly, no doubt oblivious to everything but the printed pages before me.

"There is an uncanny ability in one of the pure female hormones, to alter the lives and fate of man, and the pure male hormone—testosterone—to bring about deep changes in the sex lives of women." These facts, Dr. de Kruif stated, had been discovered by a surgeon in his search for hormone controls over certain urological diseases.

"Chemically, all of us are both man and woman because our bodies make both male and female hormones, and primarily it's an excess of testosterone that makes us men, or an excess of female hormones that makes us women; and the chemical difference between testosterone and estradiol is merely a matter of four atoms of hydrogen and one atom of carbon."

I didn't know how my own case might be related to these ideas but at that moment it seemed possible to me that I was holding salvation in my hands: the science of body chemistry. Even then, I think I knew that Providence had intervened again and opened a door on a new and shining vista.

On what was to me a fateful day in December of 1948, I left the library in a state of excitement and with a deep feeling of gratitude. I remember walking through the falling snow, passing shop windows ablaze with Christmas lights and decorations. That day, I bought myself a Christmas present—a copy of *The Male Hormone,* which was to become thoroughly worn and dog-eared before I took the next vital step toward a solution.

My total preoccupation with these new chemical theories was interrupted by the Christmas holidays, which I spent at home in the Bronx. After the holiday intermission, I returned to school and the all-consuming study of the principles of body chemistry, contained in Dr. de Kruif's book. If I wondered, hormones were to be a possible answer, which way should I turn? Should I follow the course already suggested and try to become more masculine by developing the outward physical signs of manhood? However, I reasoned, if that was possible, would I then have a man's desires, attitudes, and emotions? I felt certain, even then, that the answer to that would be "No." Then what of the more drastic measure of trying to become more feminine? Could the transition to womanhood be accomplished through the magic of chemistry? At that point, I feared the answer to that question was "No" also.

The frustrations of my very limited knowledge were seemingly endless during that period and I realized there could be only one remedy: I would simply have to learn more. *The Male Hormone* was merely a key that, hopefully, would open the doors and lead to avenues of further enlightenment.

After graduating from the photography school in New Haven in January, 1949, I returned to New York, determined to continue my search for answers. Before giving a thought to job-hunting, I visited the library of the New York Academy of Medicine, located at 103rd Street and Fifth Avenue in Manhattan. Soon I was spending many hours in that great repository of medical information, hoping to find other keys to my dilemma. My research led me to references on "hermaphrodism" and "pseudo-hermaphrodism" and I studied case histories of other sex abnormalities also. Shortly, I became steeped in a literature which I could only partially understand. Too many references were in French or German, neither of which I understood.

Also, as I remember, it was in the library of the New York Academy of Medicine that I first read of various conversion experiments in Sweden but I had no idea of their scientific importance or how they might apply to me.

At any rate, my confusion grew and by spring my search at the medical library had reached an impasse. At that point, if I'd had the money, I might have seriously considered taking a medical degree, but time was a factor to be reckoned. I was twenty-three years old and unless I could find a solution soon, I knew I'd have to resign myself to a life of frustration and despair.

About the only specific incident that I can remember from that period occurred on April 26, 1949, when I became a press photographer for a day. I was riding on a bus, on one of my many treks to the medical library, when I saw a large boat wrecked on the highway at an underpass. I got off the bus at the next stop and rushed back home to get my cameras. Then, returning to the scene of the accident, I took numerous pictures from every conceivable angle. The cabin cruiser apparently was too high to clear the underpass and pieces of the superstructure were scattered along the highway, perhaps one of the few cases on record of a boat accident on dry land. After calling the *New York Journal American,* I sent the film on to them and a few days later I had made my first photographic sale, when they sent me a check for the magnificent sum of ten dollars. Needless to say, my career as a press photographer began and ended all in one day.

Still determined to find some cure or satisfactory compromise for what I considered an emotional and sexual disorder, I enrolled at the Manhattan Medical and Dental Assistant's School, again on my GI benefits. There, I began x-ray and laboratory technician's courses which gave me a basic knowledge of bone and body structures, and I learned to perform chemical analyses of blood and urine. The standard methods of testing for sugar content in the blood, and white and red blood-cell counts soon became simple procedures to me. Also, I studied the principles of basal metabolism, which determines the rate at which the body burns up energy. However, it was the rare glandular disturbances which intrigued me more. Abnormal growth due to pituitary malfunction, steroids, enzymes, and sex hormones were all new areas of knowledge, but ones which I felt had some bearing on my problem. Avidly, I discussed glands and glandular disturbances with the doctors who were my instructors, but recalling the heartbreaking interviews with the two New Haven doctors, I tried to keep these exchanges on a completely impersonal basis. These studies occupied my every waking moment, and probably many of my sleeping ones, to become an all-consuming drive.

As the weeks passed, my work at the technicians' school unfolded into a keener awareness of the difficult road that lay ahead. Somewhat encouraged by the progress of my studies, I felt sufficiently capable of taking on a major social task. At the end of September, Askov Hall, the Danish social club, had planned a Saturday Night Barn Dance and I agreed to join the decorations committee.

In keeping with the "country" theme of the party, we filled the hall with straw and reeds and crisscrossed stout cord on the ceiling, from which we hung toy balloons, popcorn balls, lollypops, and tin whistles. Traditionally, any culprit who stole one of these prizes and was caught had to pay the penalty of a trip to "jail," a flimsy cage erected in one corner of the ballroom. There was no escape from the jail sentence, until the "prisoner" paid the exorbitant fine of ten cents into the club treasury.

We all entered into the fun of these absurdities and on the night of the party, I was assigned the role of "Deputy Sheriff," and was kept busy collecting fines.

At one point during the party, in a moment of abandon and no doubt inflated by my authority as an agent of the "law," I reached up and grabbed one of the prizes that dangled from the ceiling. An infuriated mob hustled me into the jail, amid shrieks of laughter and raucous threats to vote me out of office.

Suddenly, someone reached out and dropped a dime into the jailer's till to pay my fine and, reluctantly, the crowd released me and turned away in search of another victim.

I looked around for my liberator and found it was Eric Larsen, a Danish seaman whom I knew slightly, who had wandered over to watch the good-natured fun.

"C'mon, I'll buy you a drink," he said, in a strong Danish accent, his voice thick with alcohol.

"Why not?" I shrugged.

We moved to a dimly-lit bar on the other side of the hall and I slid onto an empty stool. Eric stood close behind me and ordered drinks and I leaned away from the strong smell of whiskey and cigars that surrounded him. Then he leaned forward and whispered in my ear, "Y'know, if I was a little queer, I could go for you!"

Even now I can recall my feeling of shock and disgust. I remember that I didn't answer him. Suddenly my throat constricted and for a moment I thought I was going to be sick. I spun away from his lumbering figure and pushed blindly through the crowd of young people into the darkness outside, heading for the beach. Sand caught at my feet and seemed to hold me back purposely, until I reached the solid boards of a pier that jutted out over the water. I leaned over the edge of the pier and vomited.

For a time, I had lost myself in the boisterous gaiety of the party but once again I'd been singled out and made to feel my strangeness anew by an unexpected and vulgar remark, which I knew to be half a statement and half an invitation.

I sat alone in the darkness, drained and limp, devoid of any feeling at all, watching the lights on the opposite shore, though that night they afforded me no comfort. The lights faded and disappeared slowly as wisps of fog began to close over the Sound. The water looked like black velvet, noiseless...motionless... peaceful...inviting. Slowly, an idea began to take form and I remember thinking that beneath the surface of the water, perhaps I could blot out the revulsion and horror I had felt. To know nothingness seemed an answer to my despair. It would be easy, I thought, to end the years of loneliness, the years of hoping and searching, by slipping quietly into the blessed release of oblivion.

I remember that I began to cry then, racked by grief and self-pity, until I was completely consumed by exhaustion and I lay quietly for a time staring into the fog.

To have even contemplated my own destruction no doubt frightened me and must have motivated my return to reason and reality, because I finally pulled myself to my feet and headed for the parking lot, slipping past the bright, noisy clubhouse. The band still played and a babble of voices poured from the windows. Somehow, I managed to drive home through the quiet streets and I parked the car and began to walk. Block after block I walked unseeing past familiar landmarks until my thoughts began to form into some sort of coherence.

I wondered why Eric Larsen had made his distasteful remark and what had made him dare to say it. He was a comparative stranger. Was it my slight build, my blond complexion? But what did bone structure have to do with it? Or had some telepathic influence been at work? Had he sensed my own censored desires that revolved around a buried love for Tom and a developing one for Jim Frankfort? Surely, these emotional indiscretions weren't so obvious. No, I thought, there had to be some physical explanation for my difficulty.

A statement from Paul de Kruif's book, *The Male Hormone,* kept returning to me: "The chemical difference between testosterone and estradiol is four atoms of hydrogen and one atom of carbon." But what is a man and what is a woman? Why do they think differently? And why did most of the men in the world seem so different from me?

If Dr. de Kruif's chemical ratio was correct, it would seem then that the relationship was very close. That being so, I reasoned, there must be times when one could be so close to that physical dividing line that it would be difficult to determine on which side of the male-female line one belonged. There was an answer—somewhere.

A pale dawn was beginning to appear when I found that I was back at the house. How I got there I didn't know, but I quietly let myself in the door and slipped into my room. I walked to the bookshelves, reached for de Kruif's volume, and for the hundredth time began to flip through the pages, wearily trying to absorb the familiar words.

"Estradiol, the female hormone and chemical sister to testosterone." Once more, I devoured the brief paragraph on the gland substance.

It must have been about that point that I began to form another idea, although at first a rather vague one: I would experiment on myself. But in order to do that, somehow I'd have to get hold of the miraculous substance known as "estradiol." I don't think I had any idea of how I was going to go about acquiring it at that moment, for I knew that I couldn't buy it legally without a prescription, but I also knew that I would have to try.

As I look back on it, I suppose it was a dangerous thing for me to contemplate, but my desperation was so great at that point that I was willing to try anything. At any rate, I seemed to find comfort in the thought that I was about to take some sort of direct action, no matter what the result.

That night, as usual in times of stress, I slept peacefully.

The next day, I awoke with a feeling of anticipation and perhaps even a vague uneasiness. Alternating between apprehension and excitement, I began to put into motion the plan I had in mind.

That afternoon, I drove to an unfamiliar section of town, entered a drugstore, and ordered several standard items from the unsuspecting clerk. Then, in a tone designed to convey my familiarity with things medical, I asked for some high-potency estradiol.

"Ethinyl estradiol is the highest potency we have," he said.

I had no idea what ethinyl meant in relation to estradiol but I was determined not to show my ignorance. "I guess that'll do," I replied. "Let me have a hundred tablets."

"That's a pretty strong chemical. We're not supposed to sell it without a prescription."

"Well, I guess I could have gotten a prescription, but I just didn't think of it. You see, I'm at a medical technicians' school, and we're working on an idea of growth stimulation in animals through the use of hormones."

The clerk hesitated. "Oh, well, in that case I guess it's okay."

As I look back on it, I have no idea why the clerk consented so easily, though present-day controls of drugs are far more stringent than they were then, but I secretly suspect that Providence again was taking a hand.

Once out of the store, I headed for the car and unwrapped the package. There, at last, the small bottle lay in my hand. How strange it seemed to me that the whole answer might lie in the particular combination of atoms contained in those tiny, aspirin-like tablets. As recently as a few years before, science had split some of those atoms and unleashed a giant force. There in my hand lay another series of atoms, which in their way might set off another explosion—one I hoped would not be a destructive force but would help to make me a whole person.

That night, as I got ready for bed, some of the echoes of the day returned to my mind. "That's a pretty strong chemical." Again, I took the small bottle in my hand and reread the label: NOT TO BE TAKEN WITHOUT THE ADVICE OF A DOCTOR. I may have had the dramatic thought that it might be poisonous, or even deadly. However, I uncapped the bottle and shook a single tablet into my hand and, trying to dismiss a nagging fear, I put it in my mouth and washed it down with water.

I went to my bed and prayed, asking God to forgive me if I had committed a wrong. I knew I hadn't tried the experiment with any thought or hope of death, but rather I hoped it might be the beginning of a life of freedom. I didn't regard it as a transgression and somehow I felt I'd be understood and forgiven.

The next morning, I awoke with the feeling that something very important was happening to me or was about to happen. I jumped out of bed and ran to the mirror. But I looked the same and I had to admit that I didn't feel any different. After all my desperate planning, I wondered why the tablet had failed to show any sign of change in me. It was a great disappointment, but I had no way of knowing then that it would take several years of constant hormone administration to finally show the physical results I had hoped to see after swallowing just one tablet.

After taking one tablet a night for a week, I believe it was on the eighth morning that I awoke with a strange, though not unpleasant feeling. Also, there was a sensitivity in my breast area and a noticeable development. Beyond the outward physical signs, another curious thing had occurred during the previous few days. The great feeling of listlessness and fatigue, which often seemed to be with me even after a full night's sleep had disappeared. I was refreshed and alive and no longer felt the need to take little cat naps during the day.

Perhaps these symptoms were psychological and my feelings of happiness resulted from the knowledge that I might be working toward a recognizable goal, that I wasn't standing still anymore. At that point, I believed I had stumbled on the first step toward a solution that would allow me to live the life my heart and mind had told me I was intended to live.

I kept the miracle that was happening within my body a closely guarded secret, but new hope had given me the courage to dream and speculate even further. If the female hormones I was taking without guidance could have such a pronounced effect on me, would it not be possible for an expert to administer them in proper proportions, so that my body's chemistry would be in complete and correct balance? Perhaps it seemed like madness or a wild dream, but I wondered if surgery could complete the process, remove what I considered a malformation and, in turn, give me the freedom I wanted; freedom to find my proper place in the world.

No doubt these were radical thoughts, based only on my own desire and emotion, half-formulated ideas from scraps of medical information, but from then on, I was even more determined to follow the dream.

CHAPTER 10

In June of 1949, I was an usher at Dolly's wedding when she married a young engineer with a major airline company. We all shared in Dolly's happiness, and had a high regard for Bill, my new brother-in-law.

Still deep in my studies at the medical technicians' school in the fall of that year, I had little time or money for social activities, except for an occasional evening of bowling with Jim Frankfort. He had frequently been in my thoughts since our chance meeting in New Haven, and when I returned to New York City and began my technical studies, we met again and renewed our friendship.

During that time, I slowly realized that the friendliness I felt toward him had been developing into a much stronger feeling. To Jim, of course, we were just two friends meeting for a few hours of bowling and casual conversation, but to me they were precious moments and part of a growing and powerful emotion. I finally had to admit to myself an unpleasant fact that I'd been carefully avoiding, and the old frustrations and distaste for myself began to mount again.

Even though I felt inexorably drawn to Jim, I knew I didn't want to be, an ambivalence that was painful and confusing. Once more, my desperation propelled me into an even greater sense of urgency and the search for a final solution.

Although my hormone experiments showed some incipient signs of change, I knew that hormones could only do so much. I wondered what I would do if I couldn't find anyone anywhere who could carry on from there. With these thoughts, I extended my pursuit by seeking help from a friend, a measure that was to have far-reaching effects.

During the period of my studies at the medical technicians' school, I had formed a close relationship with a fellow student and co-worker in the experimental laboratories. She was a young woman, slightly older than I, named Genevieve Angelo. Gen, as she was called, was a vigorous and independent person whose greatest enthusiasm and generally single topic of conversation was her husband, Dr. Joseph Angelo. "My husband, the paragon," was to her a major philosophy and one of her chief endearments.

One morning at school, probably sensing my distractions, she suggested that we have lunch together. With motherly intuition, she inferred that I looked pretty despairing and that what I needed, in her estimation, was a good, high caloric binge.

Once settled over lunch, we sipped our drinks and chatted about school and other trivia, but underneath the pleasant banter I began to wonder if I would dare take her into my confidence. Underlying that thought must have been the motive that I might be able to get additional help from her husband, the incomparable Dr. Joe.

I remember that Gen launched almost immediately into one of her customary eulogies. Dr. Joe had just pulled a woman through a critical case of pneumonia, helped a man back on his feet after a broken hip, and had done something equally noteworthy for someone else. I listened with amusement to these accomplishments, as Gen spared no praise, but I wondered silently if Dr. Joe, in some way, could help me as miraculously.

I wanted to ask Gen outright but, as usual, I was tongue tied by embarrassment and the fear of revealing myself. Finally, with a courage that was no doubt spurred by a second drink, I made the attempt. "Gen, since you're a doctor's wife, I'd like to ask you something."

"Yes?" she answered, but the words still wouldn't come.

"Well, go on, George, you were about to ask me something important."

"Terribly important to me." I paused, still reluctant to continue.

"Are you trying to tell me that you think you're different from other people?"

I remember that I was startled by her directness. Years later, Gen told me that she knew I was shy and inverted and that I had something on my mind that day I wanted to tell her. She admitted that she had been curious and felt challenged; that perhaps God had had a hand in it and placed her there to be of assistance. She somehow felt that there was something seriously wrong with me, that I was effeminate, "too dainty," as she put it, and so she asked me, directly, if I thought I was "different from other people."

I had found it so difficult to make a beginning, but once she opened the way, it was as though the floodgates parted. After that, we spent the balance of our lunchtime discussing the subject, during which Gen was calmly receptive, her attitude one of sympathy and understanding. She seemed to feel that the main factor was psychological and that what I needed was a psychiatrist.

I told her about my unhappy experiences with the physician and psychiatrist in New Haven and, also, about Jim Frankfort and the fact that for months I'd been fighting the creeping knowledge that I loved him.

"What do you want me to do?" she asked.

"Maybe I could talk to Dr. Joe."

"I'll see what I can do, George," she replied, "now stop worrying and eat!"

Gen made an appointment for me to see Dr. Joe and I was in his office in Secaucus, New Jersey, the following afternoon at three o'clock. He was a man in his mid-thirties with a relaxed, easy-going nature. He smiled his genial smile and at once made me feel comfortable and at ease. I remember thinking at the time how different the consultation was in comparison to the two previous ones, the year before. He treated me like any of his other patients, and began by giving me a complete physical examination. He noted the swelling of my breasts and asked the reason, though I was almost certain that Gen had already told him about my self-administered doses of estradiol.

"Well," he said at last, "you seem to be a man, though somewhat undeveloped. Why can't you just accept that fact and be one?"

That question opened up a series of discussions that was to last over a period of several months. During that time, I visited the Angelos' home once or twice a week and Dr. Joe and Gen became my only confidantes and my highly respected friends.

Shortly after my first interview with Dr. Joe in November of 1949, during the course of one of our conferences, I told him something of my own private theories concerning the possibility of more drastic measures. At that time, too, we discussed the limited information that was available on experiments that were taking place in Sweden.

During our visits, he tried to break down all my arguments, for though I think he respected my determination, I realize now that I was reaching for something that he, as a normal man, couldn't understand. He told me later that he was purposely cruel, in order to test my perseverance. Suddenly, he challenged me one day. "What about God? Tell me what you think about God, George."

"I believe in God, of course," I told him. "Without faith I'd have stopped existing long ago. But I don't believe God would want me to go on being unhappy, unable to present the best part of myself to the world, when there is the possibility of developing into a whole person. Even my simple hormone experiments have indicated that improvement is possible to some degree."

"But still," he countered, "God gave you the outward semblance of a man. How can you presume to go against His law? How can you reverse that law, even though you believe that emotionally you are feminine; even if you discover that the transformation you hope for is possible?"

"God gives us many chances in this world and I don't believe they're confined to a choice between good and evil, or what people think is right or wrong. Anyway, I believe my choice now is right, because if a change is possible, I will be given a chance to lead a life of greater meaning and dignity. And I think God would probably approve of that!"

"But look at yourself. Do you think that, ultimately, you'll have the same physical qualities as a woman? Look at your ears, they stick out! Of course, that can be corrected by plastic surgery. But what about your hairline? And your feet; they won't shrink, you know!"

It was true, they didn't look very feminine in my clumsy loafers, but I pointed out that they were only a size eight, which wasn't at all unusual for a tall girl.

Then, we discussed certain historical cases, one of which had occurred as early as 1930. We knew, theoretically, that what I wanted could be done, but not in this country. Dr. Joe explained that the treatments and operations I visualized were not ethical to many medical men and that there might be a legal block to them in the United States. There was a limited number of sex transformation cases in foreign countries, which he found in medical journals. Presumably, these were the "pseudo-hermaphrodite" cases, in which some outward evidence of both male and female sex organs was present, though one or the other in a rudimentary state.

In the meantime, he permitted me to continue the estradiol tablets under his direction, knowing that with careful supervision they would not be harmful. It was his plan to "retreat" and use strong doses of testosterone (the male hormone), thereby returning to my original maleness, if the estrogen injections had proven unsatisfactory, but that eventuality was never reached.

At some time during that year, I'd had some correspondence with Dr. Grayson, the Connecticut physician, who had seemed sufficiently interested to suggest that I keep in touch with him and let him know how my plans proceeded. Apparently, I had written him something of these events, for in November of 1949, I received a letter from him in which he said in part, "I understand something like the course of treatment that you requested was done at one time in Sweden."

Dr. Grayson's letter provided further fuel to fire my imagination and, as I look back on it, may have been one of those pinpoints in time that determine a person's destiny. I felt that life was passing me by. I didn't want to continue in my present state if there was even the remotest possibility of finding further help, no matter where in the world I would have to go to find it. Dr. Grayson's letter merely fortified the information I had gotten from Dr. Joe, and the few facts I had gleaned from my own research. If work of that nature was taking place in Europe, then that's where I would seek it out. Sweden, particularly, seemed to have done the most advanced research at that time. Finally, my emotional attachment to Jim Frankfort had become increasingly painful to me and, once and for all, I wanted to release myself from its stranglehold and the possibility of repeating a similar experience in the future.

Therefore, it was shortly before Christmas in 1949, that I made the decision to go first to Denmark, where I had relatives, and then to Stockholm, where I hoped I would find doctors who would be willing to handle my case.

My course at the medical technicians' school had been completed and I graduated in December, 1949. After graduation, I got a job at the school as a clerical assistant, and began to save money from my salary to add to my small savings account in order to buy my passage to Denmark.

In the meantime, whenever possible, I was still involved in my conferences with Dr. Joe and he continued his efforts to try to dissuade me. "If you're wrong in your opinion, George, have you considered the tragedy that could result? The tragedy of attempting surgery and finding it unsuccessful, leaving you in the middle of nowhere."

"Yes, I've considered that," I said, "but how could any future life be worse than the past twenty-three years?"

"Well, I guess you've examined it from every angle and you're aware of the possibly grave circumstances. You're no doubt willing to risk anything in order to have peace of mind, but have you thought of the reaction of American medical men to your transformation?"

"I'll just have to face that when and if it comes."

"There's another thing I want to warn you about. Never proceed to the point of surgery, should it even be possible, until you've made sure that you can get a new passport. Otherwise, you might find that you're a person without a country!"

That was a disquieting thought that hadn't occurred to me before, but like his other arguments, I knew I'd just face it when it came.

As I look back on it, I suppose I was living in a fool's paradise. I was going to Europe on the basis of a few scattered medical reports. I had very little money and no immediate prospects for getting more and I had no way of knowing what the cost for further treatments would be. I spoke no foreign languages, except for a few words of greeting in Danish. All of my planning had to be done in secret, for there were only two people in the world at that time who knew why I was making the trip, and it was a lonely thought. I was concealing a terrifying problem that had been insurmountable up to that point, and its solution was an unknown factor. To my friends and family, then, I was merely planning a tourist jaunt, but the Old World was to be the point of no return as George Jorgensen.

By mid-April of 1950, I had saved enough money for my passage to Denmark. With the few hundred dollars I'd collected, I was able to buy a ticket for one way only and I had a small sum left to tide me over until I could get a job.

It was a one-way ticket to a new life.

CHAPTER 11

Iremember that the first day of May, 1950, arrived in a dismal downpour of rain. It was the day of my embarkation on the liner *Stockholm,* and I wondered whether the weather was flashing an ill omen.

In my stateroom, I served drinks to twenty unsuspecting friends and relatives and it was with a concentrated effort that I made light-hearted conversation about the color pictures I was going to take and the places I would visit. My evasions, of course, weren't noticeable to anyone but me. "Yes, I'll write often. No, I didn't make a return reservation because I don't know how long my money will last. Yes, I'll remember. No, I won't forget." To friends and family, I was just another enthusiastic tourist.

My guests toasted my health in a medley of *Skoals,* and wished me a pleasant trip and a safe return, while I promised to look up relatives in Denmark and carry special greetings to friends, among whom was Helen Johnson, the girl I'd met some years before in California. Helen and her husband were to meet the ship in Copenhagen.

A short time before, I remember our delight when we discovered that my sister, Dolly, and my brother-in-law, Bill, were expecting a baby. The day I sailed, I felt a tug of regret that I wouldn't be home for that happy event.

I was disappointed that Gen and Dr. Joe Angelo hadn't arrived, but I learned later that he was delivering a baby and Gen couldn't get to the ship because of the heavy rains. However, they sent a bottle of champagne and a charming note: "To our dear George. Bon Voyage. Hurry home to us again." Among others, there was a message from Grandma Jorgensen.

Mom seemed strangely silent through all of the buzzing conversation that day, and when the gong rang, announcing that visitors must go ashore, she began to cry. Suddenly, she seemed very small and I put my arms around her and assured her that there was nothing to be upset about; I was just another square-headed tourist, off to see the world. But I knew she was very intuitive and I wondered whether she might suspect an ulterior reason for my trip.

After many more goodbyes, admonitions, and a good deal more advice, my guests departed and I stood on the deck, waving to Dolly and Mom as long as I could see them on the pier. Dad was working that day and couldn't come to the sailing, but he'd given me his advice the night before: "Take some good pictures and don't forget to keep out enough money for your return ticket!"

I made the ten-day crossing unaffected by the rolling seas, and enjoyed the ship's activities. In a state of contentment, I began to feel whole and nearly fulfilled, as if I had already projected myself into the future.

The *Stockholm* slid slowly into a berth in Copenhagen's picturesque harbor on May 11, 1950. A small band played Danish and American songs and groups of happy people were gathered along the docks. As the ship drew closer, I saw long strips of paper on which welcome signs had been printed. Even with my limited Danish, I could decipher one or two. "Welcome Home, Arne!" "We love you, Svend!" It was exciting just to be an onlooker and although I hadn't located Helen on the dock as yet, I felt that these happy people were welcoming me, too.

When I was halfway down the gangplank, I heard a cry, "Welcome to Denmark, George!" Nothing could have been more heartwarming at that moment. It was Helen Johnson, her husband, Olaf, and their four-year-old daughter, Grethe, all waiting for me. Helen introduced me to Olaf, who merely smiled warmly by way of welcome and suddenly I realized that he couldn't speak English. Immediately, I knew I'd have to get busy and learn the language.

We gathered up my luggage and were cleared through customs with very little delay. I remember that I was so overcome with the newness of my surroundings and the excitement of being in Denmark that as we left the custom's house I failed to see a parked bicycle and promptly fell over it. Helen warned me that I'd better make my peace with them, as bicycles were the only means of transportation for two-thirds of Copenhagen's population.

We piled into the Johnsons' small Mercedes-Benz and drove up the winding road that pierces Langeline, Copenhagen's harbor district, passing on the way the world-famous statue of the Little Mermaid sitting on a rock, gazing out to sea. We traveled through Strøget, the business district, and on out to the suburbs of the city, where Helen and Olaf lived in a charming one-family house. At once, they made me feel welcome and at home, and within a few days I had become accustomed to my new surroundings.

Helen showed me much of the countryside during that time. May was one of the most beautiful months in Denmark that year. The bleak winter was over and blooms had appeared in flower gardens and on trees.

One of the first letters I sent back to the United States was written to Gen and Dr. Joe. Thoughtfully, they saved all of my correspondence and gave it to me, years later. My first letter to them was dated May 27, 1950:

I have started on what I came to Europe for. Helen says there is no need to go to Sweden, they are doing similar work right here in Copenhagen. Helen took me to her doctor. He knows several big men in the field of medicine, also one in endocrinology. I am first to see a psychoanalyst. Then I will have many tests of the hormone content of my body. There may be a chance that there is some physical reason for this, I hope so. The tests will take several months before any decision can be made. First, they must be thoroughly convinced that any change would not be mentally harmful. Of

this, I am already sure, but to satisfy their minds as to
the course of action, I shall do just as they say.

Near the end of May, Helen and Olaf planned a driving trip
through Europe and generously included me in their plans. At first,
I hesitated, thinking of the expense of such an extravagant trip, but
Helen assured me that we could make it on seven hundred crowns
each; the equivalent of one hundred American dollars. I was excited
at the thought of seeing the rest of Europe and planned to take
photographs along the way, with the idea of selling them in order to
add to my small cash reserve. It is possible that I agreed so eagerly,
also, because I felt it would be like drawing a deep breath before an
icy plunge.

On a day in mid-June, after depositing Grethe with her
grandmother, we loaded the little pre-war Mercedes-Benz to capacity.
I occupied the back seat with four suitcases, my camera equipment,
and a formidable assortment of cooking utensils. A tent and
bedclothes hung precariously on the baggage rack, in addition to a
card table and three folding chairs. I'm sure there was never a tour
organized which afforded less comfort or more pleasure. In three
weeks, Helen, Olaf, and I drove through Germany, Austria, France,
and Switzerland, sometimes sleeping in the tent and sometimes in a
small, inexpensive *pensione* along the way. It was a wonderful,
rewarding experience to travel like wandering gypsies, and I returned
to Copenhagen early in July, ready to face whatever lay ahead.

Shortly after my return, I again wrote to the Angelos.

Dear Gen and Dr. Joe,
    Your very welcome letter received. How can I say
thank you for just being you. To feel needed and wanted
by people who know what I am striving for means so
very much to me now. I read *The Well of Loneliness* not
long ago. It made me more determined than ever to
fight for this victory. The answer to the problem must
not lie in sleeping pills and suicides that look like
accidents, or in jail sentences, but rather in life and the

freedom to live it. Yes, in considering the possibilities of removing and transplanting, perhaps science is reaching beyond the acceptance of current medical practice, but does that justify refusing to do it? Where would the world be without the Pasteurs and Ehrlichs to reach out and do the impossible? I believe the dedicated men I have met here are in the same league.

Love,

George

The last line of my letter indicates that I had gone slightly overboard in my enthusiasm at the time, but to me, no amount of respect and admiration for the medical profession would have seemed superlative.

On a day in late July, I went to one of Copenhagen's great medical research centers to consult Dr. Christian Hamburger, who had been highly recommended to me by one of Helen's doctors. Dr. Hamburger was one of Europe's most eminent endocrinologists and his treatises on hormone studies had been widely published in medical journals throughout the world.

The center in which Dr. Hamburger conducted his research was the Statens Seruminstitut, a group of large, immaculately white buildings, and I can remember how impressed I was at that first sight of the huge complex. It seemed to me, then, that I was about to enter Valhalla, to throw myself into the lap of the gods.

When I reached the institute, I learned from an assistant that Dr. Hamburger was vacationing at his home in the country and would not be returning for several days. Dangerously close to tears in spite of my twenty-four years, I managed to convey to him my urgency and desperation. Perhaps he thought I was an overly industrious biology student in great need of some kind, for he telephoned the doctor immediately and told me I could pay a visit to his home.

Feeling both relieved and anxious, I finally reached the address in a suburb of Copenhagen, and found a charming house, nestled in a forest. When the door opened, I was greeted personally by Dr. Hamburger, wearing paint-spattered clothes and carrying a paint brush in his hand. In perfect English, he explained that he had been whitewashing a ceiling, but he held out his hand in welcome and immediately made me feel at ease. He was a smiling man with eyes that twinkled behind rimless glasses, a narrow, rather pointed nose, and silvery hair; I guessed he was probably in his early forties. He led me out into a lovely garden where we sat chatting, while his charming and gracious wife served us cake and coffee.

When she had left us, Dr. Hamburger sat looking at me quietly for a few moments, then he said, "Well, now, just tell me about yourself." He spoke in a soft, gentle voice that I would come to know so well, and in that receptive and peaceful atmosphere, I poured out the whole story of my perplexing life. I included every major obstacle and every minor detail from early childhood to that moment. When I had finished my summary, I asked him first if he thought I was a homosexual, and I think I was surprised at my own forthrightness.

In an interview given a few years later for the benefit of a journalist who was assigned to write of these events, Dr. Hamburger recreated our conversation of that afternoon.

"No," he said, "I do not believe you are a homosexual."

"Then, what is wrong with me?"

"Why, I would believe that you are the victim of a problem that usually starts in early childhood, an irresistible feeling that you wish to be regarded by society and by yourself, as belonging to the opposite sex. Nothing is able to change this feeling."

"Do you think I ought to be treated by a psychiatrist?"

"It is possible and, eventually, I may direct you to do so, but I feel from what you have told me, that a psychiatrist couldn't do a great deal for you at present. I think the trouble is very deep-rooted in the cells of your body. Outwardly, you have many of the sex characteristics of a man. You were declared a boy at birth and you have grown up, so very unhappily, in the guise of a man. But, inwardly, it is quite possible that you are a woman. Your body chemistry and all of your body cells, including your brain cells, may be female. That is only a theory, mind you."

"Then, what can be done for me?"

"It would be possible, by hormonal treatment, to suppress the male components of your organism, by giving you female sex hormones."

"But that would be a rather expensive treatment, wouldn't it?"

"No, I would not charge you anything, but I will tell you quite frankly, that at the same time, you could serve as a guinea pig. There are several questions about the interaction of the hormone which are not quite clear now and I am very much interested in having you help me clear up these complicated matters. They can only be accomplished by observing a person over long periods of time. Since they are based on urinalysis, it will be necessary to collect specimens carefully, for several months or even a year, each and every day. You must guarantee that you will cooperate fully in this, and be very accurate."

I asked him, then, if it was possible to change me into the whole person I had envisioned.

"We can anticipate many difficulties." He paused, and said, "It is possible."

That statement struck me like an electric volt and I was so excited by then that I remember little else, except that we made an appointment for my first consultation at the Statens Seruminstitut. All I knew was that Dr. Hamburger had agreed to help me and I think I tried to express to him some measure of my enormous gratitude. He told me later that I cried, though I don't remember it.

I returned to the Johnsons' house on a crest of elation and impatience to get started. At last I had encountered someone who had offered a positive approach to my difficulties and who had not tried to dissuade me; a man of science and a highly respected one at that. Finally, I had found someone who said, "It is possible." Events no longer seemed static and, for me, it was a step forward toward some recognizable end.

That night, I wrote again to Dr. Joe and Gen.

"Just refer to me as guinea pig 0000!"

CHAPTER 12

My first tests and treatments began at Copenhagen's remarkable research center in early August of 1950, three months after my arrival in Denmark. I recall what a profoundly moving moment it was for me when I rang the bell summoning an attendant to unlock the huge wrought-iron gates. A round, moustached face appeared in the window of the gatehouse and I identified myself and gave Dr. Hamburger's name. Obviously proud of his ability to speak English, the attendant directed me to the correct location. His toothy smile and look of studied unconcern were never to change during the next two years when I applied almost daily for admittance. Later, I often stopped at the gatehouse for a cup of steaming coffee and a few minutes' conversation, for I knew he loved to talk about the United States. He witnessed the gradual change in me without any outward display of curiosity and I came to regard him as a kind of silent partner.

On that first day, I followed his directions and found myself at the entrance of the institute's hormone section. As I passed through one of the laboratories, the mixed odors of alcohol, ether, and other chemicals greeted me and I saw technicians and doctors moving about quietly in their familiar routines. It was a comforting sight at that moment.

I entered Dr. Hamburger's office and was greeted by his outstretched hand. My impatience must have been apparent, because he cautioned me almost immediately. "We must go slowly," he said, "for we don't know, as yet, just what is going on within your body, but we shall try to find out." He had no way of knowing how much that simple statement meant to me. "We shall try to find out."

"First, we are going to determine what hormones are present within your body, and how much of each the glands are producing. That is the purpose for testing your twenty-four-hour, total urine specimens. As you will recall, you have promised to be of assistance for other tests. We plan to use the specimens you submit to investigate several other problems, as well as in our search for a solution to your own case.

"You may not immediately understand all of the tests we will be making, but with time, each piece will fit into place much as the pieces of a jigsaw puzzle. Then, you will realize the great necessity for patience and caution, as we constantly recheck the facts."

I asked if the tests would be dangerous, a question that hadn't occurred to me before.

"No," he replied, "not in the sense you may be thinking of. But the human body is a very complex machine, the most complex known to mankind. It has a series of trigger mechanisms, each gland in its own way affecting the other glands in so many different parts of the body, that we doctors sometimes find ourselves far removed from the original premise. This sometimes leads to unexpected discoveries."

Then, Dr. Hamburger asked me how I felt since I had discontinued the estradiol, a request he'd made of me during my first visit to his home. I told him that for the first week, I'd felt fine, but after that, the old fatigue and sluggishness returned and I found myself somewhat depressed again.

"I rather expected you to have that result," he said. "I want you to keep from taking any more of the estrogens for a few days, until I can make my first tests. Then, I will give you a hormone injection. In the meantime, you must begin saving the urine, and that means every single drop, each day."

That began a period in my life when I was never to be without a two-quart bottle, discreetly concealed in a black bag. It may seem an excessively large bottle, but I was to learn that the human body does not excrete the same amount of fluid each day. It varies greatly and I had to be prepared at all times. Only one or two close friends were aware of its contents, the others remained in the dark about my mysterious, ever-present traveling kit. I began to refer to it jokingly as my *yor mor taske,* which means "midwife's bag" in Danish.

I visited the institute every day thereafter, and after his initial tests, which showed the balance of male and female hormones when no medication was given, Dr. Hamburger then gave me injections of high-potency estrogens, a series of perhaps fifteen or twenty. A statistical report, following the first tests, indicated a rather high estrogen (female hormone) level and a rather low androgen (male hormone) level. The report made it clear that these early tests didn't allow a definite conclusion but we knew that the first few injections of female hormones brought my energy back at a startling rate.

When he was sure that the injections were not creating a harmful effect of any kind, Dr. Hamburger changed my dosage to oral tablet form, which contained an even more active female hormone. By these methods of hormone administration, the male complement of my system was being suppressed into a slumbering state. I was undergoing what the medical experts called a "chemical castration."

It must have been rather early in our relationship when I realized that the slow, painstaking way in which Dr. Hamburger and his staff were working meant the project would be a long-term one, and I knew I'd have to find some way of supporting myself in the months to come. How provident it was for me that I came under the category of a research subject, and paid no fees to the institute for my daily medical examinations and chemical analyses. On the other hand, I had to satisfy the unbreakable habit of eating and, therefore, I selected some photographs I thought representative of my work, with the idea of presenting them to some of the local photographers.

In scanning the magazines, I'd noticed that color photography was virtually nonexistent in the Scandinavian countries at the time. I didn't sit back in fear as I had done before, but with new assurance (no doubt due to a healthier mental outlook), I gathered my samples one day and boarded a streetcar which jostled into the heart of Copenhagen. I alighted at the main street, The Stroget, which is the hub of Copenhagen's business and shopping district, a charming, narrow thoroughfare that curves from City Hall Square to King's New Square. My destination, Junker-Jensen Photographers, was located between the two squares.

I entered the studio and was greeted by a smiling young woman. I asked to see Mr. Junker-Jensen and was politely informed that he was busy, but that if I would wait, she was sure he would be happy to see me shortly. I sat on the sofa in the reception room and realized with sudden surprise that I was sure of myself in that situation of job hunting. There was none of the fear I had experienced on previous occasions, no moist hands, no rapid heartbeats. I felt that I was a thoroughly trained, very competent photographer and I knew that my work was good.

I waited for a short time, probably feeling rather pleased with myself, when a door opened and I saw a tall, slender man with dark hair and deep set eyes approaching me. "I am Jens Junker-Jensen," he said, in a brisk but friendly way. "May I help you?" He spoke in precise Oxford English.

I identified myself as an American, which must have been already obvious to him, told him that I expected to spend some months in Denmark and was looking for work in the photographic field. Mr. Junker-Jensen had no job to offer me at the time, but natural color photography was new to him and he offered me space in his studio and free use of the equipment if I would teach his staff the techniques of color photography.

I readily agreed. That association became a great source of satisfaction and pleasure to me, and several valuable friendships grew out of it. I met Edna, Jens Junker-Jensen's wife, a sympathetic young woman whose frequent invitations to dinner saved me from malnutrition. Also, I began looking for suitable models, hoping that I might land a few contracts for magazine covers. Jens introduced me to Janne Krohn, who became one of my best photographic models and a trusted friend. Janne was one of the most beautiful women in Denmark, both in looks and nature.

By then I felt that I was beginning to take my place in the world, and was happy, productive, and inspired to work in complete freedom at the studio.

Only one annoyance seemed important at the time and, finally, I decided to do something about it. For years, I'd had a complex about my prominent ears, no doubt inherited from Grandma's family, the Pedersens, and I'd been teased about them often as a child. At various times, I'd been told that I looked like a loving cup or a taxicab with its doors open, a description that wasn't really exaggerated.

Plastic surgery corrected my projecting ears by a relatively simple operation, performed in a doctor's office under a local anesthetic. In order to save money, I took the streetcar home when the job was over, clutching a small bottle of morphine. Miraculously, the complex I'd had for years disappeared almost overnight. I regarded it as a small victory, as it was the first conquest of one of the things I disliked about myself.

In October, 1950, I wrote to the Angelos, bringing them up to date on my medical adventures:

> Well, we really are progressing. The doctor said that he definitely believes the hormone injections are doing wonderful things for me, I have gained over 6 pounds, now weigh 116, and look and feel wonderful. He says that I respond to estrogens remarkably well and I feel better than ever before.
>
> Last week, I had a plastic surgery operation. I literally had my ears pinned back! I saw the results yesterday when they changed the bandages and it's a beautiful job. Completely changes my face and with some added weight, you wouldn't recognize me.
>
> Dr. Hamburger says I seem to need the estrogens. I'm not tired any more, my skin is completely cleared and my coloring is fresh. There has been some added weight in the hips and some bust development. They checked to see if the hormones are hurting the pituitary, but there was no change in the pituitary hormones. I think I am winning the battle.
>
> Love,
> George

Though I was completely engrossed in my own problem and its solution, I believe I saw, even then, the far-reaching effects that might result throughout the medical profession. Though it seems presumptuous of me now, I wrote the following in a letter of that period to Gen and Dr. Joe.

> Can you realize what success for me will mean to literally thousands of people? For I am not alone in this affliction. It may mean new hope and life to so many people. I think we (the doctors and I) are fighting this the right way—make the body fit the soul, rather than vice versa. For me, it is the heart, the look in the eyes, tone of the voice, and the way one thinks that makes the real person.

In November, I was delighted to receive word from home that I had a new little niece. Dolly's first baby girl was born November 11, 1950, and it was happy news for me.

It was sometime during that fall that I moved from Helen and Olaf Johnson's home, feeling that I had imposed on them long enough. I found a room in a large, pleasant apartment, occupied by a charming middle-aged woman, named Elsa Sabroe. I knew at once that the place would be exactly right for my needs, but I was faced with the problem of telling Elsa the truth about my medical experiments—that I might begin my tenancy as one person and finish it as another. I decided the best course was to tell her immediately, eliminating the possibility of future embarrassment to her. She was receptive and understanding and at once made me feel welcome and at home.

The rent was one hundred crowns a month, fifteen dollars in American currency. Rechecking my finances, I found that I had one hundred fifty dollars left of the money I'd brought with me. I tried to figure out a more strict budget, but there seemed to be no way I could stretch the money beyond two or three more months and I was getting awfully tired of *blod poelser* (a type of Danish salami), and yogurt.

I wrote to Dolly and Bill, telling them that I expected to land a good job and wanted to stay in Copenhagen for awhile and, without revealing any details, said that I needed a loan for some medical expenses. They promptly sent me four hundred dollars and with the few dollars that Mom slipped into her weekly letters, I managed to survive.

My first Christmas in Denmark was also my first away from home, and though I missed my friends and family, it turned out to be a memorable one. I spent a traditional Danish holiday with the Johnsons at a farm owned by Helen's parents near Roskilde, a town famous for its Gothic cathedral, and the final resting place of Denmark's royalty. I remember it was the first time I had seen a Christmas tree lit entirely by candles.

The holidays passed and with the advent of the new year of 1951, the loneliness which had been so much a part of my previous life was gradually diminishing. Each day was filled to capacity with my visits to the institute and my work at the photographic studio. I had made a few new friends and for the first time since my arrival, I began to feel content and secure.

I was suddenly shaken from my own involvements, however, when I received a letter from Dolly telling me that our wonderful Grandma Jorgensen had died on February 12. I grieved quietly for that grand old lady who had been such an inspiration in my life from my early childhood, and I deeply regretted the fact that I was so far away. Through the years, she had saved money for the expenses of her own funeral and, indomitable to the end, had made all the plans for it, including what she would wear. A gentle light had been extinguished and the world seemed not so bright a place without her.

As my own tests and injections continued at the institute and I watched the progressive results, I was confident that even without determining the cause, the scientists would find a solution. To them, the most challenging questions related to my case were: "Why did I feel certain that I was a woman masquerading in a seemingly male body?" and "Why did I form emotional attachments on two occasions with normal heterosexual men, as a woman might do?"

Dr. Hamburger had given me a theoretical answer when he said that perhaps my body cells, even my brain cells, were female. However, that theory, dating back to the 1920s and evolved by the great German sex pathologist, Dr. Magnus Hirschfeld, had never been clinically proven. As I reviewed my progress of the last few months, I wondered if proof really mattered. Results seemed to me of greater importance than the cause.

The high doses of estrogens I had received were suppressing or canceling out the effects of the male hormones which my body produced. When the male chemistry was inert, I became alive and vigorous and felt fully capable of meeting my responsibilities and problems with competence.

Professionally, things were happening also, for I began selling some of my photographs for small sums of twenty or thirty dollars each. They were color transparencies of various models, sold for magazine covers in Holland, Belgium, Norway, Sweden, and Denmark. One in particular that I remember was sold for the cover of *Vor Viden (Our Knowledge)*, a magazine which contained an article on the subject of sex hormones, written by Dr. Hamburger. Not only was the money extremely welcome, but actually selling my photographs at last was something of an achievement, and not even the dark days of that Danish winter could dim my spirits. I dreamed of a future in which I could be free from the half-life I had lived before, but the process seemed so long and I was impatient for the next step.

For five months, I'd been living successfully and happily under the doses of estrogen, and it was time to prove the correctness of these doses by eliminating them altogether and observing my reactions to their withdrawal. I remember that I was distressed at the thought of doing without them, but since I'd pledged my complete cooperation, I agreed to the next phase.

The hormone tablets were discontinued for several weeks and I was upset physically and mentally as the male hormones, no longer suppressed, took over again. Almost at once, the old fatigue and disturbing emotions returned. If I hadn't clung to the hope of final success which Dr. Hamburger had instilled in me, I might have reverted to complete discouragement and despair, but I trusted him implicitly.

I remember that he frequently impressed upon me the fact that no irreversible step, such as surgical removal of the male glands, could even be considered until all of the experts involved had thoroughly examined every possible avenue of knowledge.

He outlined my case to one of Denmark's leading psychiatrists, Dr Georg Stürup, and made an appointment for me to see him. Dr. Stürup, at the time, was psychiatric advisor to the Danish State Prison System, a foremost authority on criminal aberrations, and had been widely published with articles on neuro-physiology, children's psychiatry, and legal psychiatric subjects. He was a charming, genial, and highly amusing man. "You Americans are so childish about sex!" he said. "Operate on the brain, perform a lobotomy, create a whole new personality—but operate on a testicle and everybody explodes!"

As I remember, our series of consultations lasted for a period of several months. His main concern, of course, was to try to answer the mystifying questions of how much of my trouble was physical and how much was psychological. I suppose I must have been somewhat nervous at the prospect of these visits, because his psychological findings would be a determining factor in proceeding to surgical techniques.

He told me some years later that I had posed something of a problem for him, too. It was soon apparent to him that I was willing to undergo any risk, that I would rather be a guinea pig in a case that failed than not to try at all, to continue living as I had been. He considered my face, body, and behavior and wondered to himself how I would look as a woman. "You looked terrible as a boy! " he said, bluntly.

Notes taken during a later interview given by Dr. Stürup described some of the problems with which he was confronted at the time of our consultations.

"I was trying to get through to you," he stated, "trying to find some psychological reasons for your feeling and your desire to be transformed. Each time you came to me seemed futile, nothing I got was worth much from the psychiatric point of view and I couldn't unearth any particular childhood traumas or emotional aberrations that would give me the cause. I never reached that level where I could discover the emotional upsets.

"Once, you had tears in your eyes because you thought I was angry and wouldn't concede to surgical measures. But I had to go slowly, carefully. When you take responsibility for other people's lives, you walk on the edge of a knife, trying not to fall on either side.

"Finally, I knew it was impossible to go further and I felt you could not be cured, psychologically. After many visits, it was finally clear to me. I felt you were an intellectual type and was certain you would be able to handle your own emotional problems, afterwards.

"If it was not the success we hoped it would be then, I did not fear you would be worse than before. You see, that is what I had to decide in my own mind, 'was I going to make you worse?' You must never make things worse, but you may run all risks inside that limit. As a doctor, I wanted to help you and in the long run, I consented. Human understanding must be behind everything we do."

Having returned to the hormone injections after a hiatus of several weeks, I was approaching a crucial time. It would have been possible for me to continue taking hormones indefinitely, without harm. By then, Dr. Hamburger had proved that the male element of my body was no longer of any use to me, and Dr. Stürup felt that I was equipped, psychologically, for the move to surgery. After a consultation with the doctors and members of their staffs, it was agreed that a surgical operation was warranted.

However, such an operation, involving the removal of the sex glands, could not be performed in Denmark merely because a patient wished it or doctors prescribed it. Such a measure had to be sanctioned by the Ministry of Justice and submitted to its Medico-Legal Council, consisting of five leading medical experts.

In order to set the events in motion, Dr. Stürup made an application to the Ministry, accompanied by his reports and findings, and those of Dr. Hamburger and their other consultants. In addition, he asked me to write a letter to be sent with the reports, stating my own reasons for requesting the operation. After listing the reasons, by then so familiar to me, I concluded the summary with the following paragraph:

> I am twenty-four years of age and I know exactly what I am asking you to do in requesting this operation. Without this chance for the future, I know that I cannot go on living a good, constructive life. To return to my old way of life would destroy all my hopes and ambitions, as well as my body. This operation would not only be helping me, but perhaps open a whole new field of investigation for similar cases. If you could really realize how desperately, we, of my kind, need help. Please accept this paper with apologies for I fully realize that with these words, you shall judge the whole future of my life.

The application was reviewed by the Medico-Legal Council of the Ministry of Justice and the five council members unanimously accepted the judgment of my doctors. It was then returned to another department of the Ministry for ratification, but unaccountably was held up there by a minor official, and the events which had forged ahead so rapidly came to a complete and sudden halt. He had refused to ratify the proposal on the grounds that I was not a Danish citizen and had not been in Denmark long enough to warrant special consideration, though we had already investigated that question and could find no objection to it in the law. My disappointment was enormous but I could do nothing but sit and fret, while my doctors made countless attempts to untangle the red tape of bureaucracy, to no avail. Finally, I went to see the official, but he was very evasive and merely repeated that his refusal was final and based on my being a noncitizen.

To me, it was a long hot summer and I stewed with impatience and frustration. Dr. Hamburger and Dr. Stürup were of the opinion that the request should be granted on purely medical grounds and that the male hormone-producing system in my body was a physical liability. On that basis, they hoped to proceed as they would in the case of cancer or any other operable disease, which required no legal permission.

However, before reaching that point, Dr. Stürup had one last card to play. He approached the head of the Justice Ministry and Denmark's Attorney General, a remarkable woman named Helga Pedersen. I didn't meet Miss Pedersen but her reputation preceded her and she was known throughout Europe as a stormy petrel. At first interested in medicine, she switched to legal studies at the University of Copenhagen, after which she obtained an appointment as a State Magistrate. In 1946, she spent a year in the United States for advanced studies at Columbia University, and returned to Denmark to accept her appointment as Minister of Justice. An ardent feminist, Miss Pedersen frowned on the distinctions between men and women in the legal or social sense and was known throughout Scandinavia for her other crusades; among them, the defense of children born out of wedlock, the legalization of artificial insemination, and the psychological and other treatment of sex offenders, rather than jail sentences.

Dr. Stürup had chosen the right champion when he presented my case to her, personally. Almost overnight, she brushed aside all the obstacles and by mid-September, I had been scheduled into surgery. It seems interesting to me that I am so obligated to someone I've never met.

In anticipation of the operation, I wrote to Dr. Joe and Gen on September 17, 1951, a letter which seems to reflect my attitudes of the time:

> All papers are cleared and I was to enter the hospital today for the operation, but I developed a head cold, so it's postponed for a week. Expect to be in the Gentofte Hospital for about eight days. Incidentally, the hospital has no connection with the Seruminstitut. The whole thing will cost only thirty dollars! I repeat—thirty dollars! So you see, with room, food, and surgery, it is all incredibly inexpensive. I couldn't believe it, either, but it's true.

The more I think about this thing that I'm going through now, the less spectacular it becomes. This is a crazy world, and the word "impossible" is quite impossible to use nowadays. Newspapers here have been talking about a trip to the moon, supposedly coming in ten years or so. Is there no end to man's reaching out?

The more I talk to Dr. Hamburger the more I believe that chemistry is the whole basis of life (physical, I don't mean the soul). I think the future of life lies in the hands of the biochemists, when there won't be any cures, but rather preventives.

It's wonderful to be with a man like Dr. Hamburger. He is a scientist through and through, and yet he has the most terrific respect for life and human feelings. I tell you, if I could start over again in my education, I'd go in for biochemistry. On second thought, maybe the human race is safer with me as a photographer!

I'm in marvelous spirits. I have no feeling of fear whatever, just more impatience than anything.

Will write more later after the operation.

Love,

George

On September 24, 1951, the long-awaited surgery was performed by a surgeon of the Gentofte Hospital. It required an incision in the lower torso, through which was drawn the testicular tissue of the hormone-producing glands. The operation removed the main source of male hormone secretion and was to be the first of three operations I would undergo. Though it may sound complex, it was a relatively simple operation. It may have been one of the few times in medical annals that three physicians in widely divergent fields worked simultaneously on the same case: research specialists, a psychiatrist, and a surgeon.

October 8, 1951, I wrote to the Angelos in New Jersey:

Dear Gen and Dr. Joe:

I know I've been lax about writing, but I really wanted to wait until I could say something definite. Well, two weeks ago I was operated on. I was in surgery less than an hour and all went marvelously. I've been up and around for a week and I feel wonderful.

I saw Dr. Hamburger today, he's just returned from a medical conference in Spain. Did I tell you he went to England in July for a convention there, and took with him charts and records of my case to present information which he feels is important? My tests prove that when the estrogens are used to inhibit the androgens, it in no way affects the adrenal cortex. Apparently, there was some fear that the adrenal cortex, which produces some of the androgens in both men and women, would atrophy when estrogens were introduced.

So you see, I guess medical science has benefited from all this, too. Dr. Hamburger feels he has other important findings from my tests, but I don't know too much about it. I'll try to find out more and tell you all about it, Dr. Joe.

For now, he wants me to save twenty-four hour urines for another week before we start the hormone tablets again. Wants to check the decrease in steroids until I reach the bottom level.

As you can see by the enclosed photo, taken just before the operation, I have changed a great deal. But it is the other changes that are so much more impor-tant. Remember the shy, miserable person who left America? Well, that person is no more and, as you can see, I'm in marvelous spirits.

Half the time, people in shops call me "Miss" or "Mrs." and it doesn't embarrass me because I'm not afraid of people any more.

I have many friends here that call me constantly to join them. They like me and it makes me feel wonderful to be so much in demand. (That's not conceit—at least, I don't think so!)

All in all, everything is progressing wonderfully. Even my Danish is improving!

I thank God for the willpower He has given me, and for the friends who have been so much help thus far.

As ever,

George

P.S. I came across the following quotation just recently. It's by André Malraux, but I wish I'd written it! I'm adding it to my little notebook of favorite quotes, and thought I'd like to share it with you.

"The great mystery is not that we should have been thrown down here at random between the profusion of matter and that of the stars; it is that, from our very prison, we should draw from our own selves images powerful enough to deny our nothingness."

CHAPTER 13

By the late fall of 1951, the physical and mental changes in me had become even more pronounced and the gloom of the Danish winter that followed seemed to have no power to dampen my spirits. I continued my work at the studio, taking photographs and occasionally selling them, as the demand slowly grew for color magazine covers. I seemed to be very productive during that period and I think it was sometime late in that year that the germ of an idea first evolved for making a color motion-picture travel film of Denmark, as a project for the future.

I spent a delightful Christmas holiday with Jens and Edna Junker-Jensen, by then my very close friends, and approached the new year with the feeling that it was spring, regardless of the calendar.

Though I missed the United States and was frequently homesick, I felt secure in my life in Denmark. I loved the Danish country and the people, and I had made some very supportive friends. Although I had relatives there, I saw them rather infrequently, except for my cousin, Lona Ziegler, and her husband, with whom I shared the events of my life in Copenhagen.

All that winter and through the spring of 1952, I continued my daily visits to the Seruminstitut and consultations with Dr. Hamburger, accompanied wherever I went by my obscure black bag. Just me and my shadow.

By then, I had become so distinctly feminized that my appearance often confused people, for I still wore masculine clothes and intended to do so until my new status was officially recognized. At that point, my doctors and I agreed it was necessary to contact the American Embassy, in order to change my passport legally to a new status. I had already made the transition, chemically and surgically, in the eyes of my doctors, and it then remained for me to change my passport officially.

Shortly before my twenty-sixth birthday in May of 1952, I made an appointment to see Mrs. Eugenie Anderson, then American Ambassador to Denmark. I was still dressed in masculine clothing and I remember that I tucked my hair up under a beret. Even for the purpose of my visit, I had no intention of appearing otherwise, until I had received official sanction. For that matter, I had never signed my correspondence or credited my photographs with any name but my rightful one, until then "George Jorgensen."

The day I went to see Mrs. Anderson at the American Embassy in Copenhagen I found her a warm and gracious lady, anxious to be helpful. When I made known the reason for my visit and presented her with various letters from my doctors and the Ministry of Justice, she assured me she would handle the procedures herself and put things in motion immediately. Her first question, of course, was what name I wanted to submit to Washington for my new passport. I admit the question didn't take me by surprise, for I'd given it much thought in the previous year and, to me, the choice was a logical one.

Dr. Hamburger was the man to whom I owed so much, above all others. I transposed his first name, Christian, into the feminine, Christine, a name which I'd always thought attractive. Thus, my new name of "Christine Jorgensen."

Mrs. Anderson proceeded to relay my request to Washington and I hadn't long to wait for its approval.

By then, I had been in Denmark for two years and had told neither my friends nor family in America the true reasons for staying so long. I had started out as a tourist and was beginning to look like an expatriate.

I knew the day was fast approaching, however, when I'd have to reveal myself, and as time passed, I was even more aware of the responsibilities to my family that I'd always known I would have to face eventually. I had consistently and conveniently pushed them aside. I wasn't unmindful, of course, that my transformation was not yet complete and that further treatments and surgery would be necessary. Those future operations had been discussed thoroughly with my doctors and I considered them almost an accomplished fact.

Shortly after I had been to the American Embassy for my passport approval, "Tante Tine," Dad's aunt, arrived in Copenhagen from New York for a visit. I thought at the time that perhaps Providence had intervened once again and sent her as an emissary to help me break the news at home. Now that I look back on it, I think I've kept Providence pretty busy along the way.

My great aunt, Tante Tine, was a dear, eccentric, and delightful character and I was very fond of her. I remember that she often made me laugh with her tales about "family skeletons" and she had a disarming way of exposing her delicious gossip, usually reserving it for large family reunions.

She was a short, pixie-like little lady and when I greeted her on her arrival, I thought she had changed very little. Obviously, I had changed a great deal and at first she didn't recognize me. Once settled for a visit, I explained everything to her as clearly as I was able. She told me that she imagined something like it had taken place, when she first realized who I was, and of course she would carry back the news to my family when the time came. I had already begun to sketch out in my mind the letter I would send, and I suppose I had been composing it for two years. In the meantime, she had brought me messages and news from home and I remember how eager I was to hear it all.

Two weeks after Tante Tine's arrival in Denmark, my passport was approved by the State Department and I felt free, at last, to take my place in the outside world. However, I still had to summon up enough courage to make my first appearance in feminine dress. I'd been preparing for that time for several months, and had gotten some patterns and fabrics to try my hand at sewing. I had little or no money to spend for readymade things, and clothing was very expensive in Denmark at the time. Technically, I suppose my new clothes were not distinguished for their expert tailoring, but I managed to make them well enough so they looked presentable. Since then, I've become an excellent seamstress and for years have made most of my own personal and professional wardrobe.

I can remember the morning, early that summer, when I dressed myself in my new feminine clothing. I think I felt nervous and uneasy, for though I was secure in my own acceptance, I had no way of knowing about the reception of others.

After I had dressed in a green skirt, pale brown jacket and brown suede shoes, I looked at myself in the mirror. Quite frankly, I liked what I saw, and it seemed perfectly natural.

As I was eating breakfast that morning, Tante Tine arrived with a huge bouquet of flowers, her way of welcoming "Christine" into the world. I was very touched by her thoughtful gesture. She declared that she was delighted with the way I looked, a thought that was echoed by my landlady, Elsa Sabroe.

Later that same morning, accompanied by Edna Junker-Jensen, I went to a beauty salon, and I had what is known in those circles as "the works"—manicure, facial, permanent, and hair styling. I know that I felt awkward, it was so new to me, but I went through all the torture chambers and ended up enjoying it. As I remember, I came out looking somewhat like an unclipped poodle, with the tightest permanent in history.

To recover from that remarkable experience, Edna and I decided on some recreation in Copenhagen's Tivoli Park and that day it turned out to be an amusement area in more ways than one. We were walking leisurely through the park when suddenly I heard a long, low whistle, and undisciplined as I was at the time I looked around to find its source. Edna whooped with laughter and suddenly, I realized it was meant to be a "wolf call" in my direction. It came as something of a shock.

From then on, familiarity with my new image grew and my confidence expanded with it. I stayed within the small circle of my friends and seemed to fall into the female role gradually, and in a natural way. Those people who had not known me before accepted me in the same way that I accepted myself, and it was a period of adjustment without tension or fear.

It was then that I began to form more definite plans for making a documentary travel film, a project which I hoped would enable me to pay back my debt to Dolly and Bill and, also, to return a loan which I'd gotten from Larry Jensen. Larry had come to my rescue during one of my leaner Denmark periods, just as he had years before when he opened up a job for me at RKO-Pathé News.

I didn't expect the film to be the Hollywood extravaganza I once had dreamed of making, but felt it could be a new source of income for me by showing it on tour in the smaller Scandinavian towns. Since I planned to film it in color, I hoped it would be a more unique attraction in the outlying areas. My plan was to begin filming shortly after Tante Tine's departure for New York.

As the day of her leave-taking drew closer, I began to write the most important letter of my life, the letter to my family, which Tante Tine had promised to deliver, personally.

June 8, 1952

My Dearest Mom, Dad, Dolly, and Bill:

I am now faced with the problem of writing a letter, one which for two years has been on my mind. The task is a great one and the two years of thought haven't made it any easier. To begin with, I want you to know that I am happier and healthier than ever before in my life. I want you to keep this in mind during the rest of this letter. I suppose I should begin with a little philosophy about life and, we, the complex people who live it. Life is a strange affair and seems to be stranger as we experience more of it. It is often that we think of the individuality of each person and yet, we are all basically the same. Nevertheless, we are different in looks and temperament. Then, Nature, often for some unknown reason, steps in and adds her own peculiarities. Sometimes, something goes wrong and an abnormal child is born. These things are all a part of life, but we do not accept them. We strive, through science, to answer the great question of "Why?" Why did it happen and where did something go wrong? And last but not least, what can we do to prevent the disorder, or cure it if it has already happened? This leads to investigation and, if necessary, medical aid.

We humans are perhaps the greatest chemical reaction in the world, and therefore it is not strange that we are subject to so very many physical ailments.

Among the greatest working parts of our bodies are the glands. Several small, seemingly unimportant glands, and yet our whole body is governed by them. An imbalance in the glandular system puts the body under a strain, in an effort to adjust that imbalance. This strain, though not usually fatal, has a great effect on our wellbeing, both physically and mentally. Along with many other people, I had such an imbalance. I use the past tense, "had," because the condition has been cleared. Although a long, very slow process, a doctor in Copenhagen has managed this miracle. He is a great man and a most brilliant scientist.

Mine is an unusual case, although the condition is not so rare as the average person would think. It is more a problem of social taboos and the desire not to speak of the subject, because it deals with the great "hush-hush," namely, Sex. It was for this reason that I came to Europe to one of the greatest gland and hormone specialists in the world. This doctor was very willing to take my case, because he doesn't have the chance very often of finding a patient who can give such complete cooperation as I have. This cooperation meant months of daily tests and examinations. I do not know if you know that both men and women have hormones of both sexes in their bodies. Regardless of many outward appearances, it is the quantity of those hormones which determines a person's sex. All sex characteristics are a result of those hormones. Sometimes, a child is born and, to all outward appearances, seems to be of a certain sex. During childhood, nothing is noticed, but at the time of puberty, when the sex hormones come into action, the chemistry of the body seems to take an opposite turn and, chemically, the child is not of the supposed sex, but the opposite one. This may sound rather fantastic and unbelievable, but I think the doctor's words fit: "The body and life itself is the world's strangest thing. Why, then, should we be shocked or even surprised by anything that this strange mechanism does?" And how true those words are.

I was one of those people I have just written about. It was not easy to face and had it not been for the happiness it brought me, I should not have had the strength to go through these two years. You see, I was afraid of a much more horrible illness of the mind. One which, although very common, is not as yet accepted as a true illness, with the necessity for great understanding. Right from the beginning, I realized that I was working toward the release of myself from a life I knew would always be foreign to me. So, you see, the task was not so difficult as that; not nearly so much so as this letter is for me to write. Just how does a child tell its parents such a story as this? And even as I write these words, I have not yet told you the final outcome of the tests and an operation last September.

I do hope that I have built the letter properly so you already know what I am going to say now. I have changed, changed very much, as my photos will show, but I want you to know that I am an extremely happy person and that the real me, not the physical me, has not changed. I am still the same old "Brud." But Nature made a mistake, which I have had corrected, and I am now your daughter.

I do so want you to like me very much and not to be hurt because I did not tell you sooner about why I came over here. I felt, and still do, that it was the right way to do it. It wasn't because I didn't want you to be in on it, but rather it would have done no good for you to have spent all this time worrying about me when I was in no danger whatsoever. I knew that you must be told and it would have been easier on me if I had told you earlier, but I just knew it to be the best way. Right or wrong, it was my decision and I still stand by it.

Please don't be hurt. Tante Tine can tell you more, for we've had some good talks. She paid me the biggest compliment when she said: "My goodness, you look like both Dolly and Dorothy (a second cousin)."

I can't write more now. I seem to be all dried up for this time. Waiting at every postal delivery for your letter.
Love,
Chris
("Brud")

I labored painfully over that letter, for I knew it would cause my family great heartache and concern. At the same time, I had a deep and abiding need for their approval, though I knew even then it would be forthcoming. As I look back on it, it may seem an injustice to have kept them in the dark for so long, but I believed then they would be more protected by my silence.

I gave the letter to Tante Tine and asked her to have my brother-in-law, Bill, gather the family together and read it to them. I knew him to be a levelheaded man of intelligence, and thought his calm assurance would be helpful to them all in a time of crisis.

My great aunt promised to follow my requests and she seemed gay and confident when we said goodbye at Copenhagen's Kastrup Airport. Regardless of her air of confidence with me, however, Dad told me later that when she arrived in New York, she seemed nervous and tense when he greeted her at the air terminal. Without sharing a word of her disquieting news, she went immediately to her home in the Bronx, and remained there for nearly a week before she brought herself to call Dolly and Bill.

The news was an enormous shock to them both, but they rallied together with expected loyalty, invited Mom and Dad to their suburban home for the weekend and, finally, read the letter to them.

Mom and Dad were stunned and bewildered by facts they couldn't understand. Their immediate reaction was much the same as if they'd received word that I had died. Then, as Mom told me later, innumerable questions began to take over in their minds. How could such a thing be? What could have gone wrong? How had they failed? It was incomprehensible, it just couldn't be true. They were deeply upset and concerned for me, but in spite of their worry and confusion, they sent me the following cablegram: LETTER AND PICTURES RECEIVED. WE LOVE YOU MORE THAN EVER. MOM AND DAD.

Previously, I had written letters telling them about some of the interesting hormone experiments on animals that had been conducted at the Seruminstitut, and the color photography I had done in their connection, but those things were remote and meaningless to them when regarded in the light of my own case.

As I expected, Bill was comforting and assured them that everything would be all right. One of Mom's first thoughts, she told me later, was that she wouldn't be able to call me by my new name. Dad was so distraught, he paced the floor all night and wrestled with the thought that I may have violated the laws of my country or those of God.

Dolly called the pastor of her Lutheran Church, a compassionate friend, and when he arrived he found the family in a very upset emotional state. Dolly cried when she told him the story and when she'd finished, he said, "Now, what's all the excitement about? You people should be laughing and feeling joy for a miracle, not sorrow!"

Apparently, Dad was even more upset than Mom. "I'm sure," she told me, "that he was filled with remorse for the times he had been angry with you for failing to get or hold a job. Maybe he was remembering the times I'd told him to 'stop picking on that boy, or he'll go away some day and never come back.' " Then, that prophecy had come true, in a way that was inconceivable to them. They both feared for my future and were heartsick that they had been of no help to me at a time of need. Mainly, they regretted the fact that they had been unaware of my condition earlier, so that something might have been done to correct it.

I tried to calm those fears in a letter dated June 26, 1952:

> Your hope that I shall fit into the scheme of things and of life is unnecessary, simply because I have never been such a real person as I am today. If we all want to be truthful, I think we would admit that I never did fit into life before. But this is dragging out the old wash and since I have almost forgotten it, I hope you have, too. You both speak of being so hurt because I did it alone. I didn't want you to be worrying. As long as it all moved slowly and I knew you were calm over there, I could put more thought to the task before me. You also mention that you would have done something before, if you had known it. My answer is that you *did* do something before, namely, by giving me a good upbringing and education. You see, part of all this problem takes a pretty good head to keep from losing balance. In such a case, there is great concern over the mental shock which could follow such a drastic change. There is a human personality involved. And, to have done this thing as a child would have been extremely dangerous, because of the shock to an inexperienced young mind.
>
> I have understood every test and examination that I have been subjected to. Therefore, I could see the logic of every action. Through the doctor's eyes, I see myself as a chemical reaction, and as you know, chemical formulas are definite and lead to definite conclusions. I know you both must have taken this very hard, but I also know you are very intelligent people and that your understanding is as great as your intelligence.
>
> I have thanked God so many times for you both and all you have given me, so please don't have any post-

mortems. From here on, let's have laughter and no tears, for you must have no regrets.

I only wished that Grandma had lived to see me once more. She would have been so happy, too. Somehow I think she always knew I would have a great struggle in my life, for she had lived a long time and was very, very wise.

You've asked me about telling other members of the family. By all means, do it. I want you to feel comfortable about telling anyone you wish. It makes me feel good to know that your acceptance of me has come so far, that you wish to speak to other people about it. I can say, truthfully, with all my heart, I have no fear of meeting anyone. If you can take it, I can.

Love,
Chris

Soon after receiving that letter, Mom and Dad did tell a few friends and relatives, and the secret was kept, loyally, within that close circle. Later, Dad told me the story of those difficult moments. "I told a group of a few intimate friends at the beach club. I couldn't go down and face them with the secret in my heart, and I felt a million percent better afterward. It was a wonderful reaction from those friends. No one offered sympathy, just admiration. They were all anxious to see you, not from curiosity, just to welcome you home."

Understandably, Dad persisted in his efforts to clarify it all more fully in his mind. Perhaps, as Mom suggested, he felt that he had somehow failed me in my youth. Early in July, I received a letter from him, asking for a complete history of my case. "No technical words!" he admonished. I tried to answer in the following excerpt:

You might as well ask me to write the history of the world, without using the names and dates and, also, to do it on the head of a pin, or in three short paragraphs.

As I said in my first letter, I don't know what happened and science doesn't either, though they have some unproven theories. If they knew the answer, they could do more to keep this disorder from happening. My case began with a series of tests of several months' duration. These tests were to see my hormone content; in other words, to see my glandular output. All glands seemed completely normal, with the exception of the sex gland. My male hormone output was reduced to a point just higher than the normal female output, and the female output was higher than is found in the normal male patient. The male and female hormones act against each other; therefore, I had a bit of a chemical war going on within me, one trying to outdo the other. In the normal male person, the predominance of the one hormone keeps this imbalance at a minimum. After one year of daily examination, it was shown that the male glands were doing me much more harm than good. Consequently, the operation removing them, known as "surgical demasculinization."

Now, Dad, I don't want you to worry about my future or how I shall manage it, for everything is okay.

Love,
Chris

While these difficult family adjustments were taking place, I began the project that had been occupying my thoughts for some months, the travel film of Denmark. I had more time at my disposal by then, as Dr. Hamburger had released me from his care temporarily for the summer months that lay ahead.

I approached the National Tourist Association with my idea and they generously gave me *carte blanche* to travel anywhere in Denmark, at no expense to me, whatever. Meanwhile, Mom and Dad supplied me with sixteen-millimeter color film, which I couldn't buy in Denmark. I began filming in July, and since Denmark had no system for processing color film, I sent it to laboratories in England, editing it myself as sections were returned to me throughout the summer.

I remember that my first shots were taken at the Rebild Festival, held in the hills on the peninsula of Jutland. It is the only place in the world, outside the United States, where our Fourth of July is celebrated. Many years ago, a group of Danish-Americans bought the land, and upheld the traditional holiday of American Independence. Large numbers of Danes travel to the festival every year. Jean Hersholt was the principal speaker that year, and I also had the opportunity to renew my acquaintance with Mrs. Eugenie Anderson, the American Ambassador to Denmark, who had helpfully arranged my change of passport.

It was at the Rebild Festival that I met one of Denmark's top journalists, a charming man who seemed extremely interested in the fact that a young woman should be filming a color movie with what he regarded as such professional skill. I remember that he began a conversation by offering to carry my photographic equipment, explaining the history of the park and asking me to dinner, almost all in the same breath. Naturally, I told him nothing about myself, except that I was an American on a filming project. We were photographed together, a picture that was widely printed much later on. He had no way of knowing then that he was sitting next to one of the biggest journalistic scoops of the decade, and for that matter, neither had I. I was told later that when the story broke he was virtually suicidal. As one of Denmark's foremost journalists, he must have been, ordinarily, a man with an infallible nose for news.

My work at that time was rather like being "on the road." I spent a few days at a time in one location, went back to Copenhagen, and then moved on to a new site.

During that summer of 1952, I traveled to the beautiful island of Bornholm, which lies off the southern tip of Sweden, the small island of Fano, the shipping port nearest to England, and to the country's second largest city, Aarhus, the birthplace of Grandma Jorgensen. In Aarhus, I filmed an area known as *Den gamle By,* which means "the old town," an exact reproduction of its condition one hundred years before. Kronborg Castle in Elsinore, the legendary home of Shakespeare's "melancholy Dane," was another area rich in film subjects, and I photographed Michael Redgrave during a dress rehearsal of *Hamlet,* which was performed in the courtyard.

At sometime during my travels of that period, I met Count Einar Reventlow, who became my host for a weekend. He invited Helen Johnson and me to his castle on the island of Langland, an estate known as Rudbjergaard, which means "Redberry Garden." Helen occasionally accompanied me on these jaunts as a photographic assistant and interpreter, and I remember how excited we were to be able to film the interior of a beautiful seventeenth-century castle that was actually lived in. Count Reventlow was completely unsuspecting of my state, and I remember him as a most gracious host.

My filming chores also took me to the Royal Copenhagen factory, where I filmed the manufacturing process of some of the world's most exquisite porcelain; to Georg Jensen, the famous silver works; and to the Oscar Davidson Restaurant, known throughout Europe for its open-face Danish sandwiches and a two-yard-long menu.

In addition to the historic locations that I wanted to record on film, I was also interested in the people of Denmark: their traditions, dress, and customs, the rural and urban way of life, the working people, the family unit, and I tried to capture both the harshness and gentleness of life in the faces of those people. I look back on that experience with great pleasure, for I found charm and friendliness everywhere.

It was an extremely happy and active summer for me. Not only was I kept busy with the actual filming, but I also edited as I went along. Thousands of feet of color film gradually began to take shape in what I believed would be an entertaining and provocative travel film.

It was gratifying to feel that I was adjusting gradually to my new role in life and that I was met with acceptance everywhere I went. I was comfortable as "Christine," and I suppose that without knowing it I made other people feel comfortable as a result. Contentment and happiness are contagious, I think. The people I met during the course of filming seemed to enjoy being with me, and I was seldom at a loss for a dinner date or a pair of willing arms to carry my photographic equipment. Instead of retreating at every opportunity as I had before, I was expanding into a new eagerness for life.

Though I never shared the intimate knowledge of myself with anyone, I can safely say I had no feeling of deceit, for by then I was falling easily into the natural pattern I'd been meant to follow.

Around mid-August of 1952, I hurried back to Copenhagen to greet my Aunt Augusta, who arrived from Minneapolis. It was a momentous trip for her, for she hadn't been in her native Denmark for more than thirty years. She bustled happily off the plane and, suddenly, I was flooded with the memory of my visit to her in Minneapolis at a time when she had been such a great inspiration to me. Though only five years had passed, it seemed like a lifetime away.

After a few minutes of calm inspection, she declared her complete, unreserved approval and I laughed with relief and the joy of seeing her again.

Augusta had brought me a wealth of clothing, evidence of diligent shopping tours by Mom and Dolly. Clothing prices in Denmark were prohibitive at the time, and my mother and sister had indulged in reckless buying sprees, much to my delight. They'd sent dresses, suits, shoes, gloves and handbags, all of which helped to round out my meager wardrobe.

After several days of visiting with Augusta, I began to feel much more secure about the acceptance by my parents of the transition in my life. Though I didn't realize then to what extent, their lives had changed almost as much as mine. The anguish I had caused them was still a matter for deep regret, but I felt that with the passage of time their adjustments would be less trying and difficult.

"They still don't understand this, Chris," Augusta said, "but you are their child, and if this will bring you happiness, they're all for it."

For more than two years, I had lived with the disturbing questions of how I would affect the family I loved, and how they would reconcile themselves to these remarkable events, though deep in my heart I never doubted the answers.

After many late-hour conversations with Augusta, I was sure that the difficult times for all of us were approaching an end, and though I knew further treatments and operations lay ahead and I still faced the prospect of going home, I had no fear of the future.

When Augusta left for the United States, I eagerly returned to the fulltime job of filming again, secure in the certainty that from then on life held no more insurmountable hurdles for me. Looking back on my unruffled self-assurance, I'm reminded of a fitting phrase in Danish. *"Lad os vente,"* which means, roughly translated, "You ain't seen nothin' yet!"

CHAPTER 14

The summer passed into the autumn of 1952 and by then my film was well on its way to completion. I returned to the Seruminstitut to resume my medical treatments with Dr. Hamburger, continuing the hormone controls and daily chemical analyses. As winter approached, my doctors made plans for me to undergo a second operation, a step that would mean the removal of any remaining maleness. Specifically, the operation, termed a "penectomy," meant removal of the immature sex organs.

I entered Rigs Hospital on November 20, thirteen months after my first operation. Again, the surgery was to be performed by hospital staff members, Drs. Poul Fogh-Andersen and Erling Dahl-Iversen, both eminent plastic surgeons.

I remember that the hospital was overly crowded at the time, and out of necessity, I was given the only private room available, located near the children's ward. Since I was ambulatory for the two days preceding surgery, it was a happy choice, for it allowed me to wander about, chatting and making friends with the children. I made two good friends in the ward; one, a teenaged boy named John, hospitalized for a spinal disorder, who taught me a valuable lesson in personal courage. After spinal surgery, a blood clot had formed that pressed against his spine, leaving him permanently paralyzed, and after a long convalescence, he finally went home in a wheelchair. Shortly after, he tipped out of the chair and broke his leg, returned to the hospital, and had been there on his second trip for three months when I was admitted.

He was a very cheerful and endearing boy, with a seemingly endless fund of courage, and we played cards and other games to pass the time. He had a large collection of small clay soldiers he'd made himself, using tin foil to make their epaulettes. I still treasure the little clay soldier that he gave to me.

Another small friend from the children's ward was a blonde, blue-eyed charmer named Thora, who often tried to wheedle candy from me and was invariably successful.

The ward also held tragic victims of many other crippling diseases, almost all of which had been listed in the medical books. It occurred to me then that I was in the hospital to correct a disorder that was seldom discussed in society and that even many general practitioners were hesitant to regard openly.

Parenthetically, it seems unfortunate to me, when millions of dollars are allocated to medical research and the relief of human suffering, that little or nothing is earmarked for help of victims of sex abnormalities. It is frequently considered more appropriate to strengthen the arm of the law against people who don't fit into acceptable patterns of sexual normalcy, whatever the "norm" may be. In the face of abnormality, sometimes it's considered clever to ridicule or condemn. However, it's encouraging to note that within the past few years, the subject of deviation has not been so carefully avoided by legislative groups or medical practice, and society in general has been even further enlightened, I think, through occasional channels of mass communications media.

However, I wasn't pontificating or dwelling on social injustices on the day I was scheduled for surgery, for my problem had always seemed to me a wholly medical one. I was probably congratulating myself that I was about to reach another milestone on a circuitous road to accomplishment. At any rate, I know that I was in very good spirits and fear didn't enter my mind.

My second operation, as the previous one, was not such a major work of surgery as it may imply. The third operation was to be far more serious and complex, but that was yet in the future.

Within a few days, I was resting well and had experienced little serious discomfort. The postoperative care, however, was rather involved and I was confined to bed for a much longer time than I'd expected.

The days of convalescence were uneventful ones, following each other in the monotony of hospital routine. Typically, I fretted with impatience to be released and sent home. I'm afraid I've never been able to accept illness very graciously, especially in myself.

By then, my thoughts were centered on the hope that I'd be able to get home to Mom and Dad in time for Christmas, a little less than a month away. I was thinking, too, of the possibilities that might be open to me for exhibiting my film, either in Denmark or America, and even looking ahead to the time when I could return to a fulltime career as a photographer. New York seemed so far away, I was homesick and wanted to see my family, and the only real obstacle was our actual meeting and reunion.

In spite of almost six months of correspondence between us since my revealing letter, I wondered what they would really think when they actually saw me. I had left New York an inhibited, introverted half person and I'd soon be returning to them as a happy, whole human being.

I've had some occasion to recall since that it was on exactly the tenth day in the hospital that I awoke to see the first snow of the year outside my window. I can even remember the book I was reading that day. It was *The Robe* by Lloyd C. Douglas.

My usual reveries about home and family were ended abruptly when I heard a childish giggle outside my door, followed by a delicate knock. I was already prepared for the smiling little face of Thora. She had come for her daily raid on my candy dish, and after making her selection, she left with her usual polite response: "Thank you, Miss Jorgensen."

Shortly after, my young friend, John-of-the-toy-soldiers, was wheeled in to ask when I would be up and around again, hinting that he was in need of a rummy partner. I told him I was still a little shaky, but I hoped it would be soon. When he left, I picked up my book and began to read, soon lost in the fascinating pages of Douglas' novel. For a time, I was conscious of nothing else until I heard another light knock at the door. Expecting that it might be Thora, returning for another raid, I called out an invitation to enter. The door opened and a neatly dressed young woman entered; a complete stranger to me. "I'm afraid you have the wrong room," I said. "Who are you looking for?"

"Are you Miss Jorgensen?"

"Yes."

"I have a telegram I think you should read." It was only then I noticed a sheet of yellow paper in her hand. I felt the sudden moment of panic that often accompanies an unexpected message, and for a moment I thought there might have been a death in my family. I searched her face for some clue and wondered why she was delivering a telegram. Filled with a kind of unknown dread, I reached out to take it from her hand, and read the message: BRONX GI BECOMES A WOMAN. DEAR MOM AND DAD SON WROTE, I HAVE NOW BECOME YOUR DAUGHTER.

Nothing registered at first, I didn't even understand it. I read it again, not really comprehending, until I realized at last that it had not been addressed to me: it was a message sent over an international press-service wire, and what I held in my hand was a copy of the dispatch. It was datelined New York, December 1, 1952.

It was all so unreal, like the moment of receiving a mortal blow, and I closed my eyes hoping I could shut out the nightmare. In the first shock-waves, the world seemed to disintegrate around me with sickening finality. I know at first I felt fear for the safety of my family and horror at the disclosure of an intimate and highly personal event in my life, but the initial shock was replaced by a towering rage. I was livid with anger and I don't hesitate to admit it. To me, that message was a symbol of a brutal and cruel betrayal. A lifetime of agonizing unhappiness, two years of medical treatment and two surgical operations had been telescoped into a couple of succinct lines on a telegraph form, and I knew without being told that it would go far beyond that hospital room.

Even now, I can recall my feelings of bitter resentment, as a dozen questions raged through my mind. Who, I wondered, could have done it; of all the people I knew, who could have exposed such a totally private episode to the blinding glare of publicity and the outside world? Not only who, but why? And how had it occurred? So far as I knew then only a few friends and relatives in the United States and Denmark were aware of what had happened to me, and I was certain that the medical experts would offer no information to anyone outside their professional circles.

Finally, my fury began to subside and I turned to the young woman beside me. "Who did this unforgivable thing?" I asked.

She answered me quietly and sympathetically. "I truly don't know," she said. "You'll have to prepare yourself, Miss Jorgensen. Tomorrow's newspapers will carry this story in banner headlines. I'm a reporter for *Information*. Will you give me an interview?"

Information, I knew, was one of Denmark's leading daily newspapers. I suppose I must have agreed to her request, since I was soon aware of a barrage of questions. Her questions and my answers seemed to have no reality, and I was so distraught and preoccupied that I seemed unaware of my surroundings. Only one thought stood out clearly: "What shall I do?"

I only returned to reality when I felt something pressed into my hand and turned to see Miss Olsen, the head nurse. It was a letter from Mom, who had no way of knowing the circumstances under which it would arrive. The young Danish journalist remained, her busy pencil recording every moment, and Miss Olsen stood at the foot of my bed like a protecting sentinel.

"Dear Chris," the letter began, "This is one of the most difficult things to write. I must tell you that Aunt Edie has died." Aunt Edie was another of Dad's sisters, and we all knew that for years she had lived with a rheumatic heart which had presented a perennial threat. The news of her death was not surprising, but coupled with the shocking telegram I had just received, it created an outlet for emotional release, and at that moment I began to cry. I really let go with a good one, sparing nothing, weeping in confusion, bitterness, and unhappiness and all the time no doubt feeling wonderfully sorry for myself.

Like an avenging angel, Miss Olsen ushered the newswoman out of my room, while I tried to bring my emotional outburst under control. I wondered if, after all, it had only been a dream, if I'd really been reading a book just a short half hour before. But I knew it was real and I felt panicked and threatened.

Miss Olsen came back shortly to inform me that there were several transatlantic phone calls waiting for me, and asked what I wanted to do about them. I guess I still must have been wallowing in my own despair, for she had to ask me twice. I felt like a puppet waiting for the master to manipulate the strings that would move me into some sort of action. Something must have struck a responsive chord, however, and I asked her to help me to the nearest telephone. In my anxiety, my only thought by then was to reach Dr. Hamburger, who had been not only my medical adviser but a trusted friend and confidante.

The redoubtable Miss Olsen wheeled my hospital bed down the corridor to an empty private room that had a telephone. I dialed Dr. Hamburger's number, and he finally answered the ring himself. Somehow, I managed to gasp out the story of what had happened, and in his usual unruffled way he told me to relax and not to worry. "Now, calm down," he said, "I'll be there with you as soon as possible."

It was a great relief to hear his encouraging words and I began to simmer down a little. I recalled the old cliché that there was nothing so dead as yesterday's news, and I entertained the thought that I would pass into the limbo of old news stories, with visions of a few yellowed clippings, buried in some obscure newspaper morgue.

I was musing on my obscurity, after my heartening conversation with Dr. Hamburger, when the phone rang and the agitated switchboard operator asked if she could connect me with the first of several overseas calls. I had the impression at the time that she was beginning to look upon herself as an important cog in some international intrigue, for excitement seemed apparent in her voice. However, she managed to go through the correct motions and completed the connection. Suddenly, I heard a clear voice on the wire, saying "Miss Jorgensen? I'm a reporter from a New York newspaper. How do you feel?"

Though I'd been pretty naïve about a lot of things in my twenty-six years, I knew that solicitude for my health was not the reason for a transatlantic phone call from a strange, disembodied voice. I don't remember what I said now to his question, but since then I've thought of at least a couple of good answers. However, I was totally unprepared for his next remark, "All of America is anxiously awaiting a statement from you!"

It was, of course, inconceivable that anyone but my most intimate friends and family would be "anxiously awaiting a statement," particularly from someone who, until that moment, had been as inconspicuous as a church mouse. However, there were a few things I wanted to know myself and I countered with a question of my own, by asking how it had happened. "Well," he said, "it seems that someone wrote a letter to the *New York Daily News* about you and the reporters got to your parents."

I knew that was ridiculous and told him that my family would never have given out the story without my approval. He offered no further information as to who the "someone" might be, but continued his offensive with a barrage of questions.

I suppose I must be indebted to him for giving me my first insight into the devices sometimes used in present-day news coverage, particularly in ferreting out details of a highly personal and private nature. Several times since then I've been not only the victim but a witness to the most disgraceful, degrading kinds of behavior from the news hawks.

I realize, of course, that selling newspapers is a business, and that gathering news and presenting it truthfully must be a difficult and competitive task. However, in a story of a highly controversial nature, some newsmen are prone to alter facts and present them in an exciting, provocative way to a panting public, without always following the unvarnished truth. This is not meant to be an unqualified blanket statement, for through the years, I've known many wonderful people in the newspaper business and have enjoyed great kindnesses from them. But it was my first experience in that area, and it wasn't a very kindly introduction.

My distant inquisitor however, was no doubt merely doing his job when he asked me how tall I was, what my waist, hip, and bust measurements were and whether I slept in pajamas or a nightgown... or what? I was even then beginning to see the ridiculous humor in some of the questions. Those questions might have been pertinent to a movie star but certainly not to me.

If anyone was to be even remotely interested, it seemed to me it would be because I had gone through an unusual medical experience, which, although uncommon, was certainly not exclusive. I realized that there would be an understandable medical curiosity about my operations and their scientific details, but I also suspected, even then, that much of the interest would be excited because the controversial subject of "sex" was involved. Those suspicions were solidly confirmed that day, after I accepted several more calls from the gentlemen of the press.

Finally, Miss Olsen wheeled me back to my room and I was surprised and upset when she told me I'd been something of a disruptive force in the hospital while I was closeted with the telephone. Apparently, the corridors had come alive, the switch-board lit up like July fireworks, nurses scurried to and fro, and speculation flew like feathers in the wind. It took some time before normalcy returned.

Once in the safety of my room, I began to wrestle with the impossible thought that Mom and Dad had cooperated with a world of strangers and helped to expose me to the shocking glare of notoriety. At the same time, I knew that there must be a logical explanation, and I'd merely have to wait for word from home, in the meantime hoping against hope, that "today's newspapers would be used to wrap up tomorrow's fish."

I remember that I slept deeply that night as though I'd been drugged, but without any sedation. A psychiatrist would probably refer to it as an "escape mechanism," but whatever the explanation, I had cause to be grateful for Mom's early childhood conditioning.

It's possible that the gloom of those proceedings has colored my memory, but I think I can remember that the following day dawned into a muddy gray atmosphere. Miss Olsen woke me and began to perform the usual duties that revolved around my comfort, accompanied as always by her warm, friendly smile. Finally, I broached the subject that I knew was occupying both our minds; I asked for the newspapers. "Miss Jorgensen," she said, "I don't think you want to read the papers today." I felt a quick moment of panic and wondered if it was really going to be as bad as that. But I assured her that I was prepared for anything, and eventually I'd have to be informed anyway.

She returned in a few minutes with the newspapers. She'd borrowed them from my young friend, John, who had taken a quick look at the headlines, thrown the papers on the floor, and said he didn't want to read them that day.

It was only then, as I stared at the front pages, that I became fully aware of the magnitude of my betrayal. The stories and pictures confirmed my worst expectations. A photograph of me in military uniform was planted next to one of the more recent photos I'd sent to Mom and Dad, and the letter that Tante Tine had carried back to them was printed verbatim. There could be no question that the press had obtained a complete copy of that letter, not just a general idea of its contents. Repeatedly, as I read the papers that morning, the question of how the story was revealed and by whom returned to me like a nagging, insistent little tune. I could think of no possible answer. As for my letter and photos, I knew I'd just have to wait until I heard from Mom and Dad for clarification.

It seems to me now a shocking commentary on the press of our time that I pushed the hydrogen-bomb tests on Eniwetok right off the front pages. A tragic war was still raging in Korea, George VI had died and Britain had a new queen, sophisticated guided missiles were going off in New Mexico, Jonas Salk was working on a vaccine for infantile paralysis....Christine Jorgensen was on page one.

Nothing could have prepared me, however, for the events that followed the initial news stories. Like an avalanche, letters and cables poured into my hospital room, and I was inundated with fantastic and extravagant offers:

WIRE IF INTERESTED IN PICTURES OR NIGHTCLUBS AND
AVAILABILITY.

WARNER BROS STUDIO   HOLLYWOOD, CALIFORNIA

ADVISE IF INTERESTED IN WORKING MY NIGHTCLUB $500
A WEEK.

COPA CLUB   PITTSBURGH, PA

ADMIRE YOUR GREAT COURAGE, YOU CAN NOW HELP
THOUSANDS TELLING YOUR STORY. CAN OFFER NUMBER
OF WEEKS LECTURE, PERSONAL APPEARANCE.

46TH ST THEATER   NEW YORK CITY

CONGRATULATIONS YOUR SELECTION AS SWEETHEART OF
FRATERNITY. WOULD APPRECIATE VISIT AND AUTO-
GRAPHED PICTURE.

KAPPA DELTA KAPPA   UNIVERSITY OF HOUSTON
HOUSTON, TEXAS

REFERRING PHONE CONVERSATION WEDNESDAY AM
PREPARED TO PAY $1,000 A WEEK PERSONAL
APPEARANCES. YOUR ACCEPTANCE WITHIN 48 HOURS
REQUIRED. ALSO WOULD LIKE ACT YOUR PERSONAL
MANAGER. WILL PREPARE SPECIAL MATERIAL FOR YOU TO
USE ON PERSONAL APPEARANCES.

HOLIDAY THEATER   NEW YORK CITY

HAVING SEEN YOUR PHOTOGRAPHS IN NEW YORK PAPERS
WE FEEL YOU WOULD BE A LIKELY CANDIDATE FOR THE
TITLE OF MISS NEW YORK PRESS PHOTOGRAPHER FOR
1953 AND WOULD APPRECIATE YOUR ENTERING OUR
CONTEST TO BE HELD JANUARY 18TH.

N.Y. PRESS PHOTOGRAPHERS' ASS'N.

MIAMI BEACH'S NEW BILTMORE HOTEL OPENING
DECEMBER 20 OFFERS YOU POSITION AS CHIEF
PHOTOGRAPHER. CAN PLACE YOU IN OUR SHOW FOR THE
SEASON. SING, DANCE, OR PARADE. IF INTERESTED CABLE
SALARY WHEN AVAILABLE, ETC.

CLUB FROLICS   TAMPA, FLA.

CAN OFFER YOU $500 A WEEK NET TO CO-STAR WITH ME
IN A TWO WOMAN STRIP SHOW PLAYING FIVE THEATERS
IN THE US MIDWEST THIS COMING SUMMER.

NEW ORLEANS, LA.

I have to admit that those incredible offers left me stupefied. At the same time, my sense of humor took over. The striptease item, particularly, left me convulsed with laughter at the hysterical vision of myself in ostrich feathers. I could only shake my head in bewilderment and add each message to the mounting pile beside my bed.

It was impossible to view the offers with anything but amazement. I was, after all, a patient in a hospital, still flat on my back and convalescing from recent surgery. No matter how minor the surgery may have seemed, I was still undergoing postoperative care and had not been released by my doctors.

Foremost was the fact that I had absolutely no interest or inclination for the entertainment world, and even the idea of appearing in a nightclub or on a stage, then, was totally unthinkable. The only time I had ever considered such a thing was in connection with my Denmark film, for I knew that without a sound track I would probably have to narrate it myself. The thought had given me a lively set of nerves, but for that purpose, I hoped to overcome my fear of appearing in public.

At that point, I had no thought of a professional career other than photography, for which I'd been educated and trained. I had worked very hard on the travelogue, both on the filming and the editing, and that alone was the center of my interest. I believed I'd done a good job and I hoped to use it as the source of a badly needed income.

Of that period, one letter in particular served to counteract my critical opinion of the press. It was a charming letter of apology, sent by the attractive young Danish woman, who had brought me the first shocking news:

December 3, 1952

Dear Miss Jorgensen:

I don't like journalism when I have to pour such a lot of surprising and confusing information over somebody's head, as I had to do when I went to your room at the hospital with the New York telegram. I felt very badly about it, but although I disliked the situation itself, I certainly at the same time enjoyed meeting such an interesting and sympathetic person as you. I would like to hear how you are getting along after these eventful days. If you don't mind, I will try to drop in and say hello to you at the hospital, but if you prefer peace, I will understand and respect that.

Best wishes,

Thyre Christensen

One of my greatest concerns in that period of insanity was for my family, and I was desperately anxious to hear from home. I received a brief cable that read: ALL OKAY, DON'T WORRY, but I knew that a letter must be on its way and I had the feeling it was crossing the Atlantic by carrier pigeon instead of by airplane. Finally, the letter arrived, dated December 3, 1952:

My dear Chris,

The news has broken here, as you know by now, all over the headlines. First, the *New York Daily News* and others followed.

We do not know how he got the information or who the source was, but a reporter from the *Daily News* was the first to contact us, asking for information, and he was very threatening. I know you must be very distressed and upset that your letter and pictures have been published, but he told us if we didn't give him further material, he'd print the story anyway. After a long talk, we all decided that it would be the best way of presenting the truth, and I'm sure you must feel as we do, that it's best to have been honest, once they had the story, than to make matters worse by allowing them to slant everything badly.

Since the first *Daily News* break, the phone rings all day and night and so does the doorbell. Calls from reporters wanting interviews and pictures. We posed for no pictures, refused them all.

The calls and visits started again this morning, so we are up at Tante Tine's to get out of their reach today. It has been terrific, but don't worry, we are okay. We can't figure out how this got out or from whom. Did this break in Denmark first? We can't tell what. I sent you a cable today, but we are going to phone you within the next few days, to tell you everything in greater detail.

All will quiet down, we hope. It surprised us much and we are still in the dark about it all.

I do hope you can be as calm as possible. We are all big enough to face facts with strength and courage, as you have already shown. Do take care. We are okay, so don't worry.

Enclosed, $10.00.

Love,

Mom

Keep your chin up, everything will be all right. We are with you all the way.

Love,

Dad

Always, I'd been a very private person, due no doubt to my personal difficulties, and those problems had forced me to throw a protective covering of shyness and reticence around myself. I'd come from a hardworking, churchgoing family, proud of its long Danish heritage, and I think we had reason to regard ourselves as good, responsible citizens. We'd had our fair share of happiness, tragedy, success, and failure, but surely there was nothing to distinguish us from the millions of other families in the world.

Suddenly, without warning, my family and I had been thrust into the blinding spotlight of notoriety, through no design of our own. I think we felt rather like the Christians thrown to the lions, and the Romans were having a field day.

I could only lie in the hospital as a captive audience, watching the sordid little drama unfold, helpless to do anything about it. I didn't know it then, but the curtain would never ring down.

CHAPTER 15

Apparently, the shattering events that began on December 1, 1952, were to affect the lives of many more people than just the Jorgensen family.

Dr. Hamburger was besieged with letters, as he indicated in the following excerpts from a medical paper, published in *Acta Endocrinologica,* a scientific journal, in 1953.

> Events have put into my hands what must certainly be regarded as a unique collection of letters from a considerable number of men and women who desire to change their sex. These letters were occasioned by the sensational publicity given by the World Press to one case in which feminizing hormonal treatment and surgical demasculinization were carried out. Our patient differed from others previously reported only in that surgical castration followed a period of hormonal castration during which the patient was under careful psychiatric surveillance.
>
> Even before our patient had been discharged from the Surgical Clinic of the hospital in Copenhagen, the news of the "change of sex" had spread all over the world. As far as is known, the press succeeded in tracing the contents of a private letter from the patient to his relatives in New York—and published the story without his knowledge or consent. On December 1, 1952, a

New York paper splashed its front page with the "world beater." In record time the news had reached the remotest corners of the earth, and since my name was quoted in the reports, letters began pouring in.

Between December 3, 1952, and October 18, 1953, I have received 1,117 letters from patients, as well as numerous enquiries from the medical world.

These letters are very varied: faulty attempts at presentation in writing, mingled with stylish masterpieces; almost undecipherable bits of paper in between faultlessly typed reports of up to sixty foolscap pages. They are written in Danish, Dutch, English, French, German, Italian, Norwegian, Portuguese, Spanish, and Swedish. The majority of these letters appear to have been written by exceedingly unhappy persons who feel that life is a tragedy. This collection of letters may probably yield highly significant information of the psychological background governing the "desire for change of sex." It is probably important that these letters are spontaneous reactions, and not filled-in questionnaires. Their contents—and what can be read between the lines—may be of psychological interest. I have studied the letters carefully in order to ascertain what may be learned from them, and as endocrinological disturbances may play a part in the desire for the change of sex, it may interest the readers of this journal to know about their contents.

Dr. Hamburger summarized his treatise in the following paragraph:

> These many personal letters from deeply unhappy persons leave an overwhelming impression. One tragic existence is unfolded after another; they cry for help and understanding. It is depressing how little can be done to come to their aid. One feels it a duty to appeal

to the medical profession and to the responsible
legislature: do your utmost to ease the existence of
these fellow-men who are deprived of the possibilities
of a harmonious and happy life—through no fault of
their own.

During that period, too, Mom and Dad and I began to receive
many letters from disturbed people who believed they suffered from
the same problem as mine. Literally hundreds of tragic letters
poured in from men and women who also had experienced the deep
frustrations of lives lived in sexual twilight. Most all of them seemed
touchingly aware that some tremendous force had driven me to a
drastic solution.

The surgeons who had performed the operations were also
flooded with letters of inquiry, both from suffering people and the
medical profession.

When the story broke in New York, Dr. Joe Angelo had not
seen the newspapers that day until a patient in his office handed him
a copy and said, "Have you seen this?" Dr. Joe told me later that he
answered, "Why, that's my patient, a very dear friend of mine!" His
main concern was for me and my ability to face the publicity and
unfavorable comments. He had no concern for himself or the part
he had played, for his advice and care had been strictly ethical,
according to American medical beliefs at the time. Furthermore, he
had argued strongly against the transformation, until he realized
that my mind was set and nothing could change it.

On the day after I received Mom's letter, giving me a brief
account of the events in New York, I received her promised long-
distance phone call at the hospital. I knew that more pieces of the
confusing puzzle would fall into place. Her voice was clear over the
transatlantic wire and so was her rapid account of how the story broke.

On a Sunday afternoon, Mom and Dad had left the Bronx to
visit Dolly, Bill, and their new grandchild on Long Island, leaving
behind a house guest, my friend Helen Johnson, who had returned
to the United States shortly before. A news reporter arrived in their
absence, and told Helen it was a matter of great importance that he

speak with my parents, so she rang them at Dolly's number. He told Mom and Dad that he had a letter containing a number of details about my transformation, and that the story would be used in his paper, the *New York Daily News*. He made it patently clear that nothing could prevent the use of the story, and if they wanted the report to be accurate, they'd better talk. Then, he set an appointment to see them the following day at their home in the Bronx.

In all probability, he had only limited information at the time, or at least, just enough to present a threat. It was an old device that bordered on a little impolite blackmail, and one used on occasion by unscrupulous reporters to elicit information.

Mom and Dad spent an uncomfortable night, worried and upset, and the next morning when the newsman arrived, they faced what amounted to The Inquisition. He flashed a letter, which apparently contained some details of my medical and surgical history, and claimed it had been written by a laboratory technician in Denmark, though he used some care in concealing the signature from them.

Again, he demanded further information from my parents, repeating the fact that the story would be used, regardless of whether they cooperated or not. At first, they were adamant and told him that no power on earth could force them to say a word, in the face of more attempts to wear them down. Finally, they decided on a conference. After talking it over with Dolly, they agreed it would be better to clarify the situation in the press rather than allow them to fill the story with mythical information. With no time allowed them to contact me, and with great reluctance, they gave him my letter and photo.

"It seemed like we were in front of a firing squad," Dad told me later. "The reporter walked in with his letter and some facts, and we felt we had no choice. We had a long talk about it and finally showed him your original letter to us, and we gave him permission to publish it, because it was as clear and truthful a statement of your case as possibly could be made. Then, we gave him one of your first 'Christine' pictures, with the understanding that it was to be used once and no more. Of course, when it began to appear in newspapers and magazines all over the world, we knew we'd been tricked. I guess we didn't know much about the workings of the press!" Dad always had a great gift for understatement.

That was the beginning of what was to become a most uncivil war with the press. The day that the *Daily News* made its scoop, other papers began bombarding Mom and Dad with requests for information. One of the rivals even arrived on their doorstep with the front page of the *News* held up in front of him and that was the way they were greeted and introduced to the first coverage.

The steady procession of reporters and photographers in their lives became a nightmare, an incredible exercise in the invasion of privacy. Newsmen and photographers were parked around the house day and night, the phone calls so frequent and at such odd hours that they had to have their number changed to an unlisted one. Mom even caught one reporter trying to dig his way into the mailbox to examine the mail. Several tried to force entrance to take photos, and although they granted some interviews, Mom and Dad refused all pictures at that time.

Mom told me later, "We felt almost like we were prisoners in our own home, that we couldn't get out. We knew that if they caught us outside our own home, they had the right to photograph us. After a while, we got the system of timing their vigil at the house. When one group left before the next one came on, I'd get out to do the grocery shopping."

However, the newsmen didn't stop there. They went to the neighbors and the local tradespeople for the slightest lead to add fuel to the story, which by that time had blazed around the world.

At one point in the onslaught, in a moment of despair, Mom said, "I wish we could find Dr. Joe!" Anxious to explore any angle that presented itself, one reporter turned it into a direct appeal and printed Mom's explanation that she knew I had been a friend of a "Dr. Joe," but she couldn't remember his last name. Dr. Joe read that appeal, and when he showed it to Gen, she said, "Mrs. Jorgensen must be frantic with worry, let's call her right away!" They phoned at once and told Mom that I had discussed my hopes and ambitions before leaving for Europe; they had received letters from me relating my progress in Denmark and felt sure I could weather the storm of publicity and that all would be well. My parents were deeply concerned and bewildered by all these events, but knowing we had friends and champions close by was a great comfort to them. In that incident we can be grateful for the press interference.

In answer to their comforting phone call, Mom wrote the Angelos the following note:

> Dear Friends,
> I shall write you soon when I can compose my thoughts. Thanks, thanks, thanks to you both for your help in the readjustment of our child. You both have been instrumental in helping her find her true self. She is so happy now.
> Sincerely,
> Mrs. Jorgensen

My parents, my doctors, and I were extremely reluctant to offer much in the way of help to the newspapers, at the time. None of us wanted to seem completely uncooperative, so we did give in to interviews, but it seemed to us all that the story should be allowed to die a natural death. Since the sources of press information were therefore somewhat limited, they began to manufacture follow-up stories, culled from their own fertile imaginations, and based on speculation only. At best they were distorted facts; at worst, complete untruths. Within the next two or three weeks, there was an abundance of these stories and many of them were cause for great amusement.

For example, one of the headlines read: DOCTORS SIX OPERATIONS TURN MAN INTO WOMAN. That figure seemed rather excessive, as I had some reason to know that my operations had numbered two, at that point.

A story datelined December 4, 1952, U.S. Air Base, Bentwater, England was headlined: EX-GI WHO BECAME GIRL HAS BOYFRIEND. "A United States Air Force sergeant said today, Christine Jorgensen...is his girlfriend." The fact was that I met the sergeant in Copenhagen, had dinner with him on one occasion and received a note from him later, asking for a photograph, which I sent him. I remember our meeting as sociable, pleasant, and impersonal.

Another statement from a release dated December 2: "...there were more than 2,000 hormone injections during the two-year period." I can only say, had that been true, Dr. Hamburger and I would have engaged in an endurance contest, not a medical experiment.

Reference to me as a "World War II veteran," left the false impression that I had been in active warfare, which was certainly not true, since I entered the service after the war ended.

I was also credited with the following remark: "I'm happy to have become a woman and I think more people who are as unhappy as I was before, should follow my example." That misquote implies that I was an advocate of "instant womanhood." I never regarded my project as a cure-all or panacea for the troubles of others. Admittedly, no two people are alike, and it's possible that it could have been a dangerous solution for another, either psychologically or physically. Furthermore, I was in no position to give anyone else advice.

Another fabrication involved a picture of a young man, Joe Vacarelli, holding one of my photographs, clasping one hand to his forehead in a gesture of surprise. He referred to me as "his pal," and was quoted as saying he had known me for seven years and was "flabbergasted" at my transformation, as I'd always been "a normal guy in every way." Flabbergasted or not, Mr. Vacarelli was a total stranger to me.

That was the beginning of a long list of strangers who were to claim my acquaintance or friendship.

To me, one of the most unfair reports of the time, and one without a grain of truth, was that my parents were about to sell my story for thirty thousand dollars. More to the point, it was a blatant lie. In fact, I was the one being badgered in Copenhagen by various newspapers and magazines for the exclusive story of my life, and I had no intention, at that moment, of doing any such thing.

One newsman, in particular, was so persevering that he seemed invested with the qualities of job. His name was Verner

Forchammer, an International News Service representative, who also
held a responsible position with a Copenhagen daily paper. Perhaps
he entertained a proprietary interest because once, when I was in
need of money, I'd sold one of my cameras to his newspaper.

He first sent me the following cable: NEW YORK INSISTS SOONEST
ANSWER OUR PROPOSAL $20,000 THREE FOUR ARTICLES. SUGGEST YOU
HAND ANSWER PREPAID BY ME TO TELEGRAPH MESSENGER HANDING YOU
THIS, USING MY CABLE ADDRESS. VERNER FORCHAMMER. He sent me that
message, as an authorized agent of the *American Weekly,* a syndicated
Hearst magazine.

Then he came to see me in the hospital, a delightful little
man, with a charming, old-world manner. His visit was timed just a
few days after the first deluge of headlines and, at that point, I was
indifferent to his pleas and tried to discourage him. I simply wanted
to be left alone.

There were other offers of the same type that merely joined
an ever-growing pile of correspondence: WE ARE EXTREMELY INTER-
ESTED IN PUBLICIZING YOUR COMPLETE STORY IN YOUR OWN WORDS. WILL
BE IN COPENHAGEN WEDNESDAY AND THURSDAY AND WOULD LIKE TO
DISCUSS TERMS WITH YOU THEN. REGARDS. WILLIAM ATTWOOD, EUROPEAN
ED. LOOK MAGAZINE.

In the meantime, as I was still in the hospital, Mr. Forchammer
was being kept at arm's length by the formidable nurse, Miss Olsen,
though he managed to communicate in some way every day by
messages or gifts of flowers and candy.

The battle was on and I was being indoctrinated in the
techniques of artful dodging. Seven days after the first news break, I
was released from the hospital. I found it necessary to sneak out the
back door and seek refuge at the home of my friends and
photographic colleagues, the Junker-Jensens. Somehow, Mr.
Forchammer found my hideaway and arrived one morning, shortly
after my discharge from the hospital, bearing a large bouquet of
roses to pave the way. He proceeded to hammer the point that since
there had been so many confusing statements and recurring half-
truths in the news, I was obliged to give an honest and authentic
account of myself to the world.

I was also aware of the fact that, like most professional men, my doctors had an inherent dislike for publicity and were especially annoyed by what they called, "all the nonsense in the press." Dr. Hamburger had said, "Contrary to popular opinion, this conversion was not accomplished for the sake of headlines. It is an outstanding medical achievement and ninety percent of the questions from reporters border on the ridiculous!"

After several conferences with the doctors, I began to believe that I might be helping others, as well as myself, by an accurate account of the events in my case. By then, we had received thousands of letters from all over the world, from greatly disturbed people asking for help and information, and my doctors were as concerned as I was about those letters. They felt that a disclosure of the facts would help eliminate some of the attendant hearsay in the ever-widening publicity, and promised their cooperation.

My agreement to a factual account also promised some financial security and would enable me to repay my personal obligations and, finally, to provide for my parents, whom I knew I'd distressed and worried far beyond my wish or expectations.

All of these considerations induced me to accept Mr. Forchammer's proposal. Furthermore, I liked him personally and felt that, in addition to his professional aim, he was interested in me as a human being. The final terms of our contract provided for a series of five articles to appear in the *American Weekly* magazine, at a fee of twenty thousand dollars. Irmis Johnson, a staff writer, was assigned to the series, and arrangements were made for her to fly on to Copenhagen shortly after.

That was to be the only offer I'd ever accept from a publication, and the only one sanctioned by my doctors and me.

In the meantime, I began counting the days until Christmas, for Mom and Dad and I were secretly planning our reunion in Denmark for the approaching holidays. We felt we had the right to regard it as a private affair, away from prying eyes, and that would have been virtually impossible to achieve in New York. As a generous gesture, the Hearst publication gave my parents five hundred dollars for their trip to Copenhagen.

While I awaited their arrival and that of the writer, Irmis Johnson, I tried to collect my thoughts in the quiet of the Junker-Jensen home and plan for the Christmas gifts I would buy for the friends and family who had been so strongly supportive during my long years of struggle. By then, I had received an advance sum from the *American Weekly,* and I began to enjoy the thought that for first time in my life, I didn't have to worry about finances.

As for the publicity, I held my breath and hoped that "This too, shall pass." Almost immediately, I exhaled explosively in anger, when I read an item in *Time* magazine.

> By week's end, the Jorgensen family, which had seemed reluctant to be pushed into the spotlight, was fast learning the sweet uses of publicity. Christine's parents announced that they would sell her life story for $30,000 "in order to help others" who need similar treatment. On her part, Christine, who had protested the blizzard of page-one publicity, also made a discovery. She had been "shooting a little 16mm color travel film of Denmark...not a bad little movie." She had never really thought about it before, but now Christine said, widening her gray-blue eyes, she was "afraid that all the publicity in the newspapers might spoil her plans to tour the country showing it in schools, small towns and places like that, giving lectures."

With growing fury, I wondered if that was going to be the popular reaction to a project I'd worked on with a great deal of hope and a lot of plain hard work. I picked up the telephone and made arrangements for the Danish premiere of that "not bad little movie," with the understanding that all proceeds would go to the King Frederic and Queen Ingrid Fund for Tubercular Children in Greenland. I held a brief press conference to announce the plan, and it was the last time I gave information to any member of the press—except for the *American Weekly* writer—until my arrival at New York's airport, nearly two months later.

Actually prompted by a contractual obligation, my seeming aloofness by then may have been a costly detachment, for it created an even greater antagonism among the reporters who were kept in the dark for that period.

The showing of my film was scheduled for December 15, 1952, in Copenhagen's Odd Fellow Palae'et, a civic auditorium. It was the first time I'd ever appeared before an audience and I was extremely nervous, because I planned to narrate the film myself in Danish. Although I'd managed to get along in the language, I was still a far cry from perfection. One example of my confusion was when I said *teppe* (rug), instead of *tag* (roof). Consequently, during the narration when I described "red rugs" on the houses, rather than "red roofs," my delighted Danish audience howled with laughter.

My first review in the entertainment business appeared the following day in Copenhagen, datelined December 15.

> More than 500 Danes tonight applauded the first public showing of a color film, which Christine Jorgensen, the Bronx boy turned girl, has made during her two-year stay in Denmark.
>
> It was hard to say whether the applause was for the film, Miss Jorgensen's charming juggling of the Danish language, or the courage she showed in facing a large audience for the first time since the series of operations that changed her sex.
>
> There were many beautiful pictures of Danish scenes in her film, which showed she has a natural camera eye.
>
> Throughout the showing, she commented in a mixture of Danish and English. She began rather nervously, but when she felt the audience was sympathetic, she rallied and finished in great style.
>
> She wore a long dress of flowered greenish-gray taffeta, long black gloves and pearl earrings.

I had another cause for nervous excitement that evening because the series writer was due to arrive in time to witness my film, and I had reason to believe that Mom and Dad might be arriving with her. By then, however, our attempts at secrecy were so involved that we often merely succeeded in confusing each other.

By the time the performance was over, there was no sign of Miss Johnson or my parents, and I returned to the Junker-Jensen home with a group of friends where I'd planned my first real party. It was well under way when the doorbell rang, and I remember the feeling of elation when I thought they'd arrived at last. I opened the door to find Mr. Forchammer and a smiling woman, who turned out to be Irmis Johnson, the only welcome reporter. I liked her at once, and thought she was an engaging, intelligent, and sensitive person. Almost immediately, we were on a first-name basis, and from then on, she was "Irmy" to me.

Mom and Dad hadn't accompanied her after all, but Irmy assured me that they would be arriving within a few days.

The next morning, I met her for lunch at the Hotel Richmond, where she was staying. I'd never been in the hotel restaurant before since it was then one of the finest in Copenhagen, and I began to make up for the two years I'd subsisted on a diet of Danish salami and yogurt.

At that time, I had no knowledge of deadlines or how much work went into writing a series of articles, but I made it clear to Irmy that two things would take precedence over our interviews: my Christmas shopping and the impending arrival of my parents.

The *American Weekly* had tried to keep me posted on their arrival, but it was extremely difficult because they didn't want rival newsmen to be on the scene for the family reunion. They wanted an exclusive story and I agreed, though personally, I'd have preferred making it even more so by excluding them. Be that as it may, the magazine gave me the tip that Mom and Dad would be arriving on a Wednesday, a few days before Christmas. Their departure time was somehow discovered by a columnist, however, and they switched their flight to the following day, a change known only to them.

At five o'clock in the afternoon, I waited in a taxi at a rear entrance of Kastrup Air Terminal in Copenhagen, accompanied by my cousin, Lona Ziegler, and her son, Bent. Mr. Forchammer, who still assumed an advisory capacity on the article series, suggested that

I wear a veil and keep the curtains drawn in the taxicab. His delightful sense of melodrama no doubt was taking over, but I dressed simply and rejected the idea of going as a modern-day Mata Hari.

The terminal was teeming with newsmen, in spite of all efforts to keep them uninformed. In desperation, I spoke to one of the officials of Scandinavian Airlines, who immediately escorted me to his private office, where no reporters were admitted. He asked me if they could be traveling incognito and I remember thinking it was probable since I'd been receiving letters from Mom and Dad with mysterious return addresses and names of friends that had been reversed on the outside of the envelopes.

Their flight number was announced and I peered anxiously through a crack in the door. Over the loudspeaker system, I heard a voice say, "Will Mr. and Mrs. Chris Schmidt come to the information desk," and I thought that might be the name under which they were traveling. I wondered if Dad would be wearing a false beard, feeling like an international spy, or if Mom would be heavily veiled. Impatiently, I tried to single them out in the crowd, when a little couple stepped forward and identified themselves as Mr. and Mrs. Chris Schmidt. It was clear by then that they wouldn't be on that flight and I was deeply disappointed. Cousin Lona, her son, and I made a dash for the rear exit of the terminal, toward the waiting taxi.

Looking back to those moments of impatience, I think I also may have felt a sense of relief, as if the postponement had been a reprieve, for I knew that the first few minutes of our meeting would be difficult ones for us all. On the other hand, I'd waited desperately for their arrival, and wanted to get past any uneasy moments as quickly as possible. As a result, I felt both relieved and anxious.

By then, unwilling to impose further on the Junker-Jensens, I had moved to Lona's, where Mom and Dad had been invited to stay during their visit to Denmark. We returned to the Ziegler home and sat down to the dinner that had been prepared to celebrate our reunion, but without the long-awaited guests of honor.

The following day, a telegram arrived, addressed discreetly to Lona: LEAVE PARIS 4:20 PM FLIGHT 566 ARRIVE ABOUT 9 PM SATURDAY. G AND F.

CHAPTER 16

I was not aware, then, of all the experiences my parents had been through leading up to their flight to Denmark for that Christmas of 1952. Although less than three weeks had passed between the news break and their arrival, they had lived what must have seemed like several lifetimes.

They'd been victimized and courted by an occasionally friendly and sometimes threatening press. Having led rather circumspect lives until then, it was very difficult for them to make so many adjustments to their new circumstances. Gradually, they accustomed themselves to the strange world of celebrity, with a kind of calm and expert ingenuity.

After changing their flight schedule from the previous day to Thursday, December 16, Mom and Dad had taken several clandestine precautions before their departure. They left the Bronx two days early, and went to stay with Dolly and Bill. While news reporters were stationed in front of the house, Dad and a cousin had lowered their luggage on ropes from a back window and packed the car at night. Bound for Dolly's the following morning, they left the house dressed like a couple of refugees, trying to look casual, as if they were merely going down the street for a little grocery shopping. Mom wore an old raincoat, flat white shoes, and carried a little shopping bag. Dad put on a fishing cap and an old fur-lined jacket. Mom turned to Aunt Helga, who had stayed to see them off, and said, "Goodbye, we're going to Europe," to which Helga replied, "You look like you yust come over!"

Only later was I to know that at the very time I was waiting for my parents in Copenhagen on an erroneous alert, they were boarding a plane in a hangar at New York's International Airport. My brother-in-law, Bill, who was employed by one of the large airlines, had made secret preparations for their flight. Their desire to escape the press and for complete privacy had forced them to board the plane two hours before take-off. Mom's engaging description of their trip, was given in a later interview.

Bill called and told Dad, Dolly, and me to meet him on a back road. Two hours before take-off, we drove across a ramp in front of the hangar. I remember it was bitterly cold. There weren't any steps, so some of the mechanics brought out a big block of some kind and we all hoisted ourselves up on that and crawled into the airplane. It was very dark, and some of the personnel were up in front, testing the controls by worklights. One by one, the crew walked through and they gave us a glance, but that was all. Even so, I must say, we felt very conspicuous! A flight manager came through and asked us what we were doing there. Dolly told him that her husband was an executive with the same airline, and he'd explain it all. 'Well,' he said, 'it's a little unusual to see you folks sitting here.' Bill came back, after having talked to the Purser, and explained everything to the flight manager's satisfaction. We were then introduced to the Captain, and Bill told us that we were to fly to Boston under assumed names, but from there we'd continue on under our rightful identities. Finally the motors were tuned up and we wheeled out onto the field. Other passengers began to board and the Captain asked us to take seats up in front, so that the passengers who sat behind couldn't see us. We said goodbye to Dolly and Bill and the plane took off about seven in the evening.

At Boston, some kind of international personnel officer came in and asked us for our first names, changed his records, and we flew the Atlantic as Florence and George Jorgensen. I'm the least flight-minded person in the world, but we had a nice eight-and-a-half hour trip and neither one of us had 'butterflies.' We landed in Shannon in a downpour of rain and went into the terminal there to send off some postcards and have a cup of coffee. Then, we boarded again for the three-hour trip to Paris, where we stayed overnight. I remember we were both awfully confused by the time changes. From the airport in Paris, we went to our hotel by taxi, and it seemed to us that it certainly was a long, long drive, twisting in and out of the streets. That evening, we had a wonderful tour of Paris, and when we got back to the hotel, we found out we were within walking distance of the airport. And they talk about New York cab drivers!

We had to check in at Scandinavian Airlines at Le Bourget Airport, at four-thirty the next afternoon, for our flight to Copenhagen. While we were waiting in the terminal, Dad went into a bar to have a drink, and I noticed that he started talking to some young man. I wondered if it was someone trying to get an interview, and it turned out I was right. It was a United Press reporter and he took Dad by surprise, merely by calling him 'Mr. Jorgensen.' Dad thought, at first, that he was an airline official who just wanted to check our tickets. Well, we told him we wouldn't allow any pictures, but he marched around looking me over, and I think later he even telegraphed to Copenhagen to say what I was wearing. Dad went galloping out into the rain toward the plane, and he said, over his shoulder, 'Watch out, Florence!' By this time, the photographers were snapping away at Dad, even though we'd asked them not to, and I thought they were concentrating on him and would leave me alone. But as I began to head for the plane, they started on me and I held a scarf in front of my face. I felt like a thief. Once on the plane, we wondered how we'd ever meet Chris in Copenhagen.

We were in the front of the plane again, and I pulled the window curtains closed. Once in flight, we spent time talking to two young women with a baby, across the aisle, who had come from California and were on their way to Sweden.

Just before we landed at Kastrup Airport, the hostess came through and asked us to wait until everyone else had left the plane, because photographers wanted to take our picture. We said, 'That's just what we don't want!' Anyway, we were a little more prepared for what was to come.

When we got off the plane, I grabbed hold of a strange woman, pretending I was with her, while Dad went on ahead. A Scandinavian Airways official, Officer Kronberg, introduced himself to Dad and said, 'Chris sent me,' and they went off in front of me. I was still hanging on to the strange woman, and when I left her, I started dodging in among the baggage trucks with my scarf held over my face. We finally got into the terminal and met Chris in Kronberg's office.

Later, we learned more about the preparations that Mr. Kronberg and the police had to go through, before our arrival. No pictures of us appeared in the papers, although Mr. Kronberg felt sure he was the most photographed man in Denmark, because Dad was hiding behind him all the time we were trying to get to his office.

They'd even arranged to get us right through customs, all the way.

I'm sure the memory of our meeting on December 17, 1952, after more than two-and-a-half years of separation, will stay with me always. Irmy Johnson and Lona were waiting with me in Mr. Kronberg's office, but I was completely unconscious of anyone except my parents, as, with arms widespread, they were swept into the room. I know that Mom and I were crying, and even Dad kept blowing his nose and wiping his eyes. It was a blessed relief to know that we were together again, at last.

I can remember our joy and excitement, secure in the knowledge that we wouldn't be facing the battle separately anymore. After the first emotionally charged moments of our meeting had passed, Mom and Dad left with Lona by a side entrance and climbed into a Volkswagen, apparently the only taxi available, and too small to include their bags. A few minutes later, Irmy and I left with the luggage, aided by the ubiquitous Mr. Kronberg. Although there were many photographers and reporters at the airport that day, none of them got a picture of our reunion. Somehow, we'd managed to avoid them all, and we drove to Lona's suburban home to be welcomed by her husband, Carlo Ziegler, and their two children.

The house was gay and bright with Christmas decorations, which seemed a fitting background to our lively spirits. As it was well past dinnertime by then, we headed for a lace-covered dining table, swooning under a load of Danish delicacies. In a soft glow of candlelight, we bowed our heads in a prayer of thanksgiving. I remember thinking that no one had more reason to be grateful than I, for the awesome problems of the past had receded and I was reunited with my beloved Mom and Dad, from whom I'd separated myself for so long.

I wondered if I imagined it, or if they seemed older to me, worn by the burden I had unwillingly placed upon them. I couldn't detect any outward evidence of that, but I did occasionally catch their shyly appraising looks, and what I thought might be an unspoken apology for causing me possible embarrassment. It must have been a strange and trying time for them, but I think they began to realize almost immediately that my own happiness was real and my future was unthreatened by the fears of the past. What had been to me the barrier of their possible nonacceptance was soon dispelled in an atmosphere of love.

Our conviviality at dinner continued to mount, someone began proposing toasts and, according to Danish custom, we raised our glasses of schnapps and followed each one with a rousing *Skoal!* I remember that we tried to teach Irmy some words in Danish, an attempt that soon reduced us all to helpless laughter. Surrounded by friends and family in joyful spirits, I began to feel there was peace for me at last. I recall that we talked half the night away.

I was awakened the next morning by the sound of raised voices and the warning growls of King, Lona's German Shepherd. A small car was parked in front of the Ziegler home and four men were clustered around the front door, who turned out to be two reporters from Sweden and two from the United Press Service. Lona came to tell me that they were very insistent about seeing me, and we both wondered how they could have tracked us down there. I cautioned her not to let them in the house and a few minutes later went down to confront them myself. One man in particular was anything but winsome, when he told me they'd make our Christmas holidays miserable and would wait outside until they got a picture. I believe one of them even used the age-old plea of reporters, that he'd lose his job if he didn't get a photograph.

With what I believe was a sizable display of patience, I explained to them that I'd signed a contract with the *American Weekly* magazine and was forbidden by its terms to give any interviews or allow photographs to be taken until after the series had been published. My explanation didn't seem at all acceptable, and they proceeded to sit outside the house for several hours, quietly sulking in the freezing weather. Finally, they printed a sign in the car window that read, "Christine Jorgensen is hiding at Vejlandsalle 43—She is Unfair to the Press!" They drove around the block a few times, perhaps hoping to rouse the neighborhood to revolution by displaying their enthralling information. Having failed to incite a riot, they returned and parked outside the house again. They didn't try to come nearer for a second try, as King was taking his duties as a watchdog very seriously at the time.

On the same evening, another group of reporters waited until midnight outside the Junker-Jensen home, thinking for some reason that we might arrive there.

Naturally, I was distressed by those intrusions, but at the same time I didn't want to antagonize the press or seem uncooperative. Nevertheless, I'd pledged myself to do nothing that might detract from the magazine series, and I'd made the agreement willingly.

Although I was obligated by contract, I wasn't fully aware of the great difficulties involved for the news syndicates to keep their exclusive stories "under wraps" until publication date. I must admit, there were times during the next two months when I felt imprisoned by my promise. It was a new and irritating experience, to be told that Mom and Dad and I must never appear on the street together, for fear some lurking rival would get an exclusive picture, and when I planned for additional showings of my Danish film, I had to ask permission.

Although I appreciated Irmy's personal understanding and her efforts on my behalf, there were times when I looked on her more as a jailer than a biographer. I had no real knowledge, then, of the enormous task that confronted her, and I was somewhat resentful on occasion, when I felt controls were too rigid, or she required too much of my time each day for interviews and photo sittings. However, I soon began to appreciate and understand her requirements, and the fact she was writing toward a deadline date, and from then on we enjoyed a good and friendly working relationship, as well as a delightful personal one.

At the time Mr. Forchammer and I were negotiating, at my request, my friend Jens Junker-Jensen became our official photographer and was contracted for the series by the *American Weekly*. I have no idea what their financial agreement was but I hope it was a rewarding one for Jens, for it was a small way of expressing my deep gratitude for the many kindnesses he and Edna had extended to me during my life in Denmark.

Soon after we started to work, I gave up the opportunity to attend the state funeral of the Dowager Queen, Alexandrina of Denmark, although it was something of a disappointment to me since I'd planned to photograph the event. Instead, Mom and Dad went to Roskilde for the ceremonies, and I stayed with Irmy for the day to work on the articles.

While Mom and Dad were visiting relatives and enjoying many of the tourist attractions in Denmark, Irmy's writing chore was well under way. We began to spend a great deal of time with Dr. Hamburger, Dr. Stürup and the surgeons in my case, all of whom had generously offered their time and cooperation to help present the story as clearly and truthfully as possible. Most of the medical information she sought could only be obtained from them, and it was during one of the frequent interviews with Dr. Hamburger, that she repeated the questions asked by me so many times in the past. Though many of them had been answered and explained to me before, I was a layman after all, and it was necessary to have them clearly defined for Irmy by the experts. Since some of the important medical details were edited out of the articles when they were finally published, it's fortunate that her notes of those interviews still exist.

In the course of a session with Dr. Hamburger, Irmy asked, "Why did this happen in Chris' particular case, and how often does it happen to other people?"

Picking up a pencil, Dr. Hamburger began to sketch a diagram as he spoke. "I'm not able to give you exact figures, of course, for the number of victims of this disorder is only a matter of guesswork. It is also impossible to fix any definite borderline between what is normal and what is not. A one-hundred-percent man or a one-hundred-percent woman does not exist. We all have rudiments of the hermaphrodite (dual sex) state within us. This graph I have drawn, includes 'normal' men and 'normal' women, feminized males of varying degrees, masculinized women and, finally, the definitely abnormal 'intersexes.' Most average people, if there is an average, will range from, say eighty to ninety percent in masculinity or femininity. I like to quote Dr. Harry Benjamin, your great American sex pathologist. He says: 'Nobody knows as yet what is normal—we only know what is customary.' At any rate, there are gradual transitions before we reach the 'intersexes,' those extremely unhappy people in whom male and female characteristics are mixed to a greater or lesser degree. The closer a person is placed towards the middle of the diagram we have before us, the more likely it is that he will be a victim of the sexual difficulties, such as homosexual tendencies, sexual impotence, transvestism, etc."

Apparently, at that point I interrupted Dr. Hamburger with a question, designed to get back to the source of these problems. "Doesn't nature have a quite definite way of determining whether a child will be a boy or a girl?" Irmy asked him to explain the genetic processes more fully.

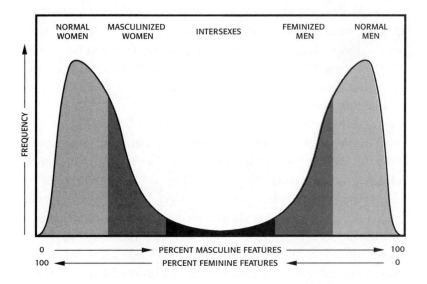

He then reviewed for us as simply as possible the complex story of the microscopic human inheritance units, called "chromosomes," which are present in every one of the body's cells. These units, passed on jointly by the parents, determine the genetic structures and factors in the child: the color of hair, eyes, facial and body characteristics. But, as Dr. Hamburger explained, we were most concerned at the moment with the chromosomes that determine gender.

"All cells in the body," he continued, contain special chromosomes, called 'sex chromosomes." The female cells possess a pair of these units that we call 'X' and the male cells, two different ones called 'X' and 'Y.' When the reproductive cells are formed, these chromosomes are split in such a way, that all egg cells (from the mother) contain an 'X' chromosome, while all sperm cells (from the father). can have either an 'X' or 'Y' chromosome. The X's and Y's are equally divided among the millions of sperm cells, and the sex of the baby depends on which of these millions joins the egg. A male sperm with a 'Y' chromosome, for example, produces a boy. This means that at the time of fertilization nature has already made up its mind what the baby's sex should be.

"But that is not the whole story. Other factors are involved in the determination of sex; for instance, the hormone-producing system of the endocrine glands. Disease or disturbances in this system may prevent the normal, harmonious development of the sex which nature intended, and may cause any one of several different stages of what we call 'intersexes.'"

Dr. Hamburger then went on to explain the renowned work of the geneticist, Professor R. Goldschmidt, of the Kaiser Wilhelm Institute of Biology in Berlin, who developed a theory about intersexes in human beings, derived from his studies of sex anomalies in plants and animals. Goldschmidt's theory held that all human intersexes were intended to be female and endowed with female cells, each containing two chromosomes. The cells would always remain female. However, disturbances could cause changes in the way body structures develop, and those changes may be so drastic that a female baby would develop male organs and glands.

"This theory needs revision," he continued, "and it is extremely difficult to prove its correctness, because at the present time, we cannot count the chromosomes in the cells with absolute certainty. Nevertheless, the possibility cannot be excluded that this 'highest degree of intersexuality,' meaning male organs in a female body, actually exists in human beings. I should like to tell you that I have developed my own private little theory in this area: that some cases of 'transvestism' also belong in this category. You, too, Chris, would fit into this category, in my estimation. It would explain the irresistible feeling of an apparently normal man that he really belongs to the opposite sex, a feeling that can be traced back to earliest childhood."

It was during these discussions, that I heard the terms "transvestite" and "transvestism" for the first time. Their application to my case didn't disturb me greatly, in the light of his explanation of the medical possibilities. It was *possible,* then, that I was an individual belonging to the "highest degree of intersexuality: male organs in a female body." The feasibility of these theories seemed to explain my feelings since early childhood of belonging, or wanting to belong, to the opposite sex.

When the term "transvestism" appeared in the above context in the *American Weekly* articles, it created a gross misconception in the minds of many readers, and one which has never been completely corrected. Countless numbers of people, as unfamiliar with the term as I had been, took up their dictionaries and read: "transvestite, a person obsessed with the desire to wear clothes of the opposite sex." In the minds of an interested, but misguided public, I was immediately placed in a narrow category which led many intelligent people to believe the stories that circulated at the time: that I had been a female impersonator before going to Denmark, and in my private life as "George," I doted on wearing feminine clothing.

Nothing could have been further from the truth and, once again, I take the opportunity to classify that story as a complete myth, clearly an invention. I had never worn, or wanted to wear, feminine clothing while I retained any evidence of masculinity. Although I was entitled in the eyes of the medical experts, I didn't wear female clothing until my legal status as a woman was established on my passport, approved by the United States State Department. I merely wanted to correct what I considered a misjudgment of Nature, so that I might physically and legally become the person I felt I was intended to be.

I was to suffer considerably from the wide acceptance of the dictionary's limited definition of the word, "transvestite." Perhaps my discomfort was not without some reason, for since then, a number of medical authorities have posed the question of whether or not it is advisable to apply new terms to cases such as mine.

The Latin words *trans* (across), and *vestire* (to clothe), combine to form "transvestism," or to use the layman's more literal term, "cross-dress." It was first used in a medical sense by Dr. Magnus Hirschfeld, a pioneer in sex pathology around the turn of the century. However, it had the disadvantage of naming a disturbance of behavior and emotions after only one of its symptoms. Havelock Ellis evolved the term "eonism," named after its prototype, the Chevalier D'Eon.* My own doctors have now adopted the use of "eonism" for severe cases, also known as "psychic hermaphroditism."

Dr. Harry Benjamin, the noted American endocrinologist, has since developed the term "transsexualism," to designate a problem that differs essentially from that of transvestism. Dr. Benjamin wrote the following comments in the *American Medical Journal of Psychotherapy* in April, 1954, two years after my transition. In differentiating between the transvestite and the transsexualist, he stated:

> The transvestite wants to be accepted in society as a member of the opposite sex; he or she wants to play the role as completely and as successfully as possible. The male transvestite admires the female form and manners and tries to imitate both, with an intensity that varies from case to case. Transsexualism is a different problem, and a much greater one. It indicates more than just playing a role. It denotes the intense and often obsessive desire to change the entire sexual status, including the anatomical structure. While the male transvestite enacts the role of a woman, the transsexualist wants to *be* one, wishing to assume as many of her characteristics as possible; physical, mental and social.

---

*The Chevalier Louis Auguste D'Eon was a French international spy, employed by Louis XV, a fearless captain in the French Dragoons, and a decorated hero of the Seven Years' War. He was a notorious figure, who frequently dressed in women's clothing, and was sent by Louis to the Russian court of Catherine the Great, where he conducted his intrigues and espionage in the guise of a woman. He died in 1810, having lived the last thirty-three years of his life as a female, by royal decree of the French king, Louis XVI.

Dr. Benjamin's article stated that much research was still necessary, but advanced his theories in the following paragraph:

An organic explanation of intersexual phenomena would have to be looked for, either in the genetic mechanism or in the endocrine constitution, or in a combination of both. Investigations into the chromosome sex have shown that it is probably contained in the nuclear structure of all body cells. It has been detected and demonstrated in the epidermal nuclei of the skin. It does not always correspond to the respective gonad (ovaries or testicles), that is to say, the endocrine sex. Future research along these lines may thus determine the dominant sex in an individual, and may do much to clarify our still incomplete knowledge of the nature of sex. To speak of a male, when there are testicles, and of a female when there are ovaries, may be the most practical way to differentiate the sexes, but it is scientifically incorrect and unsatisfactory to the geneticist. Similarly, the term 'transsexualism' answers a practical purpose and is appropriate in our present state of knowledge. If future research should show that male sex organs are compatible with (genetic) female sex, or female sex organs with (genetic) male sex, the term would be wrong, because the male 'transsexualist' is actually a female and merely requires a transformation of genitals.

My understanding of all the medical information in my case was only to come gradually. However, as the subject of some of his published reports, I was to learn a great deal more of Dr. Harry Benjamin's theories in the years following my return to the United States when he became a trusted and valuable friend. His courageous attitude toward the legal and social aspects of these problems was also cause for admiration.

Referring to various types of sex abnormalities that thrust people into lives of misery, often terminating in suicide, he wrote: "We must help them, but how? Doctors in Denmark have had the courage to apply drastic endocrine and surgical measures. Can we go as far as that?"

CHAPTER 17

The publication date for the *American Weekly* series was scheduled for mid-February of 1953, ten weeks after the first news break in the *New York Daily News*. In the meantime, the flames of speculation and rumor were being fanned in a fire of journalistic enthusiasm.

Although many of the accounts had been revealed to me during that period, I wasn't aware of all the conflicts until I returned to New York. I only hoped that with the publication of the magazine articles, the controversy would be reduced to reasonable proportions, and I would be left in peace to go about my affairs and the business of living my own life.

My work with Irmy on the fifth and final installment was finished near the end of January. We had spent the preceding six weeks in a frenzy of concentrated effort, and I think I reviewed the results then with a less critical eye than I do today. For the short length of time at our disposal, at an already hectic period in my life, I felt they were satisfactory. Because of the limitations of magazine space for each article, out of necessity, many events and facts were abbreviated, and the result was a somewhat superficial chronological history that seemed to lack a deeper human element. However, it was an honest, straightforward account and, hopefully, would help clarify the fictions and rumors that abounded at the time.

I was grateful to Irmy for all of her hard work in pulling together the mass of material and facts, and to my doctors for their generous cooperation and sacrifices of time. Dr. Hamburger put his medical stamp of approval on the articles, and sent me the following statement to be included in the first of the series:

> As a doctor, I naturally am interested in the medical significance of Christine Jorgensen's story, but I am not interested in the medical aspect alone. Important, I think, is the courageous fight Christine has made in overcoming a problem that threatened to ruin her life. Her fortitude has been extremely inspiring.
>
> Christian Hamburger, M.D.
> Chief of the Hormone Department
> *Statens Seruminstut,* Copenhagen

Once our work was finished, I breathed a great sigh of relief, and at last considered myself free from the bonds of the writing project.

I made immediate plans to take Mom and Dad to Norway for a skiing trip and they turned out to be great sports for people who, well past the half-century mark, had never been on skis before. Now that I look back on it, I didn't display any great championship form myself. We spent a glorious week in the snow and sunshine, just north of Oslo, and were dreaming of seeing Paris and Rome together, when I received what I thought was a routine telephone call from Irmy, checking revisions of her final copy. During her call, she asked if any reporters had been bothering me, and I could truthfully reply at that point that they had not. I was curious, however, and asked the reason for her question, but her reply was rather noncommittal. "Oh, Walter Winchell said something about you on the air the other night and I just wondered." I wanted to know what, and Irmy answered, "He just said you'd be returning to the United States shortly, aboard the *Queen Elizabeth,* but as a matter of fact, Chris, *American Weekly* has made all arrangements for both of us to fly back on Scandinavian Airlines, February 12."

Though I knew I'd have to return sometime, her statement came as rather a surprise. Since the beginning of all the publicity two months before, I had been toying with the idea of remaining in Europe, perhaps indefinitely. My trip to Norway had been my first

visit there, the people and country had made a profound impression
on me and I was beginning to entertain ideas of staying longer.

However, Hearst Publications insisted that my return to the
United States must coincide with the release of the first article,
scheduled for February 15. Even now, the persuasions of the Hearst
syndicate would probably snap me to attention, but at that time I was
more than eager to comply and felt obligated for the opportunities
the series had presented. I had no knowledge whatever of the
enormous preparations that were being made for my return and was
even less aware of what the public relations demands would be. In
short, I didn't know what was going on, or about to come off. Today,
I marvel at the limitations of my comprehension.

I didn't learn until weeks later that Irmy's seemingly casual
mention of our rumored return in Winchell's column was merely to
see if I'd heard a more serious report. Her concern was due to the
fact that the word "transvestite" was being circulated by the scandalmongers in connection with my case and, used out of context, was
being given the narrow interpretation, which I felt never applied to
me. Further accusations were made that no operations had ever
been performed, and that the whole case was a hoax, manufactured
by an enterprising press agent.

That remarkably untidy bit of information was promptly
refuted by the *American Weekly,* since the magazine was in possession
of photostatic copies of my medical records, in addition to
confirmation from the American Consulate in Denmark that my
converted passport was completely in order as a legal document. "It's
validity is exactly the same as yours," the Vice-Consul had told Irmy.

When I went back to Copenhagen to prepare for the trip
home, Mom and Dad stayed on in Norway, planning to follow within
a few days. Arrangements were made for us to return to New York
separately, possibly a move designed by the publication editors to
protect my parents from the tornado they knew was coming.

When I returned from the week in Norway, however, I was
totally unaware of the storm of controversy that was brewing. Had I
known it at the time, I might have gone through with my vague ideas
of staying in Europe. By then, however, almost three years had

passed. I missed my country and my home and friends in New York, and was anxious to put into effect the plans I had to continue a photographic career, the one that never quite materialized before my departure. The preparations for the trip home involved packing all of my remaining belongings into thirteen pieces of luggage, which consisted of a few well-worn suitcases and a great many cardboard boxes. Fortunately, I'd sent a trunk home ahead of me. When that raffish assortment arrived at the New York airport, a reporter discovered that one of the shipping cartons was clearly imprinted with the words: "Petal Soft Toilet Tissue," and he proceeded to publish my guilty secret. It's obvious now, I think, that I've always traveled in the grand manner.

During the last hectic days before I headed for New York, I was surprised to learn that a member of the *American Weekly* staff had arrived in Copenhagen to fly back with Irmy and me. Sending a gentleman escort seemed an extremely thoughtful gesture on the part of the editors, and I didn't suspect that he was one of their top publicity experts, who had helped to work out the frightening reception that was in store for me. Be that as it may, he proved to be a good friend, and no doubt went to a great deal of trouble to expedite matters for the flight home.

The evening before my actual departure, he asked me to go to the airport for photographs, posed on the steps of a plane, in the same clothes I would be wearing on my arrival in New York. I didn't know it at the time, but the photos of my supposed leave-taking were flown to New York, twenty-four hours before I even left Copenhagen.

I can remember the tremendous excitement that was beginning to build in me at the prospect of being home again. In the afternoon, just before our early evening departure, I gave a cocktail party for the many friends and well-wishers who had helped me through the trying, hopeful years in Denmark and I was very touched by their reluctance to see me leave. I had such a good time at my own party I almost missed the plane.

I was grateful that there was no flurry of activity at the airport, and no reporters showed much interest in my going, except for an International News Service representative who called me from

London for a final word. "What are you planning to do when you return to New York?" he asked. Later, when I saw the story in print, I apparently answered, "Oh, I'll probably just sit and think things out for awhile."

"Are you worried about your reception in the United States?"

"I'm not worried a bit. Why should I be?" It occurs to me now, I was something short of the mark.

After a few more hurried questions, I was rushed through the gates to the waiting plane. As I neared the boarding steps, I heard a voice in the distance, paging me over the loudspeaker system: "Miss Jorgensen, Mr. Verner Forchammer is calling." It was too late for the kindly little man who had besieged me with roses. As a spokesman for *American Weekly,* he'd arranged the contract that had given me financial security and started me on a struggle toward a new, unexpected career, but he never got his final interview.

I boarded the plane and settled back, little realizing that I was "fastening my seat belt," symbolically, as well as literally.

Until then, I'd been preoccupied with a great many distractions, all of them welcome: Mom and Dad's trip to Denmark, the hectic weeks spent working with Irmy Johnson, our visit to Norway and, finally, the excitement of going home. Those events had been all-absorbing, and as a result I'd found little time for introspection.

Looking back now, it's possible that I was also enjoying a sizable sense of my own importance at that point. I'd been able to bring my parents to Europe, I had made at least a minor contribution to one area of medical science, I was by then a celebrated figure, if for all the wrong reasons, and I may have been a little in awe of myself.

Regardless of what was probably a moment of self-advertisement, I realized that there lay ahead of me, at last, a few private hours in which to pause and reflect on the events of my life up to that time. As the miles of Atlantic Ocean slipped away under the wings, I remember thinking many thoughts; of the high and low points of my life and of the seemingly flat plateaus that stretched away toward some far mountain of a nameless dream. I thought, too, of God, in whom my faith had been replenished through the years,

time and again. I was, at last, the person I wanted to be and I had no
wish to alter anything. Regardless of the unknown, I knew my life was
a result of my own decisions, right or wrong, and that I alone was
responsible for them. I was twenty-six years old, returning to a
friendly, familiar world, and I faced it with a smiling confidence.
Slowly, the years of loneliness, terror and fear were slipping away into
a distant past.

In retrospect, those hours were perhaps among the most
precious I would ever know, for from then on, dictated by a curious
world, my life would never belong to me alone. I was unaware of
it then, but in my long, painful search for a normal life, I had
created a paradox; a life that was to be, for me, abnormal and uncon-
ventional.

The next morning when the hostess woke me, we were only a
short distance from New York's International Airport, and by the
time I'd had breakfast, we were nearly ready for landing. The hostess
asked if I would allow all the other passengers to leave the plane
before me. I remember thinking at the time it was a rather strange
request, but thought no more about it until we touched down and
taxied toward the terminal. It occurred to me then that newsmen
would probably be meeting the plane to interview and photograph a
celebrity on the flight, Countess Alexandra of Rosenborg, a close
relative of Denmark's king, who was making an extended visit to the
United States with her husband. I thought perhaps they would want
a clear view of the Danish Countess, without a commoner suddenly
appearing in their lenses. When the plane came to a full stop, Irmy
and the *American Weekly* escort left me abruptly with, "We'll see you
in quarantine," and I waited until I thought everyone else had
departed. Then, I gathered up my books, fur stole, hand luggage, a
shopping bag full of the last minute "leftovers," and started toward
the exit. I heard a murmur of voices, and thought perhaps the
Countess was getting her first introduction to the American press. I
stepped out of the doorway, onto the top step, and met a scene of
such chaos and utter madness that I've never been able to recall it all
clearly. I had trouble remembering the details of that bedlam the
next day, let alone years later.

I turned back to see if I had somehow, by mistake, preceded the Danish royal member, but there was no one behind me except the hostess, who seemed less bewildered than I.

I looked into a sea of faces, lined up along the ropes of "quarantine walk" and held back by a squad of determined police, then heard a roar of voices shouting my name. I reeled under the impact. I thought for a moment that I had entered Dante's inferno, as flashbulbs exploded from all directions and newsreel cameras whirred. A crowd of three hundred shoving reporters, newsreel and still photographers had converged, all jockeying for position and camera angles. I learned later it was the largest assemblage of press representatives in the history of the airport.

"Hey, Chris, look this way!" "Over here, Miss Jorgensen!" "Come down the steps a little, Miss Jorgensen!" "How about a nice, big smile?" "Just one more, Christine!" "Just one more!" Apparently, without knowing it, I was entering the Era of Just One More.

I remember little else, except the question of how I was going to run that gamut of surging humanity. I clutched my belongings more closely to me, stumbled slightly as I reached out to grasp a handrail, and started slowly down the landing stairs. Although unaware of it, at that moment I was descending into a new and alien world. The past was yesterday, and yesterday had ended last night.

Baby George, 1927.

Grandma Jorgensen was George's champion when others laughed at his "sissified" ways. This photograph was taken in 1944. She was 76.

George and his sister Dorothy with their mother, 1930

George Jorgensen, Jr., age 16, photographed at the
New York Institute of Photography, spring 1942.

With grandmother, mother and sister, 1944.

Private First Class, 1946. When George was honorably discharged from the U.S. Army, his papers read, "Recommended for further military training." His response, "They'll have to catch me first!"

Decorating the patio, Hollywood, 1947. While making the rounds of the studios to look for a job as a photographer, George was dismayed to be taken for a homosexual.

Annotation at bottom: "17. Myself, June 195[2?]." Note on back: "Hesitate to send this—It looks too much like a clothes model—but it really is for I am so proud of my handiwork—Made jacket and skirt and gloves."

"By 1950, I had saved enough money for my passage to Denmark. It was a one-way ticket to a new life." Here with Miss Denmark, 1951, shortly before George petitioned the American Embassy to change his passport legally to a new gender status.

Copenhagen, 1952. The first published photograph of Christine Jorgensen, which hit newsstands in December 1952: "I pushed the hydrogen bomb tests at Eniwetok right off the front pages."

February 13, 1953. A crowd of 300 reporters awaited Christine's arrival at New York's Idlewild Airport. "I gathered up my books, my fur stole, my hand luggage and a shopping bag full of 'leftovers,' and stepped out of the doorway...Flashbulbs exploded from all directions..."

The Scandinavian Societies of Greater New York name Christine Jorgensen Woman of the Year, March 7, 1953. "To receive a public award for something that was a transition to normalcy seemed an undue recognition, but I accepted with pleasure."

With her parents at the Woman of the Year dinner. While she was in Denmark, Christine wrote to her parents about her change. A few days later, she received a cablegram: LETTER AND PICTURES RECEIVED. WE LOVE YOU MORE THAN EVER. MOM AND DAD.

"THINK" Receiving the key to a city,
August 21, 1953.

After being cancelled by the Sahara in Las Vegas, on the grounds that
she had "misrepresented herself as a woman," Christine opens with
Myles Bell at the Copa Club in Pittsburgh on August 5, 1953.

Christine opens at Lou Walters' Latin Quarter in New York,
January 2, 1954. "She is a star who was a stare a year ago…
The audience loved her and called for more, more, more!"
—Walter Winchell

Surrounded by admirers.

Summer 1954, Bermuda, where Christine took an unexpected holiday after Boston's city fathers prohibited her appearance.

At the horse races, Shelly Bay Racecourse

Walking on the ocean floor.

Christine in her Laguna Niguel home, posing in front of a portrait of her painted by Lorraine Merrit in 1954.

At the Safari Club in Manila, Philippines, 1962. "Miss Jorgensen is the best goodwill ambassador America has sent us in years."

With Roger Moore, 1960.

Christine Jorgensen spoke on the college lecture circuit, where she drew audiences of thousands. Photo by Bob Lai, 1973.

Opening night of *The Christine Jorgensen Story*, Hollywood, June 17, 1970. Annotated with names of people in photograph.

Copenhagen, 1984.

With Mae West (left), 1984.

A series of photos that Christine hoped to sell to *Playboy:*
Nude with cigarette, 1984

Christine at home in Laguna Niguel.

With Brenda Lana Smith, Christine's last roommate and confidante. Grand Hotel, Anaheim, February 10, 1989. Brenda, a self-described "Biber Girl" had earlier transitioned from the (male) Honorary Consul of Denmark in Bermuda to an outspoken transsexual lecturing on college campuses. (Stanley Biber, one of the world's leading gender-reassignment surgeons, performed more than four thousand surgeries between 1970 and 2000 at San Rafael Hospital in Trinidad, Colorado.)

April 8, 1989. Christine at home, shortly before her death. In the last months of her life, Christine still pried herself out of her favorite armchair, put on a carefully chosen outfit, fixed up her face, and dashed out of her apartment, announcing "It's show time!" to whomever was listening.

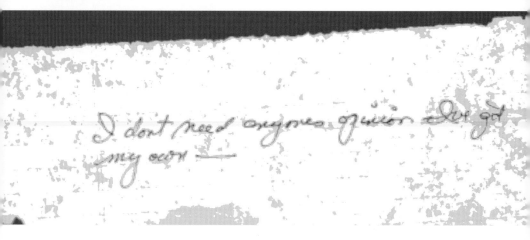

I dont need anyones opinion but got my own —

Handwritten note found in Christine's papers.

CHAPTER 18

Although some moments of February 13, 1953, are lost in a fog of faulty memory, there are others indelibly etched in my mind. If the sequence of events is not completely clear, the emotional leftovers remain. I remember that I was frightened and bewildered and I wondered why Irmy and our escort had left me so abruptly to face the ordeal alone.

I started to traverse what seemed to me was my last mile. There was a good deal of shouting and jostling as the crowd pushed against the ropes that marked off "quarantine walk," an area that separated the arriving passengers until their vaccination certificates had been validated. Three or four men crawled through the ropes, including Henry Wall, a friend who had come to greet Irmy. Almost immediately they were called to the United States Health Office at the airport, and had to submit to a smallpox vaccination on the spot.

I was rushed through the routine of customs inspection and then ushered through a long hallway into a small press room jammed with reporters, photographers, and a huge battery of blinding floodlights. It seemed to me more like a battlefield with flashbulbs popping, photographers shouting instructions, and reporters lobbing questions from the firing line. I tried to smile and answer as best I could, but I knew I was ill-equipped for that kind of exchange. Furthermore, the questions weren't designed to make me feel particularly poised or at ease. "Where did you get the fur coat?" "How about a cheesecake shot, Christine?" "How does it feel to be home?" "Do you expect to marry?" "What are you going to do now?"

"Do you think Europeans understand sex problems better than Americans do?"

The hot lights were stifling, I was still wearing a heavy fur coat, and I was physically uncomfortable and plainly rattled under the emotional tensions. Finally, in an effort to break up the session and escape, I said, "Ladies and gentlemen, thank you very much for coming, but I think this is really too much."

That comment was quoted at great length in the press. At the time, it may have sounded like a lack of cooperation, but its real implication was simple and straightforward. I truly did think the attention I was receiving was out of proportion to my importance to the world in general, and that the Christine Jorgensen story had already been magnified to a point of hysteria.

Some months later, I was told by Ben White, the *Daily News* reporter who had written the original scoop in December of 1952, that the Jorgensen story had lain on his desk for a week before he decided to use it. Apparently, at that time, a lurid sex scandal involving the trial of a wealthy playboy had run its course, the public was beginning to lose interest, and the *Daily News* was looking for another "sensation" to take its place, in order to boost its circulation. In a sense then, my notoriety was a matter of chance.

Whatever that coincidence, the press interview on my arrival home was a reality that had to be faced. Finally, the session was over and Irmy and the *American Weekly* representatives began herding me toward an exit and a waiting car. Suddenly, in the crowd, I recognized the familiar and smiling face of Madeleine Miller, my ex-boss from RKO-Pathé News, who had come to welcome me home and wish me well. At that moment, in the frightening crush of people, it was a heartwarming sight.

Once settled in the car, I asked to be taken to my sister's home on Long Island, but the *American Weekly* staff had already arranged to take me to the Carlyle Hotel in Manhattan, to keep me "incommunicado" until after the series started on the following Sunday. I balked in no uncertain terms, but when I realized we were being followed by other newsmen, I knew I'd only be involving Dolly and her family even more, so I agreed, reluctantly.

Approaching the hotel, we drove around in circles trying to elude the newsmen without success, and Irmy and I made a dash for the front door. Without stopping at the desk to register, she pushed me toward a waiting elevator, and turned to confront the pursuing reporters herself. The operator asked, "What floor, please?" Realizing that I didn't know what floor, I said, "Just up!" It seemed ridiculous when I found myself on the top floor of a strange hotel, waiting in a deserted corridor, but eventually I was rescued and escorted to a suite reserved for me under a fictitious name.

With all of the attendant excitement and tensions of the day, I decided I wanted a drink and Irmy suggested a Bloody Mary. I wasn't sure what that was, though the name was intriguing and, at that point, rubbing alcohol would have been welcome. When the drinks arrived, I found I didn't care for the combination of vodka and tomato juice and as a result I doubt if I had more than a sip or two.

At any rate, my mind was on other things and by then I had no intention of staying imprisoned at the hotel. Above all, I wanted some rest and privacy. I called Dolly and arranged to have my brother-in-law drive in from Long Island to pick me up. Irmy agreed to stay on at the hotel to keep up the pretense that I was still in residence. Bill finally arrived, we sneaked out of the hotel through a side entrance undetected by the enemy, and fled to the seclusion of their home.

For the next few days the newspapers had a field day and, once again, I was making headlines. My arrival was fully reported, sometimes in a friendly and sometimes in a hostile way: what I wore, what I said, what I looked like, my behavior, all with varying degrees of accuracy.

"Christine tosses off Bloody Mary, just like a real guy!"
"Fur collar, pearl earrings set off her beauty."
"Christine, by George!"
"Chris back home, perfect little lady."
"Christine teeters on high heels, leaving the plane."
"Christine conducted herself with dignity."
"Christine ill at ease."

"An artistically minded reporter who trailed her to the swank Carlyle Hotel, reported that Christine probably will not seek work modeling bras."

"MD's Rule Chris 100% Woman."

"Judge Wonders is Chris Real George."

"Christine is Certified as Legal Woman."

As I remember, the only paper that reported my return with any degree of conservatism was the *New York Times,* which carried a brief column containing a few pertinent facts and lived up to its motto: "All the news that's fit to print."

However, one news release that did have basis in fact was from the *New York Daily Mirror,* datelined Copenhagen, February 18, 1953.

> DENMARK CURBS CHRIS SURGERY. (INS) A top ranking medical informant said today the Danish government has turned down appeals from more than 300 persons—over half of them Americans—for trans-formation operations. The informant, familiar with the series of treatments and operations performed on Christine Jorgensen, said the requests for similar surgery and treatment were denied because the Danish Minister of Justice had decided to limit treatment of future cases to Danes.

Looking back on it, I can understand why some of the misconceptions have prevailed and how they got an early start. Except for my arrival in the United States, the *American Weekly* editors were determined to keep other newsmen in the dark to protect the exclusivity of the article series, a precaution that was understandable even then. Unable to reach me and gather the real facts, rival newspapers proceeded to enlarge on the slightest item to keep the Jorgensen story moving before the public. If I sneezed, it was duly reported as an event. Perhaps the controversies would have been minimized, had the information been shared equally.

However, I hoped the *American Weekly* series would clarify

some of that information for the public and I knew that everything possible had been done to make it a fair and truthful presentation. In a later edition of *Editor & Publisher,* a trade paper for the publishing business, an article appeared outlining some of the aims and preparations of the *American Weekly* editors:

> Numerous editorial problems had to be faced. Both the editor and associate publisher of *American Weekly* were determined that the material be presented with complete accuracy and good taste. They visualized it, not as a sensationalized bit of erotica, but as the courageous fight of a desperately unhappy person with the fortitude to overcome a seemingly hopeless obstacle.
>
> Their staff writer, Irmis Johnson, was so instructed. She was told to obtain unassailable verification for every statement in the story and to have each article read and approved by the doctors who had accomplished Christine's transformation. Complete documentation was in the *American Weekly's* files before the story began appearing. It enabled the magazine effectively to silence a number of unfounded rumors that were later circulated.
>
> Steps were also taken, with the cooperation of Miss Jorgensen and her parents who had joined her in Europe with the aid of the *American Weekly,* to make sure that no rival publication could usurp any part of her life story or obtain unauthorized pictures.
>
> The circulation increases that resulted were the greatest in the memory of circulators and were sustained throughout the series.

The *American Weekly* series was translated into fourteen languages and distributed throughout seventy countries.

Mom and Dad returned to the United States two days after my arrival, and went immediately to their home in the Bronx. Still unable to locate me, the press began to badger my parents and, again, they became the victims of the curious and the diehard reporters. I stayed in hiding at Dolly's, getting acquainted with my new niece, who had been born in my absence. At the time, Dolly was expecting her second child, another lovely daughter, born two months later.

By then, I realized that some satisfactory arrangement would have to be made to insure my family's security and peace of mind and, therefore, decided to sell our old home and leave the Bronx after twenty-six years. We rented a cottage on Long Island Sound, a few miles from Dolly's, and stayed there to rest and rally our forces, pending the time when I could buy suitable property and build a home.

I soon found some property in Massapequa, Long Island, that appealed to all of us, plans got underway for the building, and Dad contracted the house himself. The word got around that the Jorgensens were building a home and, for a time, the vacant lot became a stellar attraction. Sunday afternoons were particularly busy, and in the early building stages, people drove by slowly and photographed the empty hole in the ground or the lone bulldozer. One family even brought a picnic lunch and spent a whole afternoon at the site. Later, when the building was finished, we often saw people scanning the windows through binoculars from the opposite side of the street.

During that period, Mom and Dad and I spent some of the time reading and sorting some twenty thousand letters I had received since early December, some from countries I'd never heard of. Letters were delivered to me merely addressed: "Christine Jorgensen, United States of America," and one arrived with no other address than "Copenhagen, Germany." I could only marvel at the ingenuity of the postal department.

The letters ran the gamut of human emotions and responses, and I suppose are typical of those received by people who find themselves in the public eye. Most of them were laudatory, expressing interest and encouragement, some of them were hostile and threatening, a few were obscene. It was interesting to find that many of the congratulatory letters were sent to my parents. Also, there was the usual sprinkling of anonymous letters, a practice that's always puzzled me, for if a person has the courage to state a conviction, then surely he must have the courage to name to it.

Some of the letters, sent from all corners of the world, were from disturbed people who felt they suffered in much the same way as I had, and pathetically asked for help and counsel. I was deeply touched by these, and although many of the problems were unrelated to mine, I seemed to represent some sort of guidepost for accomplishment. Even though I was ill-equipped to advise anybody, I tried to answer some of those poignant pleas.

At least one of the letters I received from that period, however, was to net me a lasting friendship, for it introduced Dr. Harry Benjamin, one of America's most distinguished endocrinologists and sex pathologists. I had no way of knowing then that I would become the subject of many of his medical papers, or that our meeting would influence his exhaustive study of transsexualism, published some thirteen years later.

> Dear Miss Jorgensen:
>
> These lines are written to you in the interest of some of my patients and naturally also of those whose emotional problem nobody understands better than you do.
>
> Frankly, I am worried over the effect your story and publicity may have in some instances. I had a few rather frantic phone calls and letters recently. Therefore, I would be grateful to you if you would tell me how you are handling the innumerable communications that undoubtedly came to you. Don't they all indicate hopefulness yet utter frustration?
>
> In my many years of practice of sexology and endocrinology, problems similar to yours have been brought to me frequently. I need not tell you how profoundly disturbed some of these people are. Naturally, they identify themselves with you. Can I tell

them that you will answer their pleas with a personal
note, a friendly noncommittal form letter perhaps,
but—for psychological reasons—bearing your signature?
That would help enormously. Or have you formulated
another plan? Can I be of assistance? If so please feel
free to call on me.

    Most sincerely and earnestly yours,

    Harry Benjamin, M.D.

Shortly after I received that letter, I set up a meeting with Dr.
Benjamin, at the home of his good friend, the author, Tiffany
Thayer. We discussed cases similar to mine, and the problems of
answering some of my correspondence. That was the beginning of
our great friendship, inspired by mutual interests and Dr. Benjamin's
own particular brand of graciousness and charm. It was at our first
meeting, too, that he told me Dr. Alfred Kinsey had indicated
interest in interviewing me, and would request a conference in the
near future.

During my first weeks on Long Island, I bought a car and, as
my driver's license had expired in my absence, I went to the Motor
Vehicle Bureau to take the driver's tests and have it renewed. I was
met by a flood of reporters and photographers, and again became
the subject of headlines. Although I didn't think that was a
particularly newsworthy event, one newspaper called it "another step
in her famous career," reasoning which escapes me to this day.
Apparently, the slightest excuse was used to fill up newspaper space.
Even Dolly was drawn into the incident and I was beginning to get a
firsthand idea of the demands made on my family.

"…[This] reporter was sitting with Christine's sister yesterday,
while the he-turned-she was taking a driver's license test. The sister,
a pleasant woman who has been striving for anonymity, made small
talk…but absolutely refused to talk about Christine. She wouldn't
even tell the reporter her name."

Soon after my arrival, I began meeting friends and relatives,
and found that this experience which I'd somehow dreaded was, for
the most part, not really so difficult. People like Dr. Joe and Gen

Angelo welcomed me home with open arms and I was delighted to renew those friendships.

For some years, the Angelos had been interested in the research programs for cerebral palsy, and on many occasions had personally organized social events to raise money for the national fund. One fundraising project to which I was invited was an afternoon of bridge, arranged in their home and attended by a group of more than one hundred and fifty women. In a later interview, Gen recorded some of her impressions:

> Joe and I were worried most of all about Chris' ability to adjust to the storm of publicity. Before, we knew her as a terribly shy, inhibited person, but actually what we saw was a new woman coming into a world of her own. To us, she was a crusader and the thing we admired most was her personal courage and the idea that she had never wanted to cheapen or pervert herself. Undoubtedly, that was the driving force behind her, in spite of the suffering it entailed.
>
> I watched her that day of the bridge party for the cerebral palsy fund. She was perfectly poised and outgoing, charming to everyone. We had a particularly large crowd, no doubt because she'd agreed to be there. I watched those women, the real smoothie, social types and they'd get up out of their seats to get a closer look at her, not bothering to conceal their curiosity and bad manners. As a matter of fact, some of them didn't even bother to address me in my own home, they were too busy following Chris around.
>
> I can remember one of the few men present, who said, "The best looking woman in the room is Christine!" That pleased Joe very much.
>
> I was bombarded with questions right and left, people wondering why she did it, asking if her hair was naturally blonde and how she got her beautiful complexion. Oddly enough, several women came to

Joe that day, asking for hormone treatments to give
them the same smooth complexion.

Joe was furious when one guest made a comment
that Chris was still not a woman, but a freak. "She's as
much a woman as you are," he said. "She could marry,
yes, and do anything you can do, and perhaps do it
better."

Although most all of my old friends and family were as warmly
supportive as the Angelos, it would be untrue to say that all of the
reactions to my homecoming were enthusiastic. One or two of my
relatives showed their deep distress, cause for a breach in the family
that wasn't healed until ten years had passed.

However, with few exceptions, it was a time for happy reunions
and I remember it as a wonderful period when most everyone I love
was a champion. One of Dad's much quoted answers to a query from
the press made it clear what he thought about it all. "She's ours and
we love her," he snapped.

Having once overcome my initial shyness, or at least learned
to hide it, I began to feel more freedom in my ability to make new
friends. Outside of my own small circle, I met many people in the
literary and theatrical world. Elaine Carrington, a radio-TV script
writer, was the first to invite me to her home, and for the first time
among strangers, I felt nothing but friendliness and genuine interest
in me as a person. Elsa Maxwell invited me to a luncheon at her suite
in the Waldorf Hotel, and a few days later wrote in her *New York
Journal-American* column:

> I reproached Bob Hope for saying on the air not
> long ago when he was asked if he were going to
> Copenhagen, that he wasn't because he didn't want to
> come back a new Elsa Maxwell. Bob roared and said,
> "That reminds me, you had a lunch the other day for
> Christine Jorgensen." "I did," I replied, "for I was full of
> curiosity because I couldn't believe that she was real."
> Russell Crouse, Howard Lindsay, and Leland Hayward

said they would cut me dead if I didn't have them to meet her, so that is just what I will do. Cole Porter was the only man who came to see her and Cole was impressed, also Eleanor Loder and Margaret Case of *Vogue* magazine were the other two guests.

Christine is definitely on the level. Her voice is soft and low. She is quite beautiful, very intelligent, has poise and very good manners. When she left she thanked my maid who had cooked lunch, which no one else has ever done that I can remember.

The excitement in the private entrance at the Waldorf Towers was something I have never seen before. Christine is certainly a celebrity and a nice one.

Columnist Leonard Lyons also gave a party for me to which he invited Sam Goldwyn, Dr. and Mrs. Ralph Bunche, Danny Kaye, and Milton Berle, and Truman Capote invited me to a delightful Sunday brunch.

Namedropping by recounting some of those early meetings after my homecoming may seem to indicate shallow pride, but the fact of the matter was, at the time, I was flattered to think that I should be interesting and sought after, frankly charmed by the attention, and was guilty of some goggle-eyed celebrity-watching in return.

The poet, Abraham Cowley, wrote that "curiosity does, no less than devotion, pilgrims make," and there's no doubt that curiosity was the main reason why I was in demand socially, at that point. *New York Journal-American* columnist Louis Sobol commented: "Party-givers now plead with Christine Jorgensen to 'drop in.' It's a huge lift for the party—just like in other days the big feature was the huge 'pie' out of which would step unclad maidens." Now that I think of it, the simile seems questionable. Recently, one of my friends who was an interested bystander of the period, has said, "At the time, everyone in the world wanted to meet Chris and damned near everybody did!"

On the other hand, I knew that much of the curiosity and interest stemmed from the understandable fact that people were looking for answers. I had no reason to be concerned by that, for once having met me personally, they showed their acceptance with kindness and warmth.

But most important to me at the time was the fact that those were the first steps in a difficult social adjustment for a person who had been shy and introverted for so long. It was my new ability to meet people and to be accepted by them in return that was deeply gratifying to me.

It's only fair to add, however, that not all columnists regarded me with as much favor as Elsa Maxwell. I found that I was frequently the subject of attack, invariably from people whom I'd never met. One writer in particular, in the *New York World-Telegram,* became so virulent that I began to wonder what his own personal problems might be.

If it was fashionable in some instances to meet me in person, it was fashionable in others to turn out a cleverly written phrase to prove the immense wit of the writer:

"The fellow who wanted to be his own girl—Christine Jorgensen."

"Sid Caesar thinks Ralph Edwards should glorify Christine Jorgensen on *These Are My Lives.*"

"Christine Jorgensen (a regular Man-About-Town) doing the swankier boites."

"Seeing pix of Christine (George) Jorgensen reminds locals of the collegiates in the Harvard Hasty Pudding show."

"Arthur Murray has a former teacher who has a new dance named after Christine Jorgensen—the Christine is a fast shuffle."

"Christine Jorgensen has Treasury agents excitedly anticipating the surfacing of her income-tax report in the heap. Curious to know whether it was filed as male, female, or perhaps a joint return."

"With this year's Art Student League's ball using a Shakespeare theme, will Christine Jorgensen come as Romeo or Juliet?"

"Didjez see those photos of Christine arriving from Denmark? Isn't she just George-jus?"

"I have friends who doubt the complete femininity of Christine Jorgensen, the ex-GI—but I'm one who believes she's all girl. For evidence I refer skeptics to her retort when a newspaper reporter, in a baiting mood, asked a too obvious question about the fur piece Christine was carrying as she got off the plane. 'Don't you know mink when you see it?' Christine meowed. You can't mistake that, kids. That's a female talking!"

There were many other samples, of course, equally tasteful.

It may seem like feigned innocence, but I had little idea of what effect the newspaper publicity was having on the rest of the community, though I soon learned what to expect. At that point, all sorts of new experiences were cropping up daily, one of which included an invitation to attend the opening of a Broadway show, *My Three Angels*. As I'd never been to a Broadway opening before, I looked forward to it eagerly, little realizing that I was going to cause a disturbance.

I was escorted to the theater by a friend of Irmy's and once settled in our seats, we noticed a general lift in the usual pre-curtain buzz in the audience as men and women walked up and down the aisles, gaping with frank curiosity. I turned around to see what had caused the flurry, when my companion gave me a sudden nudge and whispered, "Chris, it's you!" I read in the columns the next day that "Christine almost ruined the opening of *My Three Angels* just by going," and "the disturbance caused the management to darken the house for a few minutes before lifting the curtain for each act." Apparently, too, I'd incurred the wrath of the excellent cast of the play, headed by Walter Slezack, Jerome Cowan, and Darren McGavin, a reaction for which I couldn't blame them.

After the performance, we walked to a nearby restaurant for an after-theater snack, and were followed by a dozen or so onlookers, who frankly entered behind us. What I had expected to be an evening of enjoyment turned out to be one of discomfort and embarrassment and I said as much to my escort.

"Face the music, Chris," he answered, "it can't last forever!"

I was by then beginning to get an inkling of what to expect, not only in public, but of the adjustments I would be making from then on. Apparently, I was going to have to get used to the idea of being stared at and inspected. People were going to be interested and inquisitive, I decided, and I would just have to accept it as logical, if I was going to function in the world at all.

About three weeks after my return from Denmark, I received a letter from the Scandinavian Societies of Greater New York, a charitable organization representing some seventy-five thousand Scandinavian-Americans, informing me that I had been selected as Woman of the Year—"because of your outstanding contribution to the advancement of medical science, and because of the dignified and courageous manner in which you have deported yourself through it all." To receive the citation, I was invited to attend a gathering of five thousand members on March 7, an annual event that included a concert and grand ball. Proceeds of the evening were to go to various Scandinavian charities. I must admit that I was surprised and very moved by that honor. To me, my accomplishments had seemed to be of such a highly personal nature, insignificant to anyone but me and the Danish medical men who had contributed so much to my existence. To receive a public award for something that was a transition to normalcy seemed an undue recognition, but I was grateful for their acknowledgement and accepted it with pleasure.

Accompanied by my family and friends, a citation scroll was presented to me. I made a brief speech of thanks, if somewhat timidly, for it was my first experience in front of such a large group of people.

That appearance, however, gave me sufficient courage to accept an invitation from Walter Winchell a week later, to appear at Madison Square Garden for a charity benefit. One of Winchell's pet projects, called "The Bravest and Finest" had been organized to help the families of New York policemen and firemen who had been killed in the line of duty. Entertainment was provided by a host of well-known theatrical stars, and although I had no way of entertaining, it seemed to me an opportunity to prove myself a useful member of the community. Having lived in Europe for several years, I felt a need for belonging and to satisfy that need by making some sort of contribution. I consented to appear, in spite of the fact that Winchell's personal barbs in his column had made him anything but endearing. Unsure of his reception, he offered the invitation through a friend, assuring me that my introduction would be simple and tasteful, and that I'd have little to do except to make an appearance with a brief speech.

On the performance night, I confess to being excited as I walked back stage at Madison Square Garden. There was certainly no doubt about my naïveté, when an ample gentleman named Gleason was introduced to me and I asked him if he was related to the Hollywood actor, Jimmy Gleason. He said he wasn't and I asked him if he was in show business. "Well, in a way," he admitted. "I do a weekly thing on TV." I promised to look for his program the following week, and he was called onstage to do his stint for the show then in progress.

Hank Wall, who had accompanied me that evening, promptly set me straight, much to my chagrin. "Chris, Jackie Gleason is the biggest name in television!" I'd been away for almost three years where TV hadn't existed, and the entertainers who were then making their fame in America were unknown to me.

I was very big in the *faux pas* department that night. As the star-studded show progressed, I met a slim and smiling young man whose name I didn't hear when we were introduced. He was pleasant and congenial and I was enjoying our conversation, thinking perhaps that he was an observer backstage, when someone tapped him on the shoulder to indicate he was next to perform. In a moment, the Garden was ringing with his famous number, "Cry." His records were popular in Denmark and I knew them well, but as I'd never seen a picture of him, I didn't recognize Johnny Ray.

At last, someone led me to the stage entrance, gave me a signal, and I walked out under the blinding spotlights to face the great darkened expanse of people. In a courteous gesture, Winchell removed his famous reporter's hat and said simply, "Ladies and gentlemen, meet Miss Christine Jorgensen." I know that I was nervous and frightened, but the brief speech I addressed to the audience was a simple expression of the honor accorded me at being invited, and the opportunity to be a useful citizen of New York City. Suddenly it was over and I walked offstage, followed by a deafening ovation, experiencing that peculiar excitement and stimulation that I would come to know better, later on.

For some reason that evening, I thought of the last time I had been in Madison Square Garden. Seven years before, during my army service, I'd attended the circus there and had I been asked then to do so much as get up and whisper "hello" from my seat high up under the roof, I'd have fled in terror. As a young army private, I'd had no idea I would some day make my debut as "Christine," in front of eighteen thousand people, on a stage under glittering lights, surrounded by show-business headliners.

A few weeks after the Garden benefit, Arthur and Kathryn Murray pledged five thousand dollars, to the Damon Runyon Cancer Fund if I would appear on their telecast of *The Arthur Murray Party*, an invitation that conformed to my idea at the time to appear only for charitable purposes. However, I'd already been informed several times that although many TV personalities had wanted to invite me as their guest, the network executives had banned me from appearing. The Murrays succeeded in breaking that barrier and I consented to appear and make a speech on behalf of the Cancer Fund.

On the day of the telecast, I sat in a corner of the studio, watching with fascination the preparations that went into thirty minutes of live television. Again, it was an alien atmosphere in which I felt out of place. Dancers were limbering up in corners, Kathryn Murray was rehearsing a skit with Charles Coburn, and Melvyn Douglas and Jane Pickens were listening to each other's speeches on behalf of the fund drive. Lights were set, microphones swung in from above and cameras rolled into positions looking like uneasy squids, with masses of wires trailing behind.

As I watched all of these preparations, I was struck by the thought that I didn't really belong and I wondered what I was doing there, again in the company of successful stars. I had little or nothing to offer except a sincere desire to be helpful in the cancer drive.

Though my return to the United States had been in mid-February, a little less than two months earlier, my life in that brief span had been extraordinary in many ways. I'd renewed old friendships and met a great many new and exciting personalities. I had been both attacked and applauded in the press, and known the delight of being accepted by society, as well as the anguish of non-acceptance. An amazing thing in itself, I'd found the courage to make several public appearances in front of large crowds, and most satisfying of all, I was building a new home for myself and my parents.

There hadn't been much time to pause and reflect in those full and busy weeks, but when I finally stopped to consider it, I'd faced some extremely difficult adjustments. I'd been courted, derided, admired, made the subject of off-color jokes, and clothed in the light of half-truths and controversy. Apparently, there would be no attitudes in between complete hostility and total approval. I was going to be like eggplant—one either liked it very much, or not at all.

Miraculously, the past had led me to a life of fame and notoriety, with all of its attendant frustrations, pleasures and responsibilities. By turns, I'd known delight, bewilderment, amusement, and resentment, but always supporting those personal reactions was a strong, underlying sense of happiness. In spite of all the perplexing events, in the deepest recesses of myself, I was a happy person.

Although I still had one more large medical step before total fulfillment, I had started on the new life I'd looked toward, prayed for, and knew was rightfully mine. In more ways than one, I had come home at last.

CHAPTER 19

Several times since my return from Denmark in the early months of 1953, I'd been approached by insistent agents and managers who tried to badger me into managing my affairs. However, inexperienced as I was at the time, I could recognize an opportunist when I saw one. One sharp character in particular had dreams of cashing in quickly on what he termed "the phenomenon of the century." Whatever that meant to him, to me it was a disturbing idea, as though I were some monstrosity to be ogled in a sideshow and I had no doubt that his ideas of publicity surrounding such a "phenomenon," would be sensational and tasteless.

For his services, I was assured, he would charge only the usual agent's fee of sixty percent of my earnings, whatever they might be. Although then I had no knowledge of what was a normal fee for such services, his figure seemed as excessive as his schemes. Later, of course, I learned that ten percent was the accepted fee set by the theatrical unions.

I was learning that I would be a likely prey for phonies and the unscrupulous.

Again, however, Providence was on my side. Among the many people I met in the early weeks after my return, one in particular was to yield an enduring friendship, a man whose counsel and influence would make great changes in my life. His name was Charlie Yates, one of the most astute and beloved artist's representatives in the entertainment world, who numbered among his clients Bob Hope and Beatrice Lillie. I first met Charlie socially through an acquaintance, and though our meeting was brief, I had an instinctive feeling that he would somehow be important to my life.

Probably in his early fifties when we met, he was a tall, quiet man with a thin, aquiline face and a paternal air that inspired respect and confidence.

Charlie arranged a second meeting which I accepted eagerly; I with the idea of promoting my Denmark film, and he with the thought of encouraging me in other areas.

At that point, I had to make some sort of decision about the direction my life would take toward a professional career, as by then I'd invested most of the money from the *American Weekly* series in our new house, and had no other means of income in sight.

My brief appearances in public surrounded by such shining talents had made me painfully aware that I was ill-equipped for any role in the entertainment field except that of a spectator, regardless of my childhood triumphs as Mickey Mouse, some twenty years before. I still had hopes that a photographic career lay open to me.

Charlie was very much against the idea of releasing my Denmark film, and considered it a poor venture with which to launch a career. He respected my ideas of appearing in public for charity alone, but asked me how I was going to live on it. "Comes the day when your cash is gone," he said, "who's going to throw a benefit for you?" That idea brought me up short.

"Look, Chris, you're a world-famous personality whether you like it or not, so you're either going to have to face up and join it, or turn and leave. The only thing is, you can't leave the limelight now, because they won't let you. From here on out, there's nothing you can do and no place you can go to lead a normal, quiet life. You go to the grocery store, walk your dog, get a driver's license—that's news. With the kinds of publicity you've received, there just aren't many opportunities left to you."

I knew that was true. I'd had many offers from various enterprises, everything from hat designers to burlesque houses, from beauty salons to carnival midways. I was perfectly aware that they didn't want to hire me for my abilities, but for the notoriety surrounding my name.

Charlie earnestly believed that a nightclub act was the answer. He assured me there was money to be made in clubs, and warned me again of my immediate problem of making a living.

"You've got one thing in your favor, Chris, besides the publicity. Personality—and that's a salable commodity."

"Look, Charlie, I can't sing, I can't dance and I can't give out the snappy chatter. I'm a photographer, not an entertainer. I'm a basic, simple person with my feet on the ground where they belong. Because I'm now something of a celebrity, it doesn't mean I'm suddenly endowed with miraculous gifts as a performer."

I didn't tell him at the time, but I was also suffering from a plain old-fashioned dose of snobbery. Although I'd been in a nightclub only once or twice in my whole life, I had an exaggerated idea of their low moral tone. There's no doubt that at the time, I was something of a self-righteous prude.

We argued amiably back and forth for several days and he urged me to talk it over with my family. Mom and Dad and I agreed it would be all right, only if I made an appearance in connection with my film. Charlie, of course, was still averse to the idea, but he agreed to try for a booking in a theater, cautioning me that the film would have to be cut to twenty minutes.

True to his word, Charlie arranged an engagement at the Orpheum Theater in Los Angeles for the first week in May, with a pre-engagement test run in Waterbury, Connecticut. That left me about two weeks to cut the film from one hundred twenty minutes to the specified twenty, to plan the narration accordingly, and produce the musical sound track, for which I'd chosen the music of the Danish composer, Carl Nielsen. It wasn't an easy job and I hated sacrificing the many scenes which I'd worked so hard to get. By the time I was finished, I no longer had a full-length travel film, it was reduced to a brief synopsis.

That was the start of a lasting friendship and profitable business relationship with Charlie Yates, and in spite of its drastic beginning, my career was in his hands from then on. We never had a written contract, but merely shook hands to cement our agreement. The first Christmas after our association began, he gave me two gold charms for my bracelet; a "10%" mark and two clasped hands, representing our business arrangement.

If I'd thought the controversies of my case would soon abate, I was very much mistaken, for a new storm was brewing over its medical ethics and the attitudes of the American Medical Association. Not more than a week after the *American Weekly* series had ended, the *New York Post* began a series of daily syndicated articles entitled, "The Truth About 'Christine' Jorgensen." Facts that had already been disclosed in my own story were manipulated to suit a position that was diametrically opposite. Many comments were cloaked in the mythical realm of "a reliable source," which is merely an ambiguous term that puts the stamp of approval on prevarication.

The *Post* articles consistently referred to me as "he," "Jorgensen," or "the Bronx man," as though I were some anthropological missing link. Their main point was that no sex transformation had taken place and the implication was clear that I was a charlatan, out to dupe the public and the medical profession in the United States. What was termed "a strange and tragic case," was followed up by a statement of the conflicting views between the European and American doctors.

"Interviewed at his Long Island home...he was told that the *Post* undertook to tell the whole story after exhaustive investigation, because of the worldwide misapprehensions in his case and because thousands of homosexuals and transvestites had been led—wrongly and perhaps tragically—to the belief that Denmark had discovered a surgical 'cure' for them."

Neither my doctors nor I had ever advocated these procedures as a solution for other sexual breaches of Nature. Mine was a single, highly individual case and the doctors had proceeded along the lines they felt would be most beneficial to me alone, with my full knowledge, approval, and consent. Beyond that, I had no advice for anyone. If others had seen in me a false hope for their own problems, then surely it was "wrong" and "tragic," but help for others could only come from the acceptance and enlightenment of the public and the medical profession.

To continue the conflict, the *New York Post* articles stated: "He was told that many members of the medical profession in the United States had grown increasingly outraged over his disclosures because homosexuals and transvestites were now hammering on their doors for surgical relief...whereas these American doctors believe that psychiatry or psychoanalysis holds the one real hope for the physically normal male who has strong female tendencies.

"...Jorgensen's doctors know now that many men in the U.S. medical and psychiatric groups were furious over the employment of so drastic and irrevocable procedures as castration and penisectomy in such cases because their view is that it only worsens an already deteriorated situation."

Whatever the American medical attitudes, time and again in scientific literature on cases of transsexualism, psychiatrists and sexologists have reported no psychiatric cures, either temporary or permanent. With over thirty years of experience as a sexologist, Dr. Harry Benjamin stated a positive view on the subject, in a medical paper printed in the *Western Journal of Surgery, Obstetrics and Gynecology* in 1964: "I have never heard of a cure of transsexualism by psychotherapy in spite of the fact that some patients have had psychoanalytic treatment for as long as three years. The transsexual patient simply doesn't want to change his psychological sex. I must, therefore, agree with Dr. Robert Laidlaw, chief psychiatrist at Roosevelt Hospital in New York, and with others who have studied several of these patients, that 'psychiatry has nothing to offer in these cases as far as any cure is concerned.' The patient's suffering has to be relieved by other means."

That theory was born out by Dr. Stürup, the Danish psychiatrist who had handled my case, when in a later interview he had said: "Nothing I got was worth much from the psychiatric point of view."

The *Post* also stated that my Danish doctors had advised against my giving the story to the *American Weekly,* implying that their medical sanction of the account had been withheld. That statement was totally untrue, as the *American Weekly* articles were the only ones officially certified by all the medical men involved in my case, either then or since.

I was sufficiently disturbed over this new critical attack to write an appeal to Dr. Hamburger in Copenhagen, to which he promptly answered: "Why pay so much attention to the newspapers? They are not interested in your problem, and as far as I can see, they only want to make money. Let the newspapers quarrel. You wrote your own decent story in a manner which could be understood by the laymen, and as true as it could be made."

However, the newspaper's view that no transformation had taken place, insinuating that I had perpetrated a hoax, continued to rankle. If they implied that the true meaning of "sex transform-ation," meant a complete reversal of the sexes, whereby a male becomes entirely female, then their claim might have been credible. I was never an absolute male and I shall never be an absolute female. But whatever the value of percentages in the scale of sex determinants, there are no absolutes; even the most masculine or feminine person approximates only eighty percent of the possible total. There is no one hundred percent Adam or Eve.

Although the term "sex transformation" has been used by many people when referring to my case, even by me on occasion, mine was rather a process of revised sex determination, inspired by the preponderance of female characteristics.

But what is male and what is female? Many factors predominate to determine a person's sex. In an article written for a sexological journal in 1961, Dr. Benjamin describes seven different kinds of sex to be considered in the human makeup: chromosomal, anatomical, legal, endocrinological, germinal, psychological, and social.

The fundamental chromosomal sex is the genetic constitu-tion, containing male and female genes, which are the carriers of heredity; anatomical sex includes internal and external sex structures in both primary (reproductive organs) and secondary (genitalia, body build, hair distribution, etc.) manifestations; legal sex is most often based on the visible, external anatomical structures of the individual, the sole determinant of gender on a birth certificate; endocrinological sex refers to the proportionate amounts of various hormones secreted by the sex glands and certain other glands; germinal sex is the type of germ cell produced by the gonad (sex gland); the psychological aspect of sex concerns the individual's emotional orientation and identification; and the social sex deals with the areas in which a person can best function socially and find his place in the world.

Dr. Benjamin himself admits that these concepts are arbitrary, but in his words: "The purpose of scientific investigation usually is to bring more light into fields that are obscure. Modern researchers, however, delving into the 'riddles of sex,' have actually brought more obscurity, more complexity. What sex really is, has become an increasingly difficult question to answer."

If some of the great medical minds in the world were preoccupied with those intricacies, then it was highly unlikely that a New York daily newspaper would have the answers. Nevertheless, it was a common practice for news writers to make public proclamations as to what I was, or was not. It seemed to me that the selection of sex determination should lie with the individual in an effort to live freely, so long as it was to no one else's disadvantage.

The *New York Post* series brought out a rash of pseudoscientific commentary on the subject in the rest of the press:

"Was Her Sex Really Changed? Medics Raise Query on Chris"

"AMA Denies Investigation of Christine"

"The Third Sex—The Truth About Christine"

"Sex Surgery Specialist Reports Hundreds of Boy-Girl Operations"

"Sex Shift Old Stuff to US Specialists"

"Thousands in the US Don't Know Their True Sex"

"Many Bar Surgery for Change of Sex"

"Christine—Is She He or He She?"

"All Human Beings Begin Lives With Double Sex"

"20 Sex Conversion Cases Treated Here"

"MDs Here Want to Know About Chris"

"Doctors Deny Sex Probe"

"AMA Asks Report on Chris"

In the meantime, Dr. Hamburger was preparing a report for the *Journal of the American Medical Association*, and wrote me details of the medical account in March of 1953:

As to the medical report to *JAMA*, I should like to give you the following information.

We (you and I) have previously spoken about publication of the medical facts in scientific papers, and you have given me "free hands." I would never have given you the permission to use my name to such an extent as has happened, if I were not allowed to write a medical paper on...your case.

The American Medical Association has written to the Almindelige Danske Laegeforening [Danish medical society], and directly to me. They need some information and asked for a report. Prof. Dahl-Iversen, Dr. Stürup and myself have promised Dr. Austin Smith (editor of *JAMA*) to submit a report, and it is absolutely necessary that USA medical professions are made acquainted with our motives for the treatment.

My scientific name would be completely spoiled if I refused to give a report, and the same applies to D-I and Dr. S. We have prepared a paper on..."hormonal, psychiatric, and surgical treatment of a case." As a matter of fact, you need not be afraid, as our report follows your own story closely. Your report will get a scientific guarantee, and this can only be an advantage for you. Our intentions of helping the unhappy individuals would also be destroyed if we were silent. We have submitted a Danish version for *Nordisk Medicin* [a Norwegian medical journal] and it is our intention to send *JAMA* an English edition in the course of 5-7 days (it is being translated now).

Therefore, don't worry about the coming report. It can make no harm, on the contrary—it will be an immense help for your future and probably also for the people we want to help.

I am quite sure you understand me, and that you trust me. And I know you believe me when I tell you that the medical report has to appear, and in the near future. If not, I would be scientifically a dead man!

Dr. Hamburger's article did appear shortly after, though how the medical profession in the United States reacted at the time is difficult to determine.

The *New York Post* was not the only offender in the sex crusade, but was representative of the press work that was going on at the time all over the world. Other papers were taking up the cudgels and raising controversies about my status, a pastime of which they've never seemed to tire.

Another syndicated article appeared widely in late March, and included the following statements:

> ...Girlish as all get out, but under a cloud as far as New York doctors are concerned, Christine-George Jorgensen has to do a lot of proving before he/she gets a full bill of credence. American docs think it just can't be done. Danes swear it's true.
>
> ...Critics of the transformation declare that an early, responsible determination of the true status of George-Christine is urgently needed for these reasons:
>
> Medical—If American medicine remains silent, it in effect gives tacit approval to the claim that a man can be made into a woman. Already, a number of doctors have been besieged by male homosexuals pleading to be converted into "girls like Christine."
>
> Socio-legal—Local ordinances throughout the United States forbid masquerading in the clothing of the opposite sex. What happens in the case of a "converted" defendant?
>
> ...Some sources have asked whether, under American law, Chris qualifies for marriage to a man.

...Danish law neither forbids nor specifically authorizes the operation undertaken by Dr. Dahl-Iversen. But Danish practice has been to permit it—for Danish citizens only—if a surgeon, psychiatrist, and hormonist agree in joint consultation that it should be performed. Only five or ten such cases are handled annually in Denmark.

In the first part of his task, Dr, Dahl-Iversen removed the chief source of the male hormones. Other surgery followed, including some radical plastic work. The final results caused Dr. Dahl-Iversen to tell a symposium: "Miss Jorgensen is all woman. She could live as a normal wife, except that she lacks the feminine organs necessary to have a child.

As the debates continued, I could only hope that the report prepared for the *Journal of the American Medical Association* by Dr. Hamburger and his colleagues would clarify the case for American doctors. At the same time, I realized that the general public must have been thoroughly confused by so much contradictory material, and I was virtually helpless to do anything about it. I decided to take Dr. Hamburger's advice, and "let the newspapers quarrel."

Meanwhile, I began to consummate plans for the tryout performance of the movie presentation in Waterbury, Connecticut, on May 2, a week before I was due in Los Angeles at the Orpheum Theater.

Some last-minute processing of the film had been necessary and I drove to Manhattan the day before the tryout, to pick it up at the Pathé Laboratories. I'd packed the car with my clothes, jewelry, and other paraphernalia for the performance, planning to drive immediately to Waterbury. Once parked near the film laboratories, I spent no more than half an hour inside, and returned to the car to find the window had been smashed and all my belongings were gone. I had nothing to appear in except the clothes I was wearing, and knowing it was closing time for most of the stores, I was desperate. Frantically, I called Hank Wall, always a good friend in a crisis, who suggested I meet him at the Union Square area on 14th Street. Hank was sure some of the stores there would still be open and I made straight for one of the big ones opposite Union Square.

We soon discovered that the store had little to offer in the way of evening clothes, but I bought a few other necessities before we started to leave. At the exit, which was by then locked, a large and noisy crowd was held at bay by several struggling policemen, and I was a little unnerved to find that I'd been the object of the disturbance.

The date was May 1, May Day, and a Leftist group was holding a rally in Union Square, a favorite meeting place for nonconformists and long, ranting oratory. Apparently, I'd been seen entering the store, the crowd had deserted the harangue in the square, and moved en masse across the street to get a closer look at me. Unwittingly, I'd broken up the gathering, and with the help of the police who ran interference for us, we finally made it safely back to the car.

Fortunately, Hank remembered the name of a prominent couturier whom we'd met shortly before at the New York Publicist's Ball. We called her at her home and she graciously opened her shop, where I selected clothes to replace those that had been stolen from my car. I didn't know it at the time, but all of the costly "original" gowns that I bought that night had already been worn by a famous singing star on her TV program.

In my vast inexperience, the Connecticut tryout performance was a successful one, although I had no professional critic to confirm or deny my view. Unaware of the approaching storm, Mom and I flew to Los Angeles for my first official stage appearance at the Orpheum Theater, scheduled for May 8.

As I look back on that first performance, I'm amazed at my naïve approach to it. I don't think I even knew enough to have stage fright. I thought the film would stand on its own merits, but as my manager, Charlie Yates, hadn't accompanied me, I had no friendly counsel to tell me whether or not my appearance was right, or the film commentary was sufficiently interesting to hold an audience. My only close critic was Mom, who could hardly be called severe, and as usual she could see no wrong in anything I did. She thought the performance was great and wrote postcards home saying, "Chris is packing the crowds into the theater."

Less prejudiced in my favor and rightfully critical of ineptness, the Los Angeles reviewers were merciless, and left no doubt that I was a performer of startling incapacity. "Christine's appearance proves disappointing," was the kindest reaction. Others were closer to the mark: "Christine Jorgensen's intro into the entertainment world had all the impact of a feather duster." The *Hollywood Reporter,* a show business trade paper, wrapped it up in their review: "Willie Hammerstein would have loved this—but even the old master of exploitation vaudeville would have been hard put to know what to do with Christine Jorgensen. The GI-turned-woman nixes sensationalism and insists her act must be dignified and treated decorously. Consequently, it can only be judged on the serious basis of a presentation to the public—and on that level, it's not good." In short, I had just laid one of the largest eggs in show-business history.

The week in Los Angeles was largely one of heartbreak and disillusionment and I found it extremely difficult to continue playing four performances daily for the balance of the week.

My despondency was increased by the fact that Charlie had secured a booking at the Sahara Hotel in Las Vegas, scheduled within two months. The management of the Sahara had seen a performance at the Orpheum Theater, and made it abundantly clear they would have nothing to do with me and my film as part of their floor show. As that was the only other date in view, I knew I had written "finish" to my career as a photographer-narrator.

I'd been in Hollywood eight years before, seeking a new career, and on the second time around again had failed disastrously. Apparently, the film capital just wasn't going to be my cup of tea.

I returned to New York a week older, a little wiser, and a great deal sadder. I didn't know where I'd turn next and I was convinced that my new-found agent would have nothing further to do with me. Mom and I were met at the airport, however, by the tall, gaunt figure of Charlie Yates.

"Well, Charlie, I guess I'm finished." He laughed and said, "No, as a matter of fact, Chris, you're just beginning. But you've learned one of the most important lessons in show business. You can't just sell a name, you've got to have an act to go with it!"

Only then did I realize that he'd allowed me to go through the Los Angeles experience as an opportunity to prove to myself that I'd been wrong. Nobody could teach me that lesson, I had to learn it by myself. I told him that from then on, it was all his and I'd follow his advice without argument.

Later on, Charlie gave his account of those early stages in my career to a reporter who was gathering material for a future article. Notes of that interview were recently made available to me, and I realize now why he exuded a confidence that I didn't feel. Many of his viewpoints were unknown to me then.

"When I first met Chris," he said, "I thought she was a very attractive, good-looking dame who was somewhat shy. I thought even then there was something about her that spelled talent. I'm not sure I can explain it, or why I thought so, but it was some kind of 'X' quality there. I knew eventually it would be salable, and not just on the strength of the notoriety. You know, I'm a gambler—do it every day—and to me, the odds looked good.

"Sure she'd already had about all the publicity there was to get, and as a result she was a world-famous celebrity. The thing was, she didn't know what to do with it. She wanted a career that was respected and tasteful, but all that stuff in the newspapers was pretty overwhelming, and there's no place she could have gone to escape it. The logical thing then, was to use it wisely and if she was going to be in the public eye from then on anyway, it had to be show business.

"I worked like hell to talk her into the nightclub thing. Her big argument was that she didn't have any experience, and that was true, but I kept arguing that she had enough personal charm to get by, if she'd really work hard at developing a suitable act. Plenty of performers I know in the business made it with less than she had.

"Hell, she'd been 'making believe' in a part that lasted twenty-six years, and that's a pretty long run. She must have worked very hard to convince people of her adjustment to a role she was unsuited for, before she went to Denmark. That's what I call salesmanship, and that's all show business is—salesmanship!"

Charlie was asked by the interviewer about the frequent accusations that I was an opportunist, cashing in on the publicity.

"Five will get you ten, that you can't name me three people who hate making money! If Chris could work up an act that was pleasing to the public, and if they wanted to see her, why should she do it for nothing? Up 'til then, she'd only appeared for charity and you can't put ketchup on that. Sure, I knew they'd come out of curiosity, but I had a hunch they'd go away entertained. Gambler's instinct.

"From the beginning, I knew she was more than a once-around performer, that she'd make good money in nightclubs. She had a responsibility to herself and to her parents. The world had made her what she was—she'd have been a damn fool not to pick up the ball and run with it."

Asked what his interest was in my career, Charlie answered characteristically. "Me? I get ten percent. That's my business."

But Charlie was more than a businessman, he was a warm friend and his own enthusiasm helped to build my confidence. I didn't want to let him down and I'd promised not to force the Denmark film any further. Finally, I agreed to try the nightclub circuit.

His idea was to develop an act with a professional to back me up in a series of songs and exchanges and specially written material. Charlie felt I should be teamed with someone with experience, particularly in the early stages of my career. By then, I had implicit trust in his judgement, and though I still had misgivings about my own ability to follow through, I let him continue his plans.

When I returned from the disaster in Los Angeles in mid-May, an event was approaching that had interested me for some time, the coronation of Britain's Queen Elizabeth. I had hoped to film the event with my old friend, Larry Jensen, and with the help of the King Features news syndicate, was able to acquire hotel accommodations and official papers granting me the privileges of the press. Because news coverage of the coronation was so vast, filming positions for photographers were allocated far in advance.

Charlie assured me that by the time I returned from England, he would have worked out the details for a night club act, and I left with the feeling that I was being given a slight reprieve.

Larry and I flew to Denmark for a week's visit before going on to the coronation, and American newspapers noted my departure with a headline that read: CHRIS RETURNS TO BOYLAND. One of the daily columns carried the following item: "Interest in Christine Jorgensen has faded entirely in this neck of the woods—and the plan that was brewing to build a picture around her (him) has been abandoned. I am told now that Christine, completely disillusioned with the slump in interest, has decided to settle permanently in Denmark."

Nothing could have been further from the truth. Anyone who had expected an ulterior reason to lie behind my visit to Copenhagen was vastly disappointed, as I spent most of the time visiting friends and relatives and consulting with Dr. Hamburger. This time, however, my consultations had little to do with me, but were related to the hopes and fears of other people who had read of my case, expressing a seemingly genuine desire for alteration of sex. I carried with me a briefcase full of the most challenging of the letters, to pass on to Dr. Hamburger. All of the queries contained pleas for understanding and help, and with each passing week, the number of letters increased. The tragedy of those appeals lay in the fact that there were few doctors whom they could consult with confidence. At the time, Dr. Harry Benjamin was one of the few exceptions in the United States.

As I discussed these problems with Dr. Hamburger in Copenhagen that May of 1953, he told me he was preparing a report for the medical profession, based on the personal appeals he and I both had received. He was hopeful that it would help alter some of the rigid medical and legal opinions, then current, and perhaps lead to legislative revisions.

One of the most gratifying things of my eventful week in Copenhagen, was the assurance the doctors gave of their continued faith in me and the rightness of their medical management in my case. I realized that because of the large amounts of adverse publicity, their own scientific reputations had been challenged. I set off for England greatly heartened by my visit to Copenhagen.

As our plane arrived in London simultaneously with another bearing the mother of Prince Philip, I escaped unnoticed at the airport. Caught up in the coronation activities, I enjoyed a kind of blessed anonymity, and felt free for the first time in months to move around without inhibition.

On May 18, Coronation Day, I took my appointed place in Piccadilly Circus in a building that supports the huge "Wrigley" sign, and found myself hanging precariously from the "G" to get my best film footage.

As the festivities approached an end, however, I realized I'd soon be facing a new crisis; the success or failure of a brand new career. I knew there was a great deal of work ahead of me and I still had many misgivings. Although perfectly aware of my inadequacies, I was determined to plunge on, no matter what the consequences. In looking back, I suppose there was a great deal at stake for both Charlie and me; I was gambling a whole future, he his reputation as a successful agent.

But even then, there were other things at stake, too. After my visit with Dr. Hamburger, it occurred to me that aside from my own personal aspirations, I somehow represented a concept that might possibly be important to others. Success and acknowledgement, therefore, represented something larger than my own life or ambitions. I can't say I particularly relished the idea, but it was a responsibility I felt strongly, nevertheless.

I was a controversial subject and I knew it. I also knew that there would be a great deal of criticism and opposition to my attempting a profession about which I admittedly knew nothing. Certainly, the experience in Los Angeles had prepared me for that.

I was about to throw myself into the marketplace, win or lose. I returned home with the feeling that after England and the Coronation, I was a little like the condemned who, before going to the gallows, ate a hearty breakfast.

CHAPTER 20

On the day I returned from England, I scarcely had time to unpack my luggage and settle down for a gossip session with Mom and Dad before the telephone rang. It was Charlie Yates, telling me that he wanted to set up a meeting with my new partner. As usual, Charlie had chosen wisely. Myles Bell and his wife, Nan, had appeared together for years as a variety team. She had turned from performing to writing and Myles was willing to take the calculated risk of backing me up in an act written especially for us by Nan.

We arranged a meeting within a few days and I liked my new colleagues immediately. In spite of my warning that I couldn't sing, Myles kept assuring me, "If you can count and carry a tune, you can sing!" I discovered that I could at least carry a tune, if not with brilliance, at least with determination.

After several sessions, the Bells, Charlie, and I worked out a twenty-five-minute routine of what we felt was a carefully balanced act. I was such a novice at that point, I let them do all the work and just did what I was told to do, relying on their experience and judgement.

Myles was to open the act with some of his own songs and patter, and then introduce and interview me. But working out a general format was just the beginning. There followed a long, tedious period of rehearsals which we spent in refining and shaping the material into a slick, professional unit. It was my first taste of the discipline that's required of performers and the constant repetition during rehearsals was a new and demanding experience.

It was another period of learning for me. Professionals always made the business of entertaining look so easy, as if it flowed from them automatically, but I soon realized that it was accomplished only by backbreaking work, tough discipline, trial and error. Also, I began to learn something about timing, and that the smallest fraction of a second made a great deal of difference whether or not a spoken line, a song phrasing, or a movement would have the desired effect.

I kept wondering if we'd ever get the show on the road, and if it would really fall into some semblance of order and coherence. Fortunately, I had the encouragement of experienced professionals to keep me going. Slowly, very slowly, I began to feel a sense of security in what I was doing.

When Charlie felt reasonably sure that the act was taking on some form and had value as entertainment, he started his selling job. Surely, it wasn't an easy task, because already many people in the business knew of my Los Angeles fiasco and the Las Vegas contract cancellation battle. However, Charlie announced one day that I'd be making my nightclub debut at the Copa Club in Pittsburgh on August 9, a date that had a slight sound of doom.

Early in June, I broke the schedule of rehearsals with Myles to take a short trip that was to net me a new furor of publicity, again unwittingly. A few weeks before, I had received a letter from Dr. Alfred Kinsey, inviting me to be interviewed at the Institute for Sex Research at Indiana University in Bloomington. Previously, with my permission, the Danish doctors had forwarded reports of my case for Dr. Kinsey's files at the university. His initial letter to me read in part:

> Certainly you would be contributing very materially to our research and the ultimate benefit to all the people who are utilizing the material on our research. We can guarantee, of course, that we will keep all of the material confidential. Dr. Benjamin must have assured you of this.

In order to prevent the disturbance which we are sure would occur if your name and our name were connected, we wonder if it would not be simplest to put you up in our own home...I would also suggest that I send someone to meet you at either the airport or train in Indianapolis in order to help keep your visit confidential.

You have a good deal to contribute and we shall very much appreciate the time you give us.

At the time, Dr. Kinsey was preparing material for his exhaustive report, *Sexual Behavior in the Human Female.*

I believed that since my name had become synonymous with problems of a sexual nature, it was important that a recognized scientific agency should have as much data as possible, and with my desire to contribute to the Kinsey project, I accepted his invitation.

In arranging to leave New York the last week in June, I traveled under a fictitious name, having already found it a convenience that saved a lot of trouble. I was beginning to be fairly artful at dodging reporters. My arrival at the Indianapolis airport went unnoticed and I was met by a private car and whisked off to the home of Dr. and Mrs. Kinsey in Bloomington. I spent several days in that pleasant atmosphere, and submitted myself to the complex cross-questioning at the Institute.

Probably no one would have known of my visit had it not been for my desire to spend an evening at the movies, after an afternoon of conferences. I went alone and was instantly recognized. It didn't take long to connect my presence in Bloomington with Dr. Kinsey and the work then in progress at the Institute of Sex Research. Within a few hours, newsmen from all over the country were calling the Institute for information.

Already much overworked and upset by the intrusions of the press, Dr. Kinsey suffered a heart attack and was rushed to a nearby hospital. Fortunately, the research on my case was nearly finished and I left within a day or two.

Again, the press erupted:

" 'Christine' Reported in Indiana; Hint He Talked with Dr. Kinsey"

"Christine Told All to Kinsey 'for Science' "

"Let's all hold our breath and maintain complete silence while Dr. Kinsey decides what Christine Jorgensen is."

" 'Just Like Other Women': Christine Gives a Full Report"

"Wonder which book of Dr. Kinsey's Christine Jorgensen will be in?"

"Christine Jorgensen may make a lecture tour discussing the Kinsey reports. She can take both sides."

I was afraid Dr. Kinsey would be angry at this invasion and hold me responsible, but he took it with good grace and I enjoyed a friendly correspondence with him until his death in August of 1956.

I remember him personally as a shy, quiet man and a gracious host, but in his work he was a supreme egoist, and left me with the impression that he believed his books on sexual behavior were the definitive ones, and there was not much left to be said on the subject. Perhaps his professional conceit was warranted, for above all, he was a dedicated research scientist, and I was happy to have made even a small contribution to his studies.

From Indiana, I stopped off in Chicago for a day or two to visit my uncle, whose wife, Aunt Edie, had died while I was in the hospital in Copenhagen the previous December. Due to a huge market convention, hotel rooms were at a premium in Chicago, and I stood in line to register at one of the city's big hotels. A lady in front of me asked for a room and was told by the clerk, "There might be one available in the women's section of the YWCA—if you're Christine Jorgensen." I stepped forward and said, quietly, "I'm Christine Jorgensen and I'd rather stay here, if possible." His discomfort was marvelous to behold. He flushed to a shocking pink, and after a long pause, hurried to arrange an accommodation.

I returned to New York and two incidents that afforded some amusement.

The enlisted men in a demilitarized armistice base camp in Munsan, Korea, had voted me "Miss Neutral Zone of 1953."

The *New York Daily News* carried the second story, datelined Frankfurt, Germany:

> The U.S. Army today threw the book at an American weekly newspaper publisher here who had incurred the wrath of the big brass by publishing articles about Christine Jorgensen...
>
> In an unprecedented order, Army headquarters in Heidelberg told the three year old *Overseas Weekly* that it was withdrawing the paper's license to publish, canceling its printing contract with the Army-operated *Stars and Stripes,* withdrawing accreditation of the paper's reporters and taking from the paper the right to sell to soldiers on Army newsstands.
>
> The army said stories about Christine...were bad for the 'moral welfare of the military.'
>
> GIs thought the stories about Chris were fine. The *Overseas Weekly* circulation jumped from 20,000 to 40,000 since it began the Christine stories.

As I had played no active part, personally, in this shocking demoralization of American troops in Europe, I had a clear conscience. Having been in the army myself, I didn't remember that the American GI could be so easily corrupted.

Sometime later, the Army also banned from its libraries Dr. Kinsey's book on sexual behavior in the human female, with the remarkable explanation that the Army "does not intend to spend money on that kind of a book."

Once more, I threw myself into the strict routine of rehearsals with Myles and Nan Bell, and was beginning to gain some sense of what I was doing. I found that I could sing well enough to get by, or at least "sell a number," as Myles called it. I thought probably my dancing wouldn't threaten the experts but I kept at it anyway, and I was learning about timing, pace, and the technique of using a microphone.

During my visit to England, the management of the Sahara Hotel in Las Vegas announced publicly they were canceling my contract, on the grounds that I had misrepresented myself as a woman. Milton Prell, part owner and manager of the Sahara, and Bill Miller, the hotel booking agent, sent me a registered letter rescinding the contract. The salutation in the letter read, "Dear Sir." Mr. Miller's assault was quoted widely in the news columns in mid-June:

> Before I let Christine Jorgensen mingle with women I want proof that she's a she!...I'm not going to pull a farce on my customers. I won't give them a man dressed in woman's clothing. I bought a 'she.' If the party can prove she's a woman, I'm willing to pay her $25,000 for two weeks.

By canceling the contract so publicly, they were obviously obtaining a little free publicity for the Sahara. The truth of the matter was that the agents for the hotel had seen one of the performances in Los Angeles, and based on the inadequacies of what they saw, were scared off from our contractual agreement. Had they tried to release themselves on the basis of that unfortunate truth alone, I could have understood their position, but their revelations in the press seemed reprehensible.

Angered by their public statements about me, Charlie instituted a lawsuit to hold the club to its original contract, and the negotiations dragged on for several months.

At the time, however, my main concern was to get the new act ready for the Pittsburgh opening and, inexorably, that date was drawing nearer. With the wounds still fresh from the Los Angeles fiasco and the Las Vegas battleground, I knew I was facing the supreme test. Except for the Sahara Hotel date, which had been left hanging, there were no other positive offers in sight and other club owners were standing by waiting to see what the act would do.

Myles and I kept plugging away to perfect the material, I had chosen my gowns carefully, and at last there seemed little else to do but run the frightening gamut of opening night.

We flew to Pittsburgh a day or two before the first performance, accompanied by Charlie Yates. I spent most of that time trying to calm my jangled nerves. Charlie's reaction was characteristic. "Chris," he said, "there are two things that can happen—they'll like you or they won't. Either way, it's not the end of the world or the end of your life."

I had a sudden delightful vision of a large hole opening in the earth at my feet and swallowing me up completely. It was an attractive fantasy, which faded all too quickly.

On that opening night of August 5, I stood in the entrance waiting for my cue from Myles. I felt some fleeting moments of panic, but suddenly there was no more time to indulge in the torture of stage fright. I heard Myles giving my introduction, I walked onstage greeted by a packed house, and began the routines we had rehearsed so many times before. Whatever confidence I might have mustered was short-lived, however, when I realized that there was not a sound from the people in the audience. They sat quietly and at complete attention, but made no response whatsoever to the material we'd thought was amusing and entertaining.

There was something ominous about that deafening silence. My stomach lurched around a bit and I began to get the hollow feeling that's symptomatic of abject fear. After my second musical number, however, I heard the sudden crack of spontaneous applause, and although it rocked me off-balance for a moment, I knew it was the first indication of acceptance on merit alone. I was extremely grateful for that, and from that moment on, began to enjoy myself, finishing the act with some degree of confidence.

During the following performances, each audience reacted in much the same way as the first one. I was worried about the opening silence, and wondered where I'd gone wrong. Neither Charlie nor Myles had a logical explanation, and advised me to forget it but the idea continued to nag. Several months later, I met Jimmy Durante who gave me his view on the subject, one that I gradually came to understand.

"Chris," he said, "for the first ten minutes you're onstage, you could tell the funniest joke ever written and they wouldn't laugh. People are too busy looking—all they wanna do is look!"

Immediately after the first show at the Copa Club, however, several club owners from other cities came backstage to my dressing room and, on the spot, Charlie negotiated contracts for the ensuing five weeks. As he so aptly put it, "We were in business."

Naturally, I was very much relieved for many reasons, among them the fact that my financial status would be secure. Although I was delighted at the prospect of a large salary, I was soon to learn there would be a heavy toll on the income. I not only paid the salary of my partner, Myles Bell, but there were also agent's fees, public relations services, musical arrangements, hotels, transportation, a large investment in my wardrobe, and inevitably, taxes.

As Charlie began to expand the engagements of the act, however, he discovered that there were many clubs throughout the country that refused my appearance on the grounds of "immorality." Those refusals came in spite of the fact that we'd had the good sense to keep the act free from objectionable or tasteless material. In fact, I still encounter rejections, invariably from managers who have never witnessed a performance. But at the time, Charlie was kept busy with willing offers, and I seemed to be launched successfully on a new career.

Once relieved from the pressures of opening night, I really began to enjoy my life as a performer, particularly the opportunity it presented to meet new people. Show business offered me a completely new horizon and I struggled to meet its challenges. Myles and I continued to work at refining the act and I was beginning to gain experience and grow in confidence.

In the process, many of my attitudes changed drastically. I now admit, with something of an apology, that I made my first appearance at the Copa Club in August of 1953 with the secret opinion that I was doing something slightly disreputable. I think I expected every member of the audience to be drunk, and that all chorus girls led scarlet lives. But I soon learned that life upon the wicked stage wasn't so wicked after all. I found that most entertainers were pretty average, hardworking citizens, and many of them simply went home to a husband or wife and children. They were often civic-minded, voted in elections, observed traffic laws, helped old ladies across the street, went to church, and gave innumerable benefit performances for no pay. The public only heard about the prodigals who were in the minority, as the virtues of the others simply weren't very interesting.

Today, it makes me laugh to think that I was such a great moralist, and often branded as a questionable commodity myself, that I was so abundantly guilty of being a prude.

After two exciting and rewarding weeks at the Pittsburgh Copa Club, I was feeling nothing but enthusiasm for my new career. I hoped that my development as an entertainer would warrant the encouraging notices I received from the newspapers. The reviews then were important, not because they acclaimed me a star, for they didn't, but they were supportive to my first faltering steps in a new occupation. Undoubtedly, too, they were partially responsible for its continuance and, for once, I had cause to be grateful to the press.

"...Miss Jorgensen isn't the best singer in the world, or the best dancer, but there's no denying that she has the most important ingredient of all—showmanship. This girl is no dummy."

"Christine Jorgensen, the most discussed personality of the year...presents a highly polished, amusing routine and the rest of the show backs her to perfection. Her appearance makes the gals gasp with envy, as her wardrobe is one of the most expensive and elaborate we've seen."

"...an act that surprised the cynics of the first night audience.... While it was evident that many had come out of curiosity rather than to be entertained, most of them wound up being entertained by the apparently complete femininity of Christine, as well as her adept patter with comedian Myles Bell."

"...As an attraction, Miss Jorgensen is likewise in a class by herself. What she does is done sensibly and with good grace."

But the review printed by *Variety* was the most pleasing and important to me, and as a prominent trade paper and bible for the entertainment industry, it carried the most weight in the business.

"A capacity crowd that came in for one quick look stayed to marvel at the smooth act of Christine Jorgensen in her nitery debut. Operation Big Switch sings like an off-key Greta Garbo, talks the way she looks and hesitates in her dance steps. But all in all the act moves and no one walked away disappointed. Nobody expected anything and what they got was all gravy. The act itself was tastefully written by Nan Bell whose husband, Myles Bell, is onstage with Christine at all times and carries her throughout the whole routine. Her timing is good and her jokes are funny...The gowns made the predominantly femme audience drool, but all in all, look for Christine to be more than a once around sensation. The girl has an act."

While I was lying in the hospital in Denmark when the story first broke the previous December, one of the offers I'd received by wire came from Lenny Litman, the owner of the Copa Club in Pittsburgh. I had no idea that eight months later he would be sending a telegram to Charlie Yates at the close of my nightclub debut:

1953 AUG 12
CHRISTINE JORGENSEN ACT WENT OVER BIG. AUDIENCE
AMAZED AT PERFORMANCE OF HER AND MYLES BELL.
WILL TAKE HER BACK ANYTIME. ALL PAPERS GAVE HER
EXCELLENT COVERAGE. FEEL SHE WILL HAVE A PERMANENT
PLACE IN THE TOP RUNG OF THIS BUSINESS. SINCERELY
LENNY LITMAN, COPA CLUB

From Pittsburgh we moved to Detroit for a two-week engagement and then on to Philadelphia, again playing to packed houses. In the City of Brotherly Love, I was horrified to receive a long-distance phone call from a reporter in Tennessee, informing me that a woman was appearing at the Midsouth Fair in Memphis, claiming herself to be the "real Christine Jorgensen." Apparently her act consisted of a vulgar recitation of her sex aspirations and the state of her anatomy, adding the promise of "unusual thrills" in a further intimate display. Knowing her to be fraudulent, the reporter, Paul Molloy, of the *Memphis Commercial-Appeal,* had called me for a comment. I obliged in no uncertain terms. From Molloy's exposé in the paper, the local police took action and the Fair officials closed the section in which she was appearing. Although the lady was fired on the spot, it's reasonable to guess that some people who saw her in Memphis still believe that she was the "real Christine."

Charlie was as furious as I, and threatened to sue her sponsors who claimed they'd been hoodwinked too. However, I didn't want to get embroiled in the unsavory business, or to invite further publicity from it, so Charlie settled for an apology and an explanation.

The weeks that followed were busy and productive ones. The act continued to go well and we were received by enthusiastic audiences wherever we played.

Once the Las Vegas promoters had read the reviews and taken note of the business that other managers were enjoying, they no longer seemed to have any public objections to my womanhood. Charlie dropped the lawsuit and they agreed to allow me to fulfill my original contract with the Sahara Hotel, a booking that was finally set up for the following November.

Before that, however, I was due in Washington, D.C. for an engagement at the Casino Royal, an experience that was to produce two incidents that turned out to be a study in contrasts.

About half an hour before I was to appear onstage for the opening performance, I was summoned to the manager's office and was met by a heavy, cigar-chewing character who introduced himself as an inspector of the police Morals Squad in Washington at the time. He came abruptly to the point of his visit.

"Jorgensen," he said, "I'm a police official in this city and I want to prevent any unpleasant incidents before they happen. Consequently, I'm asking you not to use the women's public toilets while you're in Washington!"

Dumfounded by that statement, I just stood there gaping at him.

"And if you dare to use a public restroom," he continued, "I'll have you picked up and examined by a board of doctors."

For a moment, I thought I'd been confronted by a madman and my first reaction was blind rage. It was difficult for me to see the relationship between public morals and public toilets, as to me those facilities had been more a matter of convenience than of sex. But his personal experience was no doubt greater than mine in those areas, and therefore he must have had some reason for his violently protective attitude.

With whatever calmness was left to me, I assured him that I'd try very hard to contain myself while I was in Washington. I know that if the incident hadn't been such a shock and taken me so off guard, I'd have been reduced to helpless laughter then and there. As it was, I excused myself as quickly as possible, and left the hygienic inspector to brood on the gravity of segregating the toilets by gender in our nation's capital.

A more attractive memory of my stay in Washington, was meeting a likable young man who approached me at the club one evening and, identifying himself as an artist, asked if he could paint my portrait. His name was Patrick Flanigan, and I had no idea then that he would become a trusted friend of long standing, in spite of the complications that were in store for us both.

Pat was a tall, lanky boyish figure with a wide, generous smile, and extended such an outgoing and warm personality that it was difficult to imagine he had ever known a stranger. His sheer enthusiasm just in being in the world was infectious, and I found him a delightful companion.

I agreed to sit for the portrait and suggested that he bring his paints and canvas to the dressing room, so that he could work between shows. It was finished by the time I was ready to leave for the next date in Havana, Cuba, and Pat gave me the portrait as a parting gift. By then, our friendship had developed into a mutual pleasure and I think we both felt some regret when the time came for me to move on. From then on, he bombarded me with his lively, informative letters wherever I went, a welcome habit he's never lost.

Myles and I flew to Havana to play the Tropicana Club. When our plane touched down, I was surprised to find myself suddenly surrounded by uniformed police. I was greeted politely by a very small gentleman in a very large white uniform who was the head of the Cuban Secret Police. It occurred to me that he might have had some trouble keeping his own identity secret, as his uniform was weighed down with what must have been fifty pounds of medals and he was about as unobtrusive as a gleaming monument. On a clear day, he could have been spotted from Miami.

However, he was very gracious in his welcome, and expressed great satisfaction that just before my arrival his department had uncovered a plot to kidnap me. I was to have no fear, the Secret Police would give me every protection during my stay in Havana, and he assigned two plainclothesmen to accompany me everywhere as bodyguards.

Privately, I thought a kidnap plot was very funny. Any kidnapper of mine would have a hard job of collecting ransom from anyone I knew, and would end up with little else but an hysterical Scandinavian on his hands. But the two bodyguards never left me during the entire week, and there were times when I wished I might have been kidnapped after all, if only to have a little privacy.

The Cuban audiences packed the Tropicana Club for every performance and showed us that special warmth that seems to come so easily to Latin Americans. Within a day or two, I was hearing a calypso song, "Christine of Denmark," which soon became the number-one tune on the Cuban hit parade.

However, the most interesting memory I carried away with me dealt with a Cuban Catholic priest, Father Hilario Chaurrondo. In an extremely candid interview with the press, he discussed his clerical position when questioned on the possibility of my marriage. His frank answers to the direct questioning of reporters was surprising to me, for until then, I'd thought the clergy would be unwilling to become involved and be quoted so freely.

The following article appeared in a Cuban newspaper in October of 1953:

> Father Hilario Chaurrondo is one of the most popular priests in Cuba. His blunt, outspoken and down-to-earth personality has won him that popularity and affection so essential to one desirous of being a good priest. And Father Chaurrondo is indeed a good priest, for he is used to seeing life in the raw. His work as prison chaplain which he is carrying out under the advocacy of St. Vincent de Paul has placed him in contact with the seamiest side of our society.

"I am familiar with the Cristina Jorgensen case right from its earliest beginnings," he said. "I have followed it in the press and I have read her memoirs. Very interesting—very. These are the things which leave us bewildered by the progress of the days we live in."

A doubt came into our mind. Should we ask him or not? Well, when all is considered, Father Chaurrondo is what one would call "a man of the world."

"Father, you are aware that Cristina Jorgensen is legally a woman with all the rights and attributes inherent in such a social condition. Would you be disposed to give your blessing to Cristina marrying a man in church?"

Father Chaurrondo doesn't flinch and he replies as if it were the most natural thing in the world.

"If her application for a Catholic ceremony carries all the prerequisites and prior dispensation by the Archbishop, I would say yes."

"Would Cristina's case involve special conditions?"

"No. Only the normal procedure. Just as for any other woman. As far as we are concerned, Cristina is a woman since she has been so designated by the United States, where they know what they are doing."

"And the Archbishop's dispensation?"

"Cristina is an alien resident, and in such cases certain requirements have to be met for reasons of diocese and parish. I repeat, Cristina's case calls for no special treatment. I can marry Cristina Jorgensen in the church once the usual and current regulations have been complied with. The procedure will be no different with her than with any other woman."

Father Chaurrondo is clear, frank, simple and definite. Cristina Jorgensen can be married by the Church.

"Look, my son, we priests nowadays have seriously to study the realities of life. We're not like the priests of sixty years ago, or as I was when I first began."

Chaurrondo's voice softened at the memory of those first years of his priesthood.

"The secret of confession is inviolable, otherwise I would tell you stories of Cristinas and Cristinos of every color under the sun. At the beginning, my soul grieved and sorrowed at the horror and shame. Now it's different. I read Maranon [a famous Spanish endocrinologist] and even dig football. Times change, but the eternal truths are immutable."

...We take our leave of Father Hilario Chaurrondo, who remains behind in the yard before his Church of Mercy, smiling in his own kindly, jolly way which somehow makes him seem Don Camillo himself.

We carry the news with us like a bomb: a Catholic prelate in Cuba is the first representative of any church, religion, or sect ever to make such a clear pronouncement on the Cristina Jorgensen case. It remains to be seen what the reactions to his statements will be amongst the Catholic congregation, not only in Cuba but throughout the world.

When we left Cuba, I was totally unaware that "Christine and marriage" would soon become an issue in the American press, also.

By the time I returned to New York, the house in Massapequa was completed and Mom and Dad and I went through the happy confusion of moving into our lovely new home. Since mid-March, each of us had contributed something to the plans, and blueprints were changed almost daily. Dad got his workshop, Mom her dream kitchen, and I settled on the solarium, which over the years became more like a small jungle.

I've always loved plants and flowers. Occasionally, I've been accused of acting like an anxious parent, and am apt to kill them with kindness. It's taken me a long time to learn that they'll do very well without so much attention from me, and now I try to keep the pruning, fertilizing, and fussing to a minimum.

As an inveterate nest-maker, I had a lot of fun during that period, though with the busy events of the previous months, I hadn't been able to spend as much time at the building site as I'd wished. Watching it grow from a hole in the ground to a beautiful ranch house, every stone and two-by-four became part of the dream come true.

Dad had contracted the house himself, since that had been his trade, and he became a close friend of each worker on the job. As a result, a lot of beer flowed into the building as they went along, and I've always had a suspicion that it's sitting on one vast mound of beer cans. The miracle was that the house was finished on schedule.

At the time we moved, in October of 1953, we were still the object of curiosity-seekers and a visiting press, so Mom suggested we get a dog as a kind of security measure. "Let's get a big one," she said. The addition to the household met even her standards. "Mark Anthony" was one hundred eighty-five pounds of lumbering Great Dane, and who walked whom on a leash became a matter of opinion.

My small nieces could impose any indignity on him, and frequently did. They mauled, hugged, pushed, and loved him unmercifully, all of which he endured with patience and great good humor. He never really knew just how big he was, and I think he always resented the fact that he wasn't permitted on the furniture or in someone's lap, a privilege allowed only to our two cats.

In one of his more trying moments, Mark nearly involved us in a small riot. On an outing one day during the fishing season, he bounded ahead of me out of sight along the shoreline. A few minutes later I heard a commotion in the distance, and rushed up to find a group of irate fishermen standing hip-deep in the water, yelling and waving their fishing poles in despair. Mark was calmly gorging himself on the lunches that had been abandoned on the shore, as if he'd found his own personal Automat. When I finally managed to pull him away from his picnic, I hurried back to the house and quickly prepared two dozen hamburgers, which I then delivered to the soaking fishermen, with apologies.

When Mark died some years later, he was succeeded by a smaller, but no less faithful friend, a cocker spaniel named Buffy. His only problem has been that he thinks he's human, and I'm still not thoroughly convinced he isn't. Buffy is still with us, though he's rather arthritic and elderly now, and as he has an age complex, it's never mentioned in his presence.

Almost immediately, we settled into the community life of Massapequa, were welcomed by our neighbors, and joined Our Redeemer Lutheran Church in Seaford, a few miles away. At last, the Jorgensens were "in residence."

In my absence, Charlie Yates had cemented plans to fulfill the engagement at the Sahara Hotel in Las Vegas. By then, the unpleasant public conflicts over cancellation of my original contract had vanished. Since the time I'd received the management's "Dear Sir" letter rescinding the contract, I'd proven that I could make money for my employers. Bill Miller, who hired the acts for the club, didn't once venture to address me as "Mister," when he met us at the plane, and when the act closed two weeks later, Milton Prell sent the following telegram to Charlie:

> 1953 Nov 14
>
> The surprise of Las Vegas was the Christine Jorgensen show...Once she hit the stage the audiences marveled at her new act her wardrobe her singing voice her personality and her warmth. Hotel Sahara had another hit. Thanks to Christine Jorgensen.
>
> Milton Prell Executive Director Hotel Sahara

As a somewhat faint-hearted gambler, Las Vegas didn't present much of a threat to my salary and I managed to stay away from the larger gaming tables. However, I did become addicted to slot machines, and spent many hours between shows plunging nickels into the "one-armed bandits."

Shortly after the opening, an article appeared describing a backstage rebellion at the club. It stated that the chorus girls in the show had refused to share a dressing room with me on the grounds that I might be a "Peeping Tom rather than a demure Thomasina."

The girls were quoted as saying, "How the hell do we know?" As I had my own dressing room at the club, it seemed to me a peculiar item, but I thought no more about it until I received the following letter, signed by all twelve girls in the chorus:

> Dear Christine:
> ...We were, if anything, more shocked and surprised than you at the contents of the clipping. At no time has any one of us made reference to your sex one way or the other to the management of the Sahara Hotel, our coworkers, or the patrons. We share a deep admiration for you as a performer and a sincere liking and respect for you as a person.
> We all wish you continued success and happiness. This letter may be used for publication.
> Most sincerely,
> The Sa-Harem Girls

Apparently, any subject at all was grist for the newspaper mill.

Our opening night in Las Vegas proved to be an exciting time for me. Not only did we play to capacity, but the club itself was a performer's dream with revolving stages, a perfect amplification system, and every conceivable lighting arrangement. There were telegrams from new and old friends and a large bouquet of yellow roses from Pat Flanigan in Washington. By then Pat and I had become good friends, if only through correspondence.

The ever alert radar of the Sahara's publicity department traced Pat's flowers through the florist, and before I knew it, I was confronted by the news report of my "engagement."

As I look back on it, I probably should have openly denied the reports at the time, but when threatened, I'm rather inclined to sit still and say nothing with the false hope that it will all just go away. Consequently, my answers to the queries of the press were neither confirmation nor denial. I simply avoided the issue.

Interviewed in Washington, Pat was equally noncommittal. "Neither of us has any statement to make," he said.

"We're just two good friends trying to find peace. I think we can, if the public will let us." Unfortunately, the damage had been done. Pat felt the repercussions at once, and lost several jobs because his name had been linked with mine. Characteristically, he wasn't resentful, however, and continued to send me letters and small gifts.

Disregarding our evasive answers, the press continued to carry the story for several days, and was no doubt responsible for the misconception that I was, or still am, married—a false impression that prevails to this day.

CHAPTER 21

Near the end of 1953, I enjoyed a brief and welcome respite from the fast pace of trouping from one city to another, a schedule I'd maintained since the first performance in Pittsburgh in early August. It had been a period of experiment and adjustment, and events had come so thick and fast, I thought I knew what it was like to be caught in a hurricane. But it was a happy time, too, for in addition to the financial security, it presented a wonderful opportunity for travel, and to meet many new and interesting people. Among them was one of the most famous painters of our century, Grandma Moses.

Driving from Montreal on my way home from a club date in early December, I stopped briefly in Hoosick Falls, New York. As a child, I'd spent some memorable summers on a farm in the country, and was anxious to visit some of my friends and family who still lived in the area. Grandma Moses lived in the next little town of Eagle Bridge, and I suggested to my cousin that we find out if we might pay her a visit. We called, and she promptly invited us to tea.

Grandma Moses was everything I'd read about her, and more: a tiny, spry and delicious lady, ninety-three years young. Totally disarming, she had no reluctance about contributing to her own legend. Almost immediately, she related the already famous story of how she once sawed one of her paintings in half to make up a specified number of works required by her art dealer for an approaching exhibition.

Eagerly, she pointed out one of her most prized possessions: a Christmas card from President Dwight Eisenhower, with one of his own paintings reproduced on its cover. The inscription read: "From an amateur to a professional."

I asked Grandma Moses what had motivated her to start painting in the first place, and she answered, "I got tired of doing the dishes." With great delight, she then pulled out several rolls of wallpaper on which some of her designs had been printed, and began blocking off various sections to show which of them would be suitable for framing singly.

She agreed to let me take some pictures of her, but added significantly, "No one ever gives me any!" Fortunately, I had a Polaroid camera with me, which was then quite a new development in photography. She was very excited about the new camera, and when I'd exhausted my own film load, she immediately sent someone out for more.

Grandma gave me one of her prints, the original of which hangs in the Museum of Modern Art in Paris, and an autographed copy of her charming autobiography, *My Life's History*.

I was, by then, approaching another crucial test in my career—a three-week engagement at the famous Latin Quarter in New York City, opening January 2, 1954.

It seems to me there is no other profession in the world in which one can rise or fall so rapidly. Incredible as it was, I'd skyrocketed from a devastating failure in Los Angeles to star status in a world-famous nightclub and my name in lights on Broadway, all in less than a year.

Broadway being the Mecca for all entertainers, I knew the Latin Quarter date would be the supreme test, and that leading news columnists and critics would be present at the opening. Among the members of the press, I could count several who had been derisive and hurtful in the past, and who would no doubt come prepared to criticize the slightest flaw in my appearance or the act. In spite of the earlier successes, I wondered if New York would accept me as a professional entertainer, rather than a news oddity.

Almost six months of nightclub appearances up to that point had prepared me for the customary silence as I stepped out onto the Latin Quarter stage on opening night. Instead of the usual lull, however, my entrance was met with immediate welcoming applause and my nervous apprehension vanished. The security I felt during that first performance, seems to have been borne out in the newspaper coverage that followed:

> Every big name in show biz showed up at the Latin Quarter last night to watch former GI Christine Jorgensen make her New York debut at the world famous club. Christine did herself proud and showed no nervousness that she was facing a celebrity packed audience for the first time...She's a star who was a stare a year ago...Incidentally, the audience loved her and called for more, more, more!—Walter Winchell

> Took the b.w. to see Christine Jorgensen at the Latin Quarter the other eve. Christine looked beautiful, her gowns are fabulous and it's pretty hard to imagine that this lovely piece of feminine pulchritude was ever able to pass as a boy!—Earl Wilson

> We dropped into the Latin Quarter tonight curious to see just what type of act Christine Jorgensen had to offer...the women in our party were fascinated by Christine's complete femininity and by the manner in which she wore her attractive gowns.—Louis Sobol

> The curiosity factor played a major role in the first big town opening January 2 of Christine Jorgensen... The Jorgensen act was good, it was well staged and the curious were tastefully taken care of.—*Billboard*

After the jitters of opening night, I settled down and really began to enjoy the Latin Quarter engagement. Each night, I particularly looked forward to the second show. Scheduled shortly after midnight, by then Broadway curtains had fallen and show people from legitimate plays and musicals stopped in to see us.

There's no doubt that I was pretty naïve and unsophisticated, that I regarded much of the period with frank and wide-eyed pleasure, and that meeting celebrities was no small part of my enjoyment. If my reactions seem impressionable, I suppose it's because they were. I was, after all, a basically unworldly person, from an unassuming, substantially middle-class family. Once I'd recovered from my initial snobbery, the entertainment world seemed a very glamorous place indeed.

Perhaps some of them came out of curiosity, some out of kindness, but whatever their reasons they were always encouraging and I was flattered and delighted to be accepted by other performers.

One of the greatest thrills to me was meeting Dame Judith Anderson, who invited me to her table for a visit. It was an especial compliment, as I was told she rarely attended nightclubs.

My appearance in New York inspired a new rash of comment from the professional gossips. They seemed to take great pleasure in linking my name romantically with various social and theatrical figures, many of whom I'd never met. While some of the gossip-mongers speculated on my love life, others manufactured more delicious morsels. Dorothy Kilgallen wondered in print: "What famous celebrity, now in a New York engagement, is going bald?" It wasn't until several days later, when Walter Winchell called me to check the truth of the statement, that I realized it referred to me. The absurdity of the item made me laugh, for not only was I not threatened with baldness then, but there's been no evidence of it in the ensuing fourteen years. Furthermore, it often comes as a surprise to people to discover that my hair is naturally blonde, and not tinted out of a bottle. As I'm of Scandinavian descent, my fair hair shouldn't seem an incredible fact.

I've often wondered why there should be some people who want everything about me to be false or masculine, or what my critics would say if I suddenly appeared with close-cropped hair, no makeup and in men's clothing. I strongly suspect that, too, would leave them unsatisfied.

Our success in New York led to a one-week engagement at the Latin Quarter in Boston and one of the most controversial scandals of my career.

The Boston opening was scheduled for February 5, 1954, but even before I left New York, rumors began to fly that I would not be allowed to fulfill the contract. Charlie Yates came across the initial notice in the *Boston Daily Globe*, three days before the opening:

> Christine Jorgensen's scheduled appearance at the Latin Quarter got top billing yesterday, in the executive, judicial and legislative branches of local government.
>
> Boston's City Council passed an order, asking the Licensing Board to force the "sex-transformed" ex-soldier to submit to a medical examination.
>
> In the House, a resolution calling for a ban on Christine was proposed, but shelved.
>
> Mayor Hynes looked askance at the situation, and labeled it, "a travesty on the entertainment profession."
>
> District Attorney Garrett H. Byrne said the grand jury would investigate "the Jorgensen case, and related matters" when it convenes today.
>
> Summoned to appear before the grand jury, is Rocco Palladino, proprietor of the Latin Quarter.

I didn't want to arrive in Boston the following day without some fortification, so Charlie asked my lawyer, Bob Sherwin, to accompany Myles and me, along with our press agent, Frances Kaye. As we stepped off the train, we met banner headlines on the newsstands:

CHRISTINE BANNED!

"Congratulations, Chris," Myles said. "You've reached the height of success—you've been banned in Boston!" I wondered how I could be banned before I'd even appeared, but apparently in Boston it was possible.

The facts were that the Boston Licensing Board had suspended the club's license to block my appearance, but within the news stories, other mysterious statements appeared, such as: "John H. Sheehan, chief New England field agent for the Federal Narcotics Bureau, threatened to 'blow the lid off Boston' and name three police captains, when he appears before the grand jury." Mr. Sheehan hinted darkly that he was going to reveal details of the narcotics racket, what he promised would be "a very interesting story." He also pledged his utmost cooperation with Boston's District Attorney to assist him in ridding the city of drug addicts and their conspirators.

District Attorney Byrne also got into the act. "We are now assembling various details," he said, "covering such matters as alleged narcotics sales, teenage liquor sales and indecent performances, and will proceed with an orderly presentation of the facts."

To thicken the plot, it was known that two investigators for the Massachusetts State Crime Commission had been working behind closed doors at the Bureau of Records in Boston's police headquarters, examining records of criminals and ex-racketeers, who were operating licensed liquor establishments. Their investigations were centered on juvenile drinking, but apparently included other sinister, though unnamed, law violations.

The *Boston Daily Record* summarized the situation in the following: "Coming on top of Sheehan's threat to 'blow the lid off' the actions of certain police officials, the activities of the investigators have made police officials jittery." Apparently, puritanical Boston had not proven to be so pure after all.

At first, I was puzzled. I couldn't understand why I'd been linked with the vice and corruption that seemed rampant in Boston at the time, but it soon became obvious that the city officials had been looking for a good excuse to make public their investigations of criminal activities. They'd found the trigger when I arrived in the "Cradle of Liberty."

One Boston columnist tied it up neatly and confirmed my suspicions: "...Most interesting details of L'Affaire Christine are those which can't be printed, many of which, however, will come out in the wash. And what a wash! It would appear that practically all of Boston's dirty linen is being hung on one line."

Although I was interested in seeing just how far the comedy would go, my main concern was whether or not we would open at the

Latin Quarter the following evening, a Sunday. Myles and Nan Bell, Frances Kaye, Bob Sherwin, and I waited at the hotel, and as information was forwarded to us, the developments began to resemble a Grade B movie plot.

The action of the officials was to bar me from performing until I had proven myself a female. The City Council passed an order demanding that the Licensing Board close the doors of the Latin Quarter, until I had submitted to a physical examination. Picking up where the council left off, Mayor Hynes also came on strong. As the mayoral office had the right to license Sunday performances, he would bar me from appearing on the Sabbath night, if he could "find the grounds to do so."

Other City Council members, however, erupted in righteous indignation. According to one account, Councilor Gabriel Piemonte stormed: "Who are you or who am I to say that any person should be subjected to a physical examination!" It is reasonable to guess that I applauded the Councilor's position.

However, in an effort to clarify my position, my lawyer, Bob Sherwin, decided to confer personally with Mayor Hynes. His Honor refused to see him, but Bob did arrange a meeting with the Chairman of the Licensing Board, Mary Driscoll, and went armed with photostats of the documents relating to my official status. Miss Driscoll released the following statement to the press: "I tried to bar her as a female impersonator. But her status is as a female. She'd been admitted to the country as a female."

Regardless of Bob's efforts and Miss Driscoll's grudging admissions, however, the Latin Quarter's doors stayed closed to the public. I decided to leave Boston's vigorous moral crusade to the professionals.

On Bob Sherwin's advice, however, I waited for a written release from Rocco Palladino, the club owner, absolving me from any future accusation of a breach of contract. The Latin Quarter was later held liable for a portion of my salary and over a year later, settled the liability through mediation by the union, American Guild of Variety Artists.

The release was immediately forthcoming and we prepared to leave for New York on the next train. I was surprised to discover that a large crowd had gathered in front of the hotel, waving cheerfully and chanting: "We want Christine!" "Don't let them chase you away, Chris," they yelled, "Stay and fight!" I laughed and waved back, then posed for one last picture under a gigantic sign that read:

WELCOME TO BOSTON.

When I returned to New York, I discovered that I had almost two weeks of freedom before the next club date. I decided to use the time to go to Bermuda for a brief rest, and to film a photographic layout which I hoped to sell for a magazine story.

While in Bermuda, I received an invitation to entertain American troops based in the area—an opportunity that pleased me very much, for though I'd offered to entertain several times before at various military bases, I'd always been turned down as "unsuitable" for the armed forces. Shortly after, I received a gracious letter from Major W. H. Kinney, the Personnel Services Officer, expressing his appreciation on behalf of the entire base. It was an experience in direct contrast to my next contact with the military, some years later.

After that brief holiday, work again claimed most of my time, and Myles and I appeared in a list of clubs for the next four months, ranging from one coast to the other.

At this point, a listing of the cities we played would only prove monotonous, but some of the funny incidents of that period have stayed with me.

In Miami Beach at the Club Morocco, I was sitting with some friends between shows, when someone from behind suddenly grabbed a handful of my hair, and gave it a hearty and very painful yank. I thought for a minute that Miss Kilgallen's prediction of baldness would come true. I whipped around in surprise to discover a woman who stood openmouthed, sputtering with chagrin, and what I suspected was a severe case of disappointment when she discovered I wasn't wearing a wig. She hurried away without an apology. As all of my hair was and still is attached to my head in the usual way, I was painfully reminded of her curiosity for days afterward, each time I combed my hair.

In Buffalo, I was approached one evening by a man who looked like a movie stereotype of a shady fight promoter, an underworld type usually portrayed by Edward G. Robinson. "Miss Jorgensen," he said, "I gotta proposition for you that'll make a million dollars. I wanna make ya the greatest lady wrestler of all time!" I had sudden visions of myself in black tights, weighing in at one hundred ten pounds, and working for two falls out of three. The following performance was spotted with sudden, unexplained giggles from me, which undoubtedly confused a lot of people in the audience and caused Myles to think I'd gone stark mad.

En route to another engagement, we stopped at a restaurant in a small Connecticut town. The proprietress kept staring at me in confusion, and finally asked me my name. When I told her, she drew a deep breath and managed to gasp out a single comment: "My God, what a wonderful job!"

Almost everybody I met had a Christine Jorgensen "joke." By then, I'd heard most of them myself, as many people, invariably strangers, seemed anxious to share them with me. Everywhere I went, someone would begin a conversation with, "Hey, have you heard this one?" Without waiting for an answer, he would launch into the story.

Comedians used Christine jokes with abandon, frequently when I was present, as even my name was good for a surefire laugh.

Many of the stories were very unappetizing, and almost always dealt with the more lewd and pornographic aspects of sex. Probably it's because I was the subject of the commentary, but I've never quite understood why it reached such levels of popularity, though I admit that the sources showed phenomenal imagination.

Without realizing it, I contributed to the fund of stories myself. One evening, I was sitting in Rubens, a well-known Manhattan restaurant, with Jan Sterling and Paul Douglas. Rubens' menu features various specialties named after celebrities: a Bing Crosby sandwich, a Frank Sinatra dessert, etc. Scanning the menu before ordering, I said casually, "All these items named after famous people, and there's not even a mixed salad named after me." There was a shocked silence at the table. I didn't realize what I'd said, until suddenly there was a great shout of laughter from my friends.

In San Francisco, the incomparable Bea Lillie was playing an engagement at one of the legitimate theaters, when I was appearing at the Ajax Club. As an ardent admirer, I was delighted to receive an invitation to meet her, and to this day she remains one of the most engaging, irrepressible personalities I've ever known. From then on, each night between shows, I went to see her perform in *An Evening With Bea Lillie,* and learned more from watching her work than I could have from reading a whole library on the subject of performing. Nightly, it was an outrageous lesson in sheer hypnotism.

In the late Spring of 1954, *Editor and Publisher,* a trade magazine for the publishing business, printed an item stating that the story which had received the largest worldwide coverage in the history of newspaper publishing had been the Christine Jorgensen story. It was frightening to think that after twenty-six years of obscurity, I had emerged in the previous year as the most written about person in the world.

With all of the evils of publicity and its causes for distress, I also realized no matter how unwilling a subject, the opportunities that it offered ultimately could only be counted on the credit side. I knew that if the sudden notoriety had catapulted me into a lucrative career and exciting new experiences, then I must use it in my life as a force for good. I hoped in the future that I would receive no more mention than my accomplishments or abilities deserved.

By the Spring of 1954, my nightclub career was well established and Charlie was booking engagements for the future, both in the United States and Europe.

The previous period had been so hectic and involved, I'd had little time to concentrate on much else but my professional life. I had, of course, known all along that the third and final phase of the surgical project still loomed ahead of me, and I decided to take time out between club dates to make it an accomplished fact. The two operations that had taken place in Copenhagen in 1952 had not entirely completed the feminine transition, and the third operation would require plastic surgery.

During the previous months, I'd consulted frequently with my good friends, Dr. Harry Benjamin and Dr. Joe Angelo. Through Dr. Joe I met one of the country's top plastic surgeons, whose reputation, views, and manner invited my complete trust. After thoroughly discussing the surgical and medical intentions, I entered a small hospital in New Jersey late in May.

The extremely complicated operation took seven hours to perform. With skin grafts taken from the upper thighs, plastic surgery constructed a vaginal canal and external female genitalia. It was a completely successful procedure.

An aftermath of the operation, however, was to cause me a good deal of panic and fright. As the lengthy surgery had proceeded beyond the anticipated narcosis period, the anesthetist began to give me ether. It was an unexpected necessity, and my face wasn't protected from the hard rubber ether mask with a lubricant. The result was a series of bad burns caused by friction.

I awoke from the operation without pain, but one horrified look in the mirror convinced me that I'd be scarred for life. The face that looked back at me couldn't have been my own—from the eyes down it looked more like charred bacon. I didn't feel any better when the surgeon came to visit me and expressed his own deep concern. When I asked him how bad it would be, he answered, "Not too bad," and after a momentary pause, added, "I hope."

Convinced my career was over before it had fully bloomed, I had awful visions of a lifetime of cosmetic patch-up jobs and lengthy lawsuits. For days I lay in a welter of fear and anxiety. Trying to keep the news from Charlie, I kept evading his offers to visit me.

I remember clearly the feelings of dread and terror, and was far more concerned about facial burns than the complex surgery I'd been through. Gradually, however, the healing process took over and the burns disappeared without leaving any scars, but before that evidence, it gave me a terrifying jolt.

Again, the problem arose of escaping notice from the press. I'd registered at the hospital under an assumed name, and when queried as to my whereabouts, my friends and family answered vaguely that I was "out of town." In spite of the precautions, news reporters somehow ferreted me out and once again, the hospital and the attending physicians took the brunt of the onslaught.

I stayed in the hospital for ten days after the operation, and during that period, one of the nurses brought me a newspaper item that had some element of humor in it for a change.

"Peter Howard, the continent-hopping, fiancée-dropping Vanderbilt heir, has a new interest—Christine Jorgensen. They've been causing heads to swivel in many an East-side-West-side bistro of late. When one of Peter's ex-loves protested vehemently that his latest capers 'are a reflection on us,' Peter told her that Christine was a lot nicer than 'all of you.' "

The heads must have been swiveling at empty air, as Mr. Howard and I had never met. Regardless of that minor consideration, rumors continued to appear, announcing everything but our engagement.

In spite of every precaution to preserve my privacy, some details of my recent surgery did leak out in the press. Again, they resorted to invention and speculation. But as it was an extremely personal and intimate procedure in my medical history, I had no wish to share its details with the rest of the world, any more than a complete hysterectomy would be advertised by another woman.

At that point, I felt at last that I'd completed the transition to womanhood, and except for the inability to bear children, was as complete a person as I'd dreamed of being, both emotionally and physiologically.

After ten days, I was spirited out of the hospital and taken to Dr. Joe and Gen Angelo's home, where I stayed in hiding for almost two weeks, and then to my home in Massapequa for another period of recuperation.

I hated the enforced inactivity, and was anxious to get back to my work and the engagements that Charlie was arranging for the time when I'd be well enough to fulfill them. I fretted with impatience, and kept thinking of the advice given to me by Sophie Tucker, when I'd met her earlier in the year during a club date in Toronto: "Keep busy, save your money, and never let time eat up your capital!"

CHAPTER 22

By the time I was well enough to go to work again, Charlie had scheduled some bookings in the United States, England, and Sweden, and once I'd fulfilled those, I planned a few months' vacation in Europe.

Playing the final date in Dallas before leaving for England, I was sitting with friends in a late-hour restaurant after a performance, when one of the men from the club rushed in to tell me that it was on fire. Since all of my theatrical wardrobe, furs, and jewelry were in my dressing room at the time, I sprinted for the scene in a wild, frantic dash, and arrived to find the firemen pouring water into the smoke and flames. I stood hopping on the sidelines until the fire was under control and I was allowed to enter.

I discovered that although the flames hadn't reached the dressing room, the smoke had turned my entire wardrobe into a fine charcoal gray color. Every single one of the costumes abundantly reeked of an odor that belonged, more appropriately, to the treatment of ham. It was obvious they'd never be suitable for stage wear again.

A day or two later, I flew to New York to replace my clothes and prepare for the trip to Europe.

The Atlantic crossing on the liner "United States" in mid-August was rather rough and I was feeling a trifle pale and shaky when we arrived in Southampton.

A press conference had been set up for later in the day at the Mayfair Hotel in London when I would be more comfortably settled and, hopefully, less green around the gills. However, many of the

British journalists jumped the gun and came out to meet the ship in a tug before it was actually berthed. To me, they all seemed charming and polite. I thought the ship interviews had been extremely satisfactory, and had no reason to feel uncomfortable about my reception in England. Therefore, it came as a severe shock when I awoke the next morning, to find I'd been unanimously smeared in the British press. Not only did they show a violent personal dislike, but they attacked the act before I'd even performed in it.

"...But those who go to see her will not be going to see an act; they will go with the same unhealthy appetites of people who queue to see murderers."

"...British *Variety* is rocking. If Miss Jorgensen is the answer to its prayer, it deserves to topple."

"Christine Jorgensen is the only GI who went abroad and came back a broad."

One of the most curious complaints appeared in the *News Chronicle* of London, in which my engagement at the Hippodrome Theater in Manchester was contrasted to an appearance of Emlyn Williams, originally scheduled for a Sunday.

The article classified me as a spectacle, "appealing to the more squalid recesses of the human mind." Mr. Williams was commiserated for having to cancel a reading of Dickens' works because he refused to appear without makeup and a false beard, in opposition to a peculiar British law which does not permit performers to wear disguises on Sundays.

"What an amazing country is ours," the journalist wrote, "for six days of the week, in a music hall, an act can be presented in which the prime attraction is the performer's sexual abnormality. But on the other day (Sunday) the law forbids one of our finest actors to impersonate one of our greatest authors in a recital which is stimulating both mentally and morally."

The comparison was absurd, and seemed more a reflection on the ridiculous British law, but I failed to see the reason why I'd been included in the idiocy. I wondered when I was going to see some evidence of the famous British reserve, and thought how easy it would be to turn into a dedicated Anglophobe.

At this point, I'm reminded of Oscar Levant's reply when he was asked the difference between American and British newspapers. "We have better funnies," he said.

My initial reception and several other unkindnesses that followed had made me apprehensive about our first performance in Manchester. But my fears were soon left behind when the British public, if not the press, welcomed us with great enthusiasm and warmth. The press attacks continued, however, and rather than repeat the experience, I canceled plans to appear in London after the week in Manchester, and left for Stockholm.

By then, I felt pretty depressed by it all. Charlie was ever-supportive, even from a distance, and sent me a cheerful letter of encouragement. "Don't forget, Chris," he wrote, "you have been in the business approximately one year and I think you have done wonders with both your talent and the theatrical knowledge you have acquired. Bigger stars than you have flopped in England, so you must put it down to experience, profit and loss."

In direct contrast to the reception in England, Sweden rolled out the welcome mat and we remained in Stockholm for a three-week run, although the act had been scheduled for only two weeks originally.

It's interesting to note that the response to me in the Swedish press held no ridicule or personal animosity. The Swedes indicated their affection and acceptance of me on the basis that I was a human being first and, second, a scientific marvel instead of an oddity. It probably was the first time that the press had not taken it upon itself to decide what I was—a circumstance that had prevailed from the time the story first broke. In general, news journalists had thought it their right to make decisions in print; facts were ignored and personal reactions were substituted for medical truths, thereby successfully creating distortions.

The immigration officials in Stockholm delighted in holding up my passport an extra week, to show their reluctance to let me leave the country. We played the added performances with pleasure, after which I went to Denmark for a brief visit, and Myles returned to the United States.

In Copenhagen, I met Helen Johnson, my old friend from the early days in Hollywood, who was to be my traveling companion on a tour of Venice, Rome, and Capri. The day after we arrived in Venice, I received a phone call at the hotel from Peter Howard, the Vanderbilt heir whose name had been connected with mine in the New York gossip columns a few months before.

"If our names have been linked, Miss Jorgensen," he said, "at least we should meet." Peter invited Helen and me to dinner and we spent several pleasant evenings together after that.

The exposé magazines, for a time, held open season on the Jorgensen story. A later invention described a clandestine meeting with Jimmy Donahue, the young Woolworth scion, in which I reportedly performed a private striptease in his Fifth Avenue apartment, after having been plied with large quantities of liquor. The truth of the matter was, I met Mr. Donahue and his secretary after a performance in a nightclub in New Jersey. He offered to drive me back to Manhattan after the show and, en route, courteously invited me for a drink at his apartment. Since his secretary was present, I accepted, and after an hour's visit I was driven back to my hotel by his chauffeur.

Some of the headlines in the scandal magazines of the time may give further evidence of their caliber.

WHAT MADE CHRISTINE DO IT?

CHRISTINE TO BECOME A MAN AGAIN!

IS CHRISTINE SLIPPING BACK?

GOODNIGHT CHRISTINE, WHICHEVER YOU ARE.

EYEWITNESS REPORT: PRIVATE PEEK AT CHRISTINE

The exposé type of magazine plays infinite variations on a single, very old theme—SEX. Almost every well-known figure in the literary, theatrical, and political world, at one time or another, has been the target of a salacious blast. By innuendo and the use of unrelated facts, fictions, and photographs, the subject's character is drawn and quartered. Murder, rape, mayhem, adultery, sadism, and masochism run rampant through the pages. No corruption or debauchery is considered too extreme, so long as it meets the publications' high levels of obscenity.

If a saint could come to life, he would not be immune to the slaughter. A movie star ordering a drink before dinner in a public restaurant may well find himself branded as an alcoholic in the next issue; a politician shakes hands with a diplomat's wife and the implication is clear; a famous writer interviews a homosexual playwright, and is equally suspect.

Written in the most provocative terms, these magazines merely titillate the dark corner of suspicion in the reader's mind. Without penalty, they go far beyond the normal freedoms of the press, and with fine art, practice what they think is the inalienable right of character assassination.

Most of the victims of these purveyors of filth have been asked, as I've been, why they don't institute lawsuits for defamation of character, invasion of privacy, or whatever. The fact is, a few people have resorted to legal means, and were accorded restitution, but those measures are often very costly. Furthermore, most people are unwilling to embroil themselves publicly and interminably in the courts. Probably uppermost, however, is the thought that any public protest will lead to the common, if often invalid view: "Where there's smoke, there's fire." Consequently, the tendency is to lie low and ignore the whole thing, an attitude that suits the publication perfectly.

The vagaries of the press, however, in no way marred my enjoyment of that wonderful holiday in Europe. Helen and I sailed for home shores from Naples on the *Andria Doria,* a few months before its final tragic voyage. The trip home was a great delight, for I had the opportunity to meet Anna Magnani and Tennessee Williams, both en route to Hollywood for the filming of *The Rose Tattoo.*

As the ship plowed toward the United States, the carefree pleasures onboard held no clue that I was heading for a disastrous personal and professional blow.

Ever since I'd met Charlie Yates, I was aware of my limitations in background and experience. But as he'd always acted as a kind of friendly and benign Svengali in my career, I allowed him to push, pull, and encourage me in any area he thought right for me.

As a representative in the entertainment field, Charlie's experience was vast. After breaking into the agency business in his native Chicago, he became associated with some of the biggest offices in the country before establishing his own a few years before I met him. Almost at once, he put his son, Steve, to work in his office to learn the business in partnership.

Once, as an executive with the Frederick Brothers Agency, he had the unusual distinction of being the center of a lawsuit, on which the court had to rule whether or not he was "unique." Although he had a long-term contract with the agency, he was determined to leave because of differences of opinion involving company policy. The Frederick Brothers went to court asking to restrain him from working anywhere else, on the grounds that he was "unique and indispensable." Everyone agreed that Charlie was unique, but the court ruled that he could have the freedom to work elsewhere, because he wasn't classified as an artist.

He was the favorite agent of many of the big club and theater managers in the country, and they often threw business his way on the strength of his honesty and personality alone. In a field in which competition is so keen that agents regard each other as natural enemies, he was undoubtedly one of the most well-liked among his own colleagues. In addition to Bob Hope and Beatrice Lillie, at various times his client list included Bing Crosby, Jerry Colonna, Gypsy Rose Lee, and Phil Spitalny.

Personally, he was an easygoing, quiet man with a wry sense of humor. An inveterate gambler, he often said he had enough inside racetrack information "to lose a fortune." Frequently, he did just that. He had a rather unusual calling card which he always left in newly decorated offices: a postage stamp pasted on the ceiling.

Next to gambling, his greatest passion was golf, and he was one of the few amateurs who played in the low seventies. His incurable addiction to gambling, particularly horse racing, caused a permanent professional break with Bob Hope, although they remained great personal friends. Feeling that perhaps his business was being neglected, Hope said, "Charlie, you'll have to decide between the horses and me. Now, what's it going to be?" Charlie replied, "I'll see ya at the race track!"

I also had an opportunity to see his compulsion for gambling in action. I was in Puerto Rico, and Charlie had used my club date there as a good excuse to accompany me and head for the gaming tables. One night I stood watching him gamble at the casino in San Juan. In his intense concentration, the usually gentle look vanished and his face broke into harsh, cruel lines. It was like watching two different people. Finally, I left him to return to our table and he rejoined me shortly after. For the first time since I'd known him, he spoke to me with severe anger, and was fuming with indignation. "Why did you leave me?" he said. "You changed my luck by leaving!"

A great family man, Charlie was extremely devoted to his wife and children, and was particularly proud of his brother, Sidney, a U.S. Congressman from Illinois.

Even though he had attained great success in his own field, he continued to explore the unusual paths of show business and his one dream was to revive Vaudeville. Also, he had hopes of building me into a personality that would transcend the freak headlines. His formula was to have me play the nightclub circuit for a time, and once having made a success there, to make the transition to the legitimate theater. It was ambitious, but that was characteristic of Charlie.

With that in mind, he arranged for me to play a small role in a production of *To Dorothy, A Son,* at a regional theater in St. Louis, the Empress Playhouse. Wisely, he had selected a small part, so that I could gain some badly needed experience without carrying too much responsibility at the beginning. It was to prove a good opportunity for me to watch acting techniques, and to learn some of the fundamentals of a performing art about which I knew nothing.

I arrived in St. Louis for rehearsals a week before the opening, which had been scheduled for January 9, 1955. Bruce Laffey, Bea Lillie's sometime secretary, accompanied me for moral support.

It must have been obvious to everyone in the company that I was a real novice in the theater. When I was asked by the director to "move upstage a little more, please Chris," I looked at him blankly.

"I can tell left from right," I said, "but I'll be damned if I know up from down!" I guess my frank admissions were disarming, because the cast and director were extremely kind and helpful, and should have shown more impatience than they did. I also found it difficult to memorize cues and lines in what seemed to me was so short a time.

Nevertheless, opening night arrived and my nerves were doing pushups. I remember that I spent the morning feverishly studying my lines, and alternately wishing I was on the moon or could break a leg. I was just about to leave my hotel for the theater and the final dress rehearsal, when the telephone rang. It was Mom calling from our home on Long Island. She was crying and at first I couldn't make any sense out of what she was trying to tell me. Finally, it came through. Charlie Yates was dead.

I sat there staring into space as Mom explained that he had been in Palm Springs, playing golf with Bob Hope. Stricken with a heart attack, he'd died on the golf course.

I replaced the receiver, but my thoughts just wouldn't jell. I completely forgot about the play and the opening. I couldn't think of anything but the dread, recurring thought: "Charlie is dead."

I was deeply fond of Charlie Yates and I knew he returned my affection. Not only was the future of my career then in doubt, but I had lost a dear and gentle friend and I knew I'd never find a suitable substitute in either area.

For the moment, I wanted no part of the entertainment world. I was simply too sick at heart to function properly, and I called Bruce Laffey to tell him that I couldn't go on for the opening that night.

Almost immediately, Bruce appeared at my door and he quickly realized, I think, that I was on the verge of hysterics. He knew I was vulnerable, and didn't give me the slightest opportunity to fall apart by offering me sympathy. Instead, he let me have it with both barrels.

"Come off it, Chris, and be realistic. Charlie created your career and he created this opportunity for you, as the beginning of a new phase in that career. You have no right to throw away something that he worked hard as hell to get. Save your dramatics for 8:30!"

Of course, he was right. His abruptness brought me up short, and I reached for my coat and said, "Let's go."

I was in no way fostering the traditions of the theater by appearing in the show that opening night in January of 1955. It was only through a sense of responsibility to Charlie and, in a small way, it was all I had to offer to his memory.

Somehow, I managed to get through the dress rehearsal and the opening, though my performance must have been automatic, and I felt no special thrill at my first attempt in the legitimate theater. I knew I wasn't brilliant, though the critics were kind enough, and the play reasonably well received. I finished out the run in a kind of dull haze.

Feeling defeated and emotionally drained, I returned to New York, wondering what I would do about my future to prove that Charlie's estimate of me hadn't been entirely wrong. I began to take stock of myself and the prospects seemed frighteningly dim. There were a few club dates which he'd set up previously, but once those had been fulfilled, I knew I'd be at loose ends, not knowing which way to turn. It was imperative to keep my career going forward, but I had no idea how to book an engagement, negotiate a contract, or arrange the multitudinous details that I'd always left to Charlie's good judgement. It was a lonely and disturbing dilemma.

Occasionally, when I was away from New York and felt troubled about something, I'd call him long-distance and regale him with the problem, for which he always had a solution. "Remember, Chris," he had once said, "I'm always back here doing your worrying for you."

CHAPTER 23

On the night of April 26, 1955, the opulent Stork Club in Manhattan, then located in the east fifties just off 5th Avenue, was the scene of greater activity and excitement than usual. Martha Raye, one of the most beloved of entertainers, had taken over a room in the club for a private party and celebrities from every branch of show business comprised the guest list. I'd been the delighted recipient of an invitation to Martha's party, and had looked forward to it eagerly for several weeks.

I remember that evening clearly. Bruce Laffey and I drew up to the brightly lit awninged entrance of the Stork Club at the appointed time; a doorman stepped smartly to the door of our car, opened it, and leaned forward with a smile. Suddenly the smile vanished, his face frozen in disbelief, the practiced greeting cut short. After a moment's hesitation, he turned and scurried for the door of the club.

Bruce and I shrugged at the odd display of discourtesy, and as he helped me from the car, we started across the sidewalk toward the entrance. At that moment, the door was flung open abruptly to reveal the tall, commanding figure of Sherman Billingsley, the club's owner. He didn't speak, but only raised an admonishing hand to bar our entrance.

"Miss Raye is expecting me," I said quietly.

Mr. Billingsley looked somewhat like a mechanized toy as he slowly shook his head back and forth in a silent gesture of refusal. After another brief moment in which our eyes locked, he still did not address me, though I think I half expected him to say, "Off with her head!" Bruce and I drove away without further comment.

Referring to the incident later, Sherman Billingsley was quoted in the newspapers as saying, "Christine Jorgensen's presence might have offended the parents of my younger college customers, by providing too bizarre a touch." He seemed to imply that my very presence would corrupt the young, like a kind of one-woman vice ring. On the other hand, from his Olympian heights as an ex-Bronx druggist, he may have felt his rudeness was justified as a prescription for wickedness.

I had no wish to dispute his authority to decide who was to be received, or who was turned away. It was a privilege held by all managers, and one from which I'd benefited myself during the course of a nightclub career. On a few occasions, obnoxious customers had been forcibly removed during a performance by irate club owners.

At the time, however, I realized I wasn't alone on the Billingsley black list. Famous names that illuminated theater marquees the world over had held the same dubious honor. Although a fistfight headed the list of unpardonable sins in the Stork Club moral code, a patron could also be drummed out of the corps for such indiscretions as offensive language, overindulgence in alcohol, or consorting with foes of the management. Apparently, there was no appeal from his restriction; the excommunicated joined a long list of the condemned, and was invited to exercise his thirst and hunger elsewhere.

In my case, there had been no such imprudences. I had been refused from the sacred portals solely because I was Christine Jorgensen.

Earlier in the year, Myles Bell and I decided on a parting of the ways, and amicably dissolved our partnership after playing the few dates that Charlie had set up previously. That presented the problem of finding a new partner and fortunately I met a young comedian named Lee Wyler, who agreed to take up where Myles left off, using the same material. My first booking with Lee was late in January in

Dayton, Ohio, and although our association was brief, it was a very pleasant one.

Sophie Tucker had often advised me to keep changing my material. "People don't want to see the same thing all the time," she said, and I thought it was time I took her advice. In April, I decided to try my wings alone, and after playing half a dozen engagements with Lee, I returned to New York and started to work on forming a single act.

I hired someone to re-stage it for me, and included several lightning-fast wardrobe changes, done onstage behind a large fur-covered screen. The trick was accomplished by what is called "under-dressing," and the use of breakaway costumes. I also inserted impersonations of Tallulah Bankhead and Marlene Dietrich. Cindy Adams, the reviewer and columnist, wrote some splendid song material especially for me, and by the time it had been put together and thoroughly rehearsed, I felt secure as a solo performer.

It was during this period that I found myself the subject of one of the most shocking pieces of news reporting to date. The item was carried by the *New York Enquirer*, a journalistic monstrosity that specializes in epic squalor. Incredibly, this monument to obscenity continues to appear on the newsstands week after week.

By now, it's redundant to say that my personal life had invited an enormous amount of comment in the news columns, but I was unprepared for the depths to which it would sink: "The 'lady' thrown off the Madison Avenue Bus (Number 10759) at 54th Street for annoying another femme's little boy was Christine Jorgensen!" I imagine that including the serial number of the bus was supposed to indicate authenticity.

For the first time since the muckraking began, I was tempted to bring legal action against a publication, and contacted my attorney, Bob Sherwin, with that in mind. The only deterrent was Bob's advice when he said, "If we sue, Chris, it will probably turn into an even bigger story, which is exactly what this rag wants to boost its circulation."

At the time, he was no doubt right, but today I almost wish I'd followed it through. The most frustrating and difficult part of such an accusation is that the writer has a column at his disposal, and the victim has no such public platform from which to retaliate. One can only sit back in anger, and let the scandalmongers play the same old insistent tune on their pornograph.

Unfortunately, this type of character defamation often follows the victim doggedly, and on occasion, has done irreparable damage. If retractions are printed, which is rare in the offending newspapers, they are seldom noted by the reader. I think it can be compared adequately to taking a bag full of feathers to a high hill and throwing them into the wind—retrieving them all would be an impossible job.

Naturally, I've not been the only victim of libelous statements, but I think that most people do not understand the basic reason for the drastic decisions I'd once felt compelled to make: namely, my inordinate fear of what for me would have been an immoral way of life.

On May 5, 1955, I opened my new single act in Indianapolis. It was very well received by the audience, and the manager of the club was happy with his box-office receipts. In fact, he was so happy that some of my salary checks bounced, and I had to go through a drawn-out legal process in an attempt to get paid. A few years later, he declared bankruptcy and I was number one on the loser's list.

Late in May, Steve Yates, Charlie's son, booked an engagement for me in Caracas, Venezuela, an event that remains in my memory as the "all-time unbelievable week." Several days before my departure, I received a phone call from the Venezuelan Embassy in New York, and a heavily accented voice said, "Miss Jorgensen, prior to entering Venezuela, it will be necessary for you to submit a copy of your police record."

"My *what?*"

"It is a government law," he answered, "for all foreigners to present their police records."

"But I don't have a police record! I can't very well go to the police and ask for a record that doesn't exist."

"I cannot help that, Miss Jorgensen, it is the law."

"It may be the law in a dictatorship like Venezuela, but I can't give you a police record if I don't have one."

I could almost feel his disappointment in the silence that followed. Finally, he said, "Well, if you say you don't have a record, I suppose it will be all right. But remember, Miss Jorgensen, my country is a democracy, not a dictatorship."

Privately, I thought he could tell that to the Marines. I suppose the call should have rung a warning bell of things to come, but it didn't, and I thought no more about it. I had previously performed in Cuba, which was both a dictatorship and Latin American, but there I had found nothing but courtesy and precautions for my safety in a kidnapping threat. Therefore, I was unprepared for the severities that were in store for me in Venezuela.

Bruce Laffey accompanied me on the trip, and our plane landed in Caracas at 9:00 in the morning of the day I was to open. I'd had almost no sleep during the night flight, and didn't particularly relish the long day of rehearsals that lay ahead, to be followed by the opening.

The first demand from the authorities was for photographs. A month before, Bruce and I had sent a dozen photos of ourselves to the embassy—not only single ones, but several taken together. Apparently, however, they were insufficient, and we were rushed to a nearby photographer and sat bleary-eyed for another set. From the photographic sitting, we were then taken to the police station and fingerprinted. Also we submitted to interminable questions, put to us with ill-mannered rudeness, and I remember that they had little to do with the purpose of our visit.

Finally, a nervous little man who seemed to be in charge, ended the interview by saying, "Now, you must sing for the Censorship Board." Bruce and I looked at each other, and with a shrug, I agreed. After more bustle and confusion, we were ushered onto the stage of an auditorium in the same building, with a large and elderly upright piano in the orchestra pit. The Venezuelan accompanist took my music arrangements and began to play "Getting to Know You," one of the numbers I used in the act. As I remember, he played with good-natured abandon, but any similarity to Rodgers and Hammerstein was sheer coincidence. As I'm not considered in the same league with Maria Callas, our discord was total and deafening.

Suddenly, a door flew open and several women, followed by a group of squalling children, came down the aisle and sat in the front row of the theater. One of the women opened the front of her dress and began to nurse a small baby. I watched the entrance of this group without missing a beat, but finally the competition was too great to overcome, and I stopped and asked who they were. I don't think I was too surprised to learn that they were the Censorship Board.

Regardless of the realities of that moment, neither Bruce nor I really believed it was happening, but unable to carry it further and to avoid a case of hysterics, I said, "Bruce, take the music and let's get out of here!" He picked up the music from a startled accompanist and we marched firmly out the door.

Fatigue was beginning to set in, and my only thought was to get settled into a hotel. We made it, finally, by mid-afternoon. By then, I'd thrown up my hands in desperation, and thought the manager who had gotten me into all this madness would just have to smooth it out on his own.

Thus far, I'd been dragged through the city of Caracas without any rest; photographed, fingerprinted and questioned, to say nothing of the pinching and grabbing that seemed to be the principal sport in Venezuela. I must admit the Venezuelans had pretty good aim, but apparently they'd had a lot of practice.

By six that evening, it was obvious that I wouldn't be opening in Caracas, and at that point, the idea suited me perfectly. Bruce and I were preparing to leave the hotel for dinner when the deluge hit. The press swarmed everywhere, overcome by the report that I would not be appearing. "You cannot get permission to entertain without the okay of the Censorship Board," a reporter said, "and you refused to sing for the Board!" I had to admit to them that I'd refused to sing for a group of howling children and nursing mothers. Later, I learned that even dancers had to sing for the censors. The law said, "Sing," and everyone had to sing, even if he was a pantomime artist.

Bruce immediately started to arrange transportation out of the country, only to find that we couldn't leave until we'd been fingerprinted again and signed out by the police department. Consequently, I had another day of questioning, fingerprinting, and pinching to look forward to, not necessarily in that order. Also, it was pointed out that the official government bureaus would be closed for the weekend, and we were forced to wait over until Monday.

The press thought all of this nonsense was a huge joke, and there was little for me to do but agree with them. When flashbulbs exploded during one of our many photo-interviews, the reporters roared with laughter. "You should see what happens when a bulb explodes in the President's office," one of them told me. I suppose even a simulated gunshot was cause for alarm in that country.

It was then that I discovered a useful and infallible method for keeping people and pressmen at arm's length. I had only to point my movie camera at someone, and he immediately turned away. I recalled that even in Havana where people were so friendly to visitors, they preferred not to be photographed. In a revolutionary dictatorship, I suppose there was always the possibility that a photo might be useful to the opposition, whatever it might turn out to be.

From then on, I always had my camera handy and, in fact, used it to bore a path to the plane when our departure time finally arrived.

Venezuela had been in the throes of a military dictatorship virtually since its independence from Spain in 1821. Having overthrown a corrupt administration in 1958, however, it has since been occupied with establishing a democratic government, and I'm sure that since my visit in 1955, visitors are welcomed more cordially and with fewer complications.

Leaving Caracas for Port of Spain, Trinidad, for a brief visit, was a welcome relief, in spite of the fact that a quarantine officer boarded the plane with an odd request. He asked that we all remain seated and close our eyes, while he proceeded to spray the entire interior, including the passengers. Bruce and I broke up with laughter when we realized we were being disinfected. In our relief to have escaped Venezuela in one piece, even fumigation seemed preferable.

In August, I was approached to play a role in *The Little Hut,* an English play that was to have a road-show production in the United States after a successful run in London. I was excited at the prospect as a wonderful follow-up to my first theatrical experience the previous year in St. Louis. Several days after the initial offer, however, I was informed by the producer that the star refused to appear with me, and that I'd have to be dropped from the company. It proved to be my first but by no means last rejection by someone in the theater. I was to encounter other similar refusals in the future, though they were in the minority, as for the most part I've been welcomed graciously by my professional colleagues.

I had another curious experience about that time, when I was given the opportunity to meet, socially, a New York State Representative, a man who was then involved with an investigation of alleged Communism in the theatrical world. I remember that I was fascinated by his conversation, and to some degree, my own ideas coincided with his on the investigational procedures. However, I found it impossible to accept his idea that the state commission had the right to announce ahead of time the names of witnesses who were requested to appear. It seemed to me that the press could brand a witness, simply by noting his entrance into the building in which the hearings were held. The press had already exhibited a talent for political witch-hunting. "We cannot control the press," he answered.

I countered with the thought that it might be more fair to have the investigation committee visit a witness privately in the confines of his home, to avoid a public prejudgment of "guilt by association." "That is simply not the procedure we adhere to," he said.

His next statement came out of nowhere, and left me gaping with surprise. "Miss Jorgensen, are you aware that you have been investigated, too? You made a pro-Communist statement on the day you returned to this country from Denmark."

I stared at him in disbelief and my mind rushed back over the statements I'd made when I returned to the United States three years before. I wondered what I possibly could have said that was misconstrued as un-American or Communist-inspired. Suddenly, I recalled a question from one of the reporters at the airport, the day I returned: "Christine, do you think Europeans have more understanding about sexual problems such as yours, than Americans do?" I remember I answered quite truthfully, "Yes, I think they do."

When I repeated the incident to the state representative, I needed only the smirk on his face to tell me it was that to which he'd referred. Today it's laughable, but I found it inconceivable then that my simple statement of fact could have been twisted into an anti-American point of view. A comparison of understanding problems of a sexual nature seemed something less than treasonous.

During 1955, I had the opportunity to appear as a guest speaker at the Men's Club of the Massapequa Jewish Center and the Farragut Masonic Temple in New York City. During my visit to the latter, the Masons weren't aware that in my high-school years I'd been a member of the Demolay, a junior Masonic order, until I told them that I was undoubtedly the only woman in the world who knew the secret rituals of the organization. I invited both laughter and consternation, but they all settled down when I promised to keep the rituals an eternal secret.

In mid-November, I flew to Las Vegas for an appearance at the Silver Slipper. Previously, I'd told Steve Yates to get me a Las Vegas date, even if I had to play the middle of the street. Charlie had been negotiating for the engagement and had, in fact, planned to complete the contract immediately after his golfing trip to Palm Springs, when he was stricken and died.

At that point, without a proper guide, my career was in the doldrums and I'd resorted to freelancing a bit on my own and working through one or two smaller agents.

Although my date at the Silver Slipper was successful, I had no other engagements lined up beyond that. There was no doubt that my career had taken a dip, not only in salary but in the caliber of the clubs I'd played since Charlie's death, and I was on the brink of giving up. "I'm through," I thought, "I'll finish this date and then make another try at photography, and chalk all this up to experience." In defense, I tried to make myself believe that I didn't want the entertainment world any more, but the fact of the matter was that the offers simply weren't there.

Underneath the defenses of indifference, I had come to love and enjoy show business. What had begun as a move toward financial security had grown into great pleasure and respect for the business and the people in it. I knew, too, that I had grown into more than just a "once-around" act, based on the appeal of my name alone. I'd learned the difference between just standing in front of a microphone and talking, and presenting a real performance. I'd learned techniques and entertainment values the hard way, and I knew I was equipped to follow the craft as a true performer.

Be that as it may, I was floundering and ready to call it quits. There's no doubt that I was open for any kind of influence in my career, either good or bad.

Dad had accompanied me on the Las Vegas engagement, and as Thanksgiving of 1955 approached, we were invited to a family dinner by one of my coworkers in the show at the Silver Slipper. As we were separated from the rest of the family, both Dad and I wanted to avoid Thanksgiving dinner in a restaurant, if possible, and eagerly accepted the invitation to spend the holiday in a family atmosphere.

It was there that I met a small, vital woman whom I will call Betty Walton. She appeared to be in her mid-thirties. I remember that she brightened the dinner party and regaled us with her British background and life in England. I enjoyed talking to her, and although a stranger, she showed interest in my career. Gradually, she began to appear backstage during the ensuing weeks, and before long, was in constant attendance at the club.

One day, I mentioned to her my decision to leave show business, which by then had become a positive idea in my mind. Betty said that with her many contacts, she would find it easy to arrange some bookings, and before long, proceeded to do just that. She became my personal manager, handling virtually every aspect of my professional life.

As I look back on it, she had eased her way into a position of guide and mentor at a time when I was most vulnerable. My career was wallowing at a low ebb and I suppose I was ripe for any form of guidance.

According to her story, which varied from time to time, she was born in Pueblo, Colorado, and taken to England by her parents when she was very young. She married and went to live in Liverpool. As a member of the British women's army, she served as a radar operator in London during World War II. Her husband was killed in Burma; her parents and two children were killed in a street shelter in Liverpool during the blitz. She had worked for the J. Arthur Rank film organization and, apparently, was on close personal terms with all of its leading players.

In Hollywood, she had worked as a "leg" woman, gathering items for a leading columnist, and had become a close friend of many Hollywood celebrities.

I must say, Betty had a very positive approach to everything she undertook, and I responded to the fact that she immediately assumed all of my professional problems. Sometimes to my detriment, however, she became arrogant and opinionated, and I found myself having to smooth down the feathers of irate nightclub owners when her demands became unreasonable. "But I'm not supposed to be pleasant to the management," she said. "If they like me, I'm not doing my job!"

I closed my eyes to many of these difficulties because she filled a professional need, and once the business relationship had taken hold, it was almost impossible to dissolve it. Her persuasiveness was enormous.

With time, she became more and more possessive, and it was rather like having a theatrical mother. I made quite a good living during those years, but I often ended up with almost nothing, though she always had a logical explanation for the disbursement of funds. Today, my gullibility seems incredible.

Her desire to separate me from my family is now clear, for it was at her urging that I changed my base of operations to Hollywood, and for several years I saw my family infrequently. Of course, all I had to do was say "no," but she had a way of wearing people down, and I have to admit to giving in to avoid argument. It was another example of my low threshold for confrontation.

I spent Christmas of 1955 in Phoenix, Arizona, the first holiday I was to be away from home. Since then, I've made it a rule to spend Christmas with my family, if at all possible. In Phoenix, I offered to visit the Veteran's Hospital to entertain the patients, but was told by the authorities they had already completed their Christmas program. Later, a newsman informed me that nothing special had been organized for the veterans, and again it was clear that I was "unsuitable."

January of 1956 dawned more brightly than the previous year. Betty had been busy lining up dates, and it wasn't until April that I finally returned home. She had also come up with the idea that I should be surrounded by a group to round out the act, and with that in mind, we returned to Las Vegas to hire entertainers. I thought it a good idea at the time, but soon learned it was a terrific drain on my income, as I had to pay the new additions out of my own salary.

We engaged three girls and a young singer, Bob Renfrew, in Las Vegas. The girls were to work first in a routine of their own, then introduce me, and Bob was to fill in with songs while we made costume changes. The act formed slowly, but finally we had it all worked out to our satisfaction, and piled into a station wagon, headed for the first engagement in Portland, Oregon. Shortly after, Bob was hit by a serious illness, and after placing him in a hospital, the three girls, Betty Walton, and I took off for Vancouver, British Columbia. Salaries, hotel bills, and other expenses mounted astronomically, and I had visions of working my head off and ending up with nothing but thanks.

February brought us back to San Francisco, and then my first trip to Hawaii. I still feel a bit guilty when I think of the Japanese-American club owner in Honolulu, who suddenly was faced with five roundtrip air fares from the mainland. She had made an offer for Christine Jorgensen, and ended up with a cast of four, plus a manager. But Marian Harada was a grand and hospitable lady, and went to great lengths to make our stay in Hawaii a memorable one.

The trip, however, did pose some interesting problems. The three girls who had joined the act in Las Vegas went completely native. The combination of idyllic weather, palm trees, beautiful beaches, and the other blandishments, was too much for my high-spirited troupe. Most of their time was spent getting into and out of the native mumu, a loose-fitting "Mother Hubbard" type of garment.

My responsibility, of course, was to my work, but as the islands are like a small village in many ways, it was impossible to escape the fact that we were all professionally associated. I suddenly found myself playing the role of den mother.

Happily, the girls decided to stay in Hawaii after our eight-week engagement, and I breathed a sigh of relief, vowing that from then on I'd concentrate on a one-woman show.

I adored Hawaii, but in addition to the escapades of the irrepressible trio, the performances proved to be hectic. The show comprised a dozen or so other acts in addition to mine, almost all of them imported from Japan. Listening to the Samisen players pluck at their whining instruments for three shows nightly was a violation to my uneducated Occidental ear, and at a point when I began to like it, I knew it was time to leave.

Marian Harada, the club owner, had been delighted with the sensational business during the engagement, and asked if I would consider playing one night at the Civic Auditorium in downtown Honolulu. I agreed to appear at an evening entitled "Christine's Aloha Performance." It was a huge barn of a place with a seating capacity of thousands, used mainly for sporting events. Arriving at the auditorium, I was confronted by an immense blazing marquee that read: "Wrestling Every Tuesday—Christine Jorgensen March 29th."

By April, I returned home in a happier state, as the world of entertainment was beginning to open up again. One date followed another, all engaged by Betty: Florida, New York, Atlanta.

In May, I made my first television appearance since the *Arthur Murray Party*, three years before. Hy Gardner, the syndicated columnist, asked me to appear on his show *Hy Gardner Calling*. Until then, I'd remained the subject of a TV boycott by the executives in the industry, though why they felt I was to be shrouded from the general public is still unclear. No doubt they felt that all sexual realities (other than exaggerated bust lines), should remain concealed, though they seem to have had no such hesitation about showing violence, murder, dope addiction, and infidelity on the home screens.

However, Hy Gardner had no similar sense of limitation, and skillfully led me through a sociological and scientific discussion of the problem. The show was a great success, and the beginning of a lasting friendship with Hy and his wife, Marilyn. People still comment enthusiastically on that particular show, some ten years later.

The day following the interview, Jack O'Brian, then TV columnist for the *New York Journal-American,* wrote a scathing review of the broadcast:

"Hy Gardner had Christine Jorgensen on TV last night at 11:30 for frankly sensational reasons (to get an audience) but it was just as frankly offensive.... Among the items divulged was that La (Le) Jorgensen tells 'Christine jokes' more willingly and better than anyone else.... We see why Hy paraded Christine into view, but don't understand NBC's suddenly descending standards of taste."

Hy countered in his own column a day or two later with: "...May I point out to Jack that if parading Christine before the public constitutes 'descending standards of taste,' the publisher who pays his salary is the trailblazer in that department. On Feb. 15, 1953, Hearst, in the *American Weekly,* published the first of a series of five articles titled 'The Story of My Life,' by Christine Jorgensen. Since it is obvious that the people who read newspapers are the same people who watch television (particularly 11: 30 P.M. to midnight), it would appear to me that O'Brian is talking out of only one side of his typewriter."

Early in May, I met the great Irish playwright, Paul Vincent Carroll, and after a few minutes' conversation, he asked me to play a featured role in his new play, *The Wayward Saint,* co-starring with Paul Lucas. The knowledge that I might be performing with the great Paul Lucas frankly produced waves of apprehension. Scheduled for a Broadway production, it was a far cry from my previous experience with the stock company in St. Louis, a year and a half before. I was terrified at the prospect, and although Mr. Carroll seemed to have enough faith in me to offer me the script for consideration, I was still unsure of myself in the theater medium. One week of *To Dorothy, A Son* was scarcely enough experience to break into the Broadway theater in an important play with one of the world's finest actors. Regretfully, I turned down the opportunity, knowing I wasn't ready for such responsibilities.

It was almost seven years to the day when I appeared next in a legitimate play. Those years were to change, to some extent, the attitudes of my critics who were still asking, "What can she do?" In the meantime, I would try to develop my abilities as a performer, and when the next opportunity in the theater arrived, I hoped I would be ready for it.

In July, some of my photographs were published in the United States. Although I'd known some success in European magazines, it was the first time I'd contributed to an American publication since my photograph of the damaged cabin cruiser on the highway used in the *Journal-American* many years before. The magazine was called *Photographer's Showplace,* and along with Joshua Logan and Sammy Davis, Jr., I was asked to submit my pictures as a guest photographer.

The balance of 1956 held little to distinguish it, except for some long-forgotten nightclub engagements. However, late in the year, I began to hear a few ominous rumblings from the United States Department of Internal Revenue. I wasn't aware of the eventual magnitude of those first little messages, but it was the beginning of a tiresome and endless waltz with the tax department. I think I did have a slightly uneasy premonition of things to come, but I tried to shrug it off with a nervous laugh and hoped for the best. I'd have been closer to the mark had I remembered Dorothy Parker's classic lines:

> *Three be the things I shall have 'til I die*
> *Laughter and hope and a sock in the eye*

CHAPTER 24

In my memory, 1957 is merely a hazy string of nightclub dates up until June, when I returned to New York City to fulfill an engagement at the Cafe Society. My contract at the famous old landmark was abruptly ended in July when the Internal Revenue Department locked the doors to satisfy a tax lien on the club. I had to go through a lot of red tape to retrieve my wardrobe, and after many phone calls and endless pleas that my livelihood was threatened without my costumes, I was allowed to remove them from the dressing room. Though I was collecting my own belongings, I felt a little like a thief under the constant surveillance of the revenue agents. Maybe they thought I was going to walk off with the bar or a spare chandelier.

After that, I played a number of spots in the East, which happily allowed me to be with my family more frequently. My arrival was always a disruptive element in the household, surrounded by luggage, gifts, and boxes of things I'd bought for the house along the way. I looked like I'd just come in off a safari, which prompted Mom's observation that it was always good to see me come home, but a relief when I departed, so the house could return to some degree of serenity.

By then, Mom and Dad's lives had returned to the routine of day-by-day living in a contented family atmosphere. From time to time, incidents arose that distressed them, but long before, they had adopted the extraordinary course of events, and placed them within a framework of tranquil acceptance and normality. The only change in their material lives was that they had a somewhat nicer place to live and enjoy the family, surrounded by grandchildren, a garden, dogs, cats, and assorted visitors. Dad always had a cabinet-making project going in his workshop; Mom busied herself with church affairs, puttered with flower pots, cooked enormous meals, and lavished affection and supervision everywhere.

For the past year, I'd noticed that my nightclub dates were becoming shorter in duration, and my salary had diminished somewhat during that period, too. I often wondered if I was really progressing or simply treading in one spot, making just enough money to keep the wolf from the door of my Massapequa home.

Betty kept copious records of my finances, and seemed to feel the need of several dozen ledgers, all roughly the size of a baseball field. She had a particular affection for office equipment, and bought everything by the gross: imprinted envelopes of every size and description, letterheads, staplers and staples, pencils and pens, mimeograph stencils, various business machines, paper clips, labels, file folders, and rubber stamps. General Motors was not better equipped than I. As a matter of fact, after ten years, I still have several gross of everything, though the packing cases of envelopes, with the help of humidity, have sealed their own flaps long ago. I think I can say with certainty there are just so many things in this world that can be stapled together, for I've been stapling my way through life ever since.

It was about that time, too, that the United States tax officials began to show ever greater interest in my records and income, and decided that I was a likely subject for investigation. The federal tax bureau had been flirting with me for some time, and we finally came to grips over the fact that I couldn't prove my three-year residence in Europe. At that time, if a taxpayer was absent from the United States for more than eighteen months, he was tax-exempt to a great degree. Although I'd been in Denmark for almost three years, I hadn't purchased property there to establish foreign residency, and since residency is an "intention," it was a difficult issue to settle.

I went wearily from one accountant and legal source to another, and managed to build up some sizable bills for legal help, but little else. I must admit, it was a nerve-wracking time. Tax liens were placed against the house and my bank accounts were garnished. What with the polite insistence of the Internal Revenue Department, I was in deep financial trouble. The total sum of retroactive taxes was close to thirty thousand dollars, and it was merrily gaining interest for the government as time went on. Every once in a while, the tax officials would help themselves, and I was in a state of constant fear that I'd be left high and dry with no chance to come out of it.

In November, I was approached by two high-pressure promoters to make a recording that would "sell millions," according to them. It was an interview-type of long-playing record, to be entitled *Christine Says,* and the interviewer was Nipsey Russell, who later become a well-known comedian. Nipsey and I made the recording, a candid and truthful presentation of the circumstances surrounding my transformation. But when the record was sent to me, it bore the title *Christine Reveals,* which seemed to me a trifle more provocative than necessary, and I took immediate steps to restrain its release under that title. However, I could have saved the effort, as the promoters proceeded to do very little promoting, with the excuse that they didn't have enough money to coax the disc jockeys into playing it on the air to stimulate sales. It was a rather ridiculous view. As a nonmusical recording, it simply wasn't the type of thing that announcers would push or sandwich in between Frank Sinatra and Elvis Presley. The result was that I never received a cent of royalty from it, though I still believe it was a very good interview, and covered the subject extremely well from my standpoint.

I experienced my only cancellation of a club date when I played the Chez Gerard in Quebec City, Canada, in February of 1958. After the first performance, I left the stage in a state of shock at the total lack of response from the audience. Neither the management nor I had realized that the French-Canadian's inability to understand English would make any difference, but we soon discovered how wrong we were. They simply couldn't understand me, and we mutually agreed to cut the engagement short.

I spent the balance of the week skating and skiing at the nearby Chateau Frontenac, and at the time gave an interview to the *Quebec Chronicle-Telegraph,* which contained the following statement:

"...She smiled when asked whether she intended to marry. 'I can,' she said, 'but it would take a man among men to live down the banter.' "

Five years had passed since my return from Denmark. Thankfully, by then, the insane kinds of publicity that had followed me around the world had somewhat subsided, and slowly I was beginning to notice a more accepting attitude, both in the press and among the people I met. The initial disturbed views of my transformation were beginning to wear off, and there were occasional references in the newspapers to other conversions that were taking place in Holland, Casablanca, Germany, Denmark, and Mexico. Each time a case came up in the news, the press came running to me for a comment, but I had little to contribute beyond a philosophical answer.

About that time, in describing a case similar to mine, Dr. Walter C. Alvarez, Emeritus Consultant in Medicine at the Mayo Clinic, made the following summation in a news article in the *Herald-Tribune:*

As I often say to these persons who have the body largely of a man, and the personality of a woman, it is very hard for a normally sexed person to conceive of a man's hoping desperately that he can find a surgeon who can help him. I could not understand it until I had talked to a number of these people and had come to see that psychically they were very feminine. Naturally, their male body and male dress was abhorrent to them.

The decision to have the operation performed was easy because the change in sexual status was so logical and so greatly desired. One reason why we are reluctant to help these unfortunate people is that we always have a fear that after the operation, the person might change his or her mind, and might want to go back. This, I should say now, is most unlikely.

I know that for having written this column, I will get
a number of letters from people who will think that I
am foul-minded. No, I am just talking about these
people dispassionately and scientifically. Let all of us
who tend to look on these people as vile, remember
that their mix-up was obvious in early childhood when,
surely, there was no vileness. We must all learn to have
sympathy for these persons who were so badly gypped
by Nature. But for the grace of God, we too might be
caught in the same cruel trap.

Aside from a few individual doctors like Walter Alavarez and
Harry Benjamin, the American Medical Association was extremely
reluctant to sanction these operations openly, or to take any public
stand regarding them. However, in the United States, doctors in New
Orleans, Los Angeles, Pennsylvania, New York, and Johns Hopkins
University were quietly working on cases of transsexualism, either in
surgeries or in the laboratories and clinics. Also, they were
encountering the same kinds of public and medical resistance that
had been experienced in my case, though perhaps with lessening
degrees of intensity.

It's more than probable that fear of legal complexities or
reprisals, in some instances, acted as a deterrent to public
acknowledgement. My friend, Attorney Bob Sherwin, discussed these
medico-legal aspects in a symposium on transsexualism by Drs. Harry
Benjamin, Emil Gutheil, and Danica Deutsch.

Again, despite great protestations to the contrary,
there is no law which specifically prohibits a doctor
from performing this operation with the consent of the
patient. Nevertheless, there is hardly a district attorney
in the country who would not inform a doctor that it
would be illegal for the doctor to perform such an
operation. When asked for proof of his statement, the
District Attorney would point to the Mayhem Statute.
Rarely has the law been used in such a ridiculous and

unscientific fashion. The Mayhem Statute has no
connection, even in its origin, with anything remotely
related to the subject under discussion. It was a king's
device [Henry VIII] in the days of yore to prevent his
men from becoming useless as fighters in his army. He
therefore made it a serious crime for a man to
dismember in any way any limb or part of the body that
would make him less able to fight. It has been held
many times that cutting off an ear would not be
mayhem. And, as a matter of fact, there seems to be
little doubt that the cutting off of the male genitalia
would not be mayhem either. And yet, it is this statute
which is cited as the reason why such an operation
would be a crime on the part of the doctor.

Dr. Benjamin enlarges on the subject in his book, *The
Transsexual Phenomenon:*

I know of a surgeon who refused to operate after
being warned by a district attorney. I too have received
a letter from another district attorney's office with the
same warning, after I had asked for the respective
information. While no case of actual prosecution under
this law has come to my attention, it has undoubtedly
served to intimidate doctors who otherwise might have
been willing to operate upon an occasional transsexual
patient. Whether fear of actual legal complications, or
fear of blackmail, or fear of being criticized pre-
dominated is a matter for conjecture. Eventually a
Supreme Court decision may be required to ban the
specter of the mayhem statute for surgeons and allow
them to act in accordance with science and their own
consciences.

Legal reforms notoriously take place at a snail-like
pace. J. W. Ehrlich, famed San Francisco attorney, said
in his recent book, *Reasonable Doubt:* "...if medicine had

remained as backward as the law, the chief remedial aid of today's doctor would still be bloodletting."

But there is another point that should not be forgotten. Many of the objections against a sex conversion are rooted in religion, as are most sex laws and legislation of morals. One may ask whether such legislation is justified in a society in which church and state are supposed to be separated.

Often, the country in which my conversion had taken place was stated variously as Holland, Finland, Sweden, Norway and even Lapland, though I suppose the geographical designation was of no importance. I noticed, too, that almost invariably when my name was mentioned, it carried the added phrase, "an ex-GI." There seemed to be something fascinating about the fact that I'd been in the army, and I wonder now if that paradox wasn't a large contributing factor in the mountains of publicity that followed. I think most people still find it difficult to understand why and how I was accepted in the United States Army.

The slow and gradual beginnings of acceptance, however, were not entirely true of professional circles, particularly television or motion pictures. At that point, too, no other offers were forthcoming in the theater, and I was becoming increasingly dissatisfied with the nightclub circuit. I looked around for a way to broaden my career in other areas, and decided that a lecture tour might be an answer. I based those lectures on my own experiences and the problems involved in the understanding of any child that is born with an infirmity, either curable or incurable. Several invitations were extended to me and I spoke at the Torah Lodge B'nai Brith in Baltimore, a cerebral palsy meeting in Harrison, New York, and the Temple Shalom in River Edge, New Jersey.

I hoped that lecturing on the "knife and fork circuit," as the service clubs are called, would open a new horizon, but not many speaking dates could be arranged and I returned to my old performing grounds, the nightclubs.

April of 1959 produced a curious incident in my life, and I'm not sure it's clear to me, even now, why I allowed it to magnify itself. Again, it created a storm of publicity and controversy—a storm that I must admit I had a hand in creating.

At that time, several friends from Washington, D.C., were visiting in our home on Long Island for an extended weekend. Among them was a man whom I'd dated several times before and had come to know well during my frequent visits to Washington. He was a labor-union statistician named John Traub. A charming and handsome man in his mid-thirties, I liked John mainly for his warmth and honesty, and we had enjoyed a friendly relationship for some time.

I remember clearly that day at the house when John and I were chatting about this and that, and suddenly our conversation turned to marriage. "Good grief, Johnny," I said, "last year I was just a single girl, this year I'm an old maid!"

"There's a remedy for that, Chris," he answered. "Will you marry me?"

Although for a minute I thought he was joking, he soon made it clear that he was not. In retrospect, I must now admit that I was at a point when I thought life was passing me by. On occasion, I suppose I had thought fleetingly of marriage when I saw the relationships enjoyed by many of my friends, but I'd never really regarded it as a serious measure for myself. Now, however, it was different; I was confronted by a serious offer of marriage. I suppose, too, I was thinking of the companionship it would mean in my life for the years that stretched ahead, and at thirty-three, I'd reached the point where I thought every woman should be married.

Perhaps it was the onset of early middle age, or possibly the excitement of a new and fulfilling adventure. Certainly, I did not regard it lightly. I couldn't agree with Sarah Bernhardt that "marriage is only a friendship sanctioned by the police." I felt that it was not only a legal contract between two people, but a spiritual sacrament. Furthermore, I was enormously fond of John and I have no doubt that I tried unconsciously to stretch that affection into a larger emotional frame.

Whatever the combination of reasons, the thought of marriage seemed enticing and I said yes to John's proposal. I tried to make it clear, however, what such an involvement would mean to him: the probable censure, the personal criticism and public dispute, but he brushed those considerations aside. Half expectantly, we entered the lion's cage.

When John and I went to City Hall to apply for a marriage license a few days later, we threw the bureau clerk into a state that was close to nervous prostration. After a great deal of jittery hesitation and clearing of throat, he disappeared into a back room, and finally emerged with a request that we go to the Commissioner's office. We were met there by Assistant Corporation Counsel Albert Cooper, and he in turn called five of his assistants who specialized in interpreting Supreme Court decisions.

After another lengthy conference, they finally found the loophole they were looking for. We were informed that as the gender designation on my birth certificate had not been changed to read "female," they couldn't issue us a license to marry.

By then, the press had descended on City Hall and Counsel Cooper gave me the following statement to present to the reporters:

"After considering all the elements of this application, it is my opinion that public policy, in the light of existing law, requires my rejection of the application at the present time, without prejudice to the submission to this office of legally competent evidence that the applicant, Christine Jorgensen, may qualify for a marriage license in accordance with the purpose and provisions of the Domestic Relations Law."

The ambiguities of that statement are self-evident. I read it over several times, and still didn't understand it. I'd already presented other documents attesting my status, including a statement written by Dr. Benjamin which read: "This is to certify that I have known Miss Christine Jorgensen for over six years. It is my opinion that she must be considered female. I have today examined Miss Jorgensen and have found her in a condition that would fully enable her to have normal marital relations."

It was, of course, a grave dilemma for Mr. Cooper, and one with which I could sympathize, for he simply had no precedent as a frame of reference. However, he found a more valid reason for denying the license. John, who had been married previously, had forgotten to bring his divorce papers with him. Visibly relieved, Mr. Cooper later explained to the press: "The law requires that any applicant who is divorced must submit proof of a valid divorce before a marriage license may be legally issued. We told the groom he would have to return with his divorce papers so we could give him a ruling." When asked further, "What about Chris?" Mr. Cooper replied, "Ah, yes, that is one of the things we have to consider. You know, sometimes you have to be a King Solomon in this job."

The following day, the story exploded in headlines: "BAR WEDDING FOR CHRISTINE."... "Bar a license for girlish Chris, all because of her boyish past."... "Six assistant Corporation Counsels bent to the task of deciding whether she was legally a lady." Pictures of John and me appeared widely, and the controversy was off and running.

The main issue, of course, centered around the problem of changing my birth certificate. However, several years before, when I'd asked my lawyer, Bob Sherwin, if it would be necessary to change it, he advised me to forget it. His reasons seemed to me as valid then as they are now, and I have left the document as it was on the day I was born.

My birth certificate was a report of a happening some thirty-three years before. It was in no way a legal sex-determining document. If I'd gone through the red tape of having it changed to read "female," I would simply have received a newer piece of paper and the original would not have been destroyed, but merely sealed in permanent files. The same holds true in the case of adoption when a new certificate is issued to the adopting parents—the old one is sealed in a vault, and can be reopened by the parents or the child on request.

Bob convinced me that there was no reason to go through a legal procedure which would, to say the least, mean nothing. In his view, a birth certificate is just that: the certification of a birth.

Dr. Benjamin has encountered similar problems and relates them in his recent study of transsexualism:

In practice, and in the United States, much depends upon the state in which the applicant for a legal change of sex status had been born. In some states, it proved to be easy and merely required filling out some form and sending it to the respective Bureau of Vital Statistics, with a doctor's certificate....

Some few states promptly issued a new birth certificate with the name and gender changed accordingly. In other states, a more complicated procedure was required, namely a court order. Sometimes that took so much time and money that the applicant gave up and continued to live in his or her "new sex" illegally, hoping there might never be the need for a birth certificate, for instance, for the purpose of getting married...Again, in other states, the request was such a novel and unprecedented one that delaying tactics were resorted to or the application was denied, unless proof could be rendered that the original certificate had been issued in error....

I know of one wise official who issued a new birth certificate if a physician could furnish some laboratory proof indicating abnormal values in the male-female balance....He helped a few operated-upon transsexuals in this way in their new life pattern until, alas, bureaucracy, ignorance, or a combination of these caught up with him and forced him to ignore or reject applications for a legal sex change.

One thing seems certain. While great conservatism should prevail in advising, consenting to, and performing a conversion operation, all possible help should be given those who present a *fait accompli* by having undergone the irrevocable step of surgery. It seems to me to be the duty not only of physicians, but also of the community, to pave the way as much as possible for such persons so that they can succeed in their new pattern of life as members of the opposite sex.

And so, the transsexual's plight exists in the legal field as it does in the medical. That may be partly because there is actually no legal definition of "male" and "female." Such a definition hardly seems necessary since everyone knows the answer, or thinks he does...I asked a well-informed and prominent San Francisco attorney, Mr. Kenneth Zwerin, how the law defines the two sexes and his answer is so clear and striking that it is worth recording here:

"As far as my research discloses, there has never been a judicial decision determining what is meant by the words 'male' and 'female.'

"There are many cases that deal with rape committed on the body of a female and other cases which construe the meaning of the term 'male issue' for inheritance purposes, but the decisions are silent as to what these words specifically mean.

"Our Civil Code permits marriage only between a male and a female, but our court has never been called upon to pass on the meaning of these designations.

"Since the Courts do not render advisory opinions, I must conclude that the problem has never been judicially raised."

As a layman, I can only conclude that the time may not be far away when the courts may be called upon to decide the actual significance of the male or female genitalia for the determination of one's sex. Neither the genetic nor the psychological sex could then be ignored.

It was somewhat disconcerting for me to be refused a marriage license on the basis of my birth certificate alone. Aside from the medical designations, the United States State Department had issued me a passport as a female, and I was recognized as such by the World Health Organization. I carried a driver's license from the State of New York as a female. The Police Department of the City of New York had granted me a cabaret card as a female entertainer. Entitled "Cabaret and Public Dance Hall Employment Identification," it is a license required by all nightclub performers to show they have no police record of drug addiction. Female designations also appeared on my insurance applications and the ownership papers of my house. Surely, I thought, these documents were as legal as any other.

It seemed to me that it was not within the domain of the Marriage License Bureau to establish itself as a sex determining agency, yet that's what it had become on that April day in 1959. Recently, I asked Bob Sherwin why he thought the bureau had made such an issue of the certificate of my birth, when legally they had not the right to do so. He summed it up with the brief reply: "Hysteria!"

Ostensibly, there are only two reasons on which a refusal may be based legally, if a person is single: application by a minor, and failure to pass a blood test for communicable diseases.

The ruling on our application was therefore held in abeyance for several weeks until John could obtain and present his divorce papers and I could decide what further steps to take that would be acceptable to the Marriage License Bureau. In the interim, the press played havoc.

Fortunately, the hiatus gave us both a period in which to pause and reflect on the step we had contemplated. I'm sure that both John and I had cause to be grateful to the red tape of bureaucracy, for giving us the opportunity to think sober second thoughts. I think we both realized that we were play-acting at a relationship that was based on strong affection and the desire for companionship, rather than one based on love alone. The publicity surrounding our engagement also made it abundantly clear that notoriety would be an ever-present factor, and an increasingly painful one for him. Already he had felt the repercussions and had lost his job as a statistician with the labor union.

We both agreed we were propelling ourselves into a situation from which it would be difficult, if not impossible, to extricate ourselves. A matrimonial failure involving me would be far more disastrous than for the average person. Finally, after some weeks had passed, we decided to end our relationship, and parted as warm friends.

As I look back on that experience, I am still wondering at my willingness to enter into marriage, particularly as I had always held to the conviction that I would never marry simply to prove that it was possible. It strikes me that perhaps I was testing after all, and am grateful that both John and I escaped the possibility of disaster without any visible scars.

Late in 1959, I was offered a date at the Interlude Club in Hollywood and it was with some hesitation that I accepted. Memories of my unsuccessful attempt to break the barriers of the film industry in 1946, and the debacle of my Denmark film in 1953, had made me regard Hollywood as a kind of nemesis, and as the jet landed at the Los Angeles airport, some of the old fear returned.

Betty had flown ahead to settle details at the club and make living arrangements, and we headed for the great old apartment hotel in the Hollywood Hills district, the Chateau Marmont.

One day soon after my arrival, friends began to gather for a visit, all of them highly irritated that they'd been stopped on entering the grounds and regarded with suspicion. I called the front desk and was told that Errol Flynn's wife, Patrice Wymore, was my neighbor in the next cottage, and as Mr. Flynn had died that day, she had requested complete privacy and seclusion.

For several days after his death, the news photographers sneaked across my lawn in the hope they could catch a quick photo of his widow. My cocker spaniel, Buffy, proceeded to have a running battle with the press, and although he hadn't met Mrs. Flynn personally, he defended her with a vengeance. He also enjoyed the constant stream of animals that came through the fence daily; cats, dogs, even a rabbit, and all pets of my neighbor's. With the thought that Mrs. Flynn might be in the mood for some company, I sent her a note that said: "We've had your cat, your dog and your rabbit as guests; when can we expect you for a cocktail?" Within a few minutes she called and joined us for a drink, and made it clear that she needed that brief interlude of escape from the unhappiness of the moment.

Fortunately, the opening at the Interlude was a success, and fear of the past Hollywood disasters began to fade. Frankly, I was no less delighted than the tourists when I was visited by many of the great names in the film industry. To indulge in a little namedropping, they included Judy Garland, Franchot Tone, Esther Williams, Natalie Wood, Robert Wagner, Betty Grable, and Ann Miller.

One night at the club, I was invited to Judy Garland's table between shows, but was cautioned ahead of time not to mention the fact that she was overweight. "What do you think I'm going to say," I replied, "Hello, Fat Lady?" A few minutes after our introduction, it was Judy herself who mentioned her weight problem, and wasn't at all reluctant to discuss it. After admiring my wardrobe, she asked me what I thought of her costuming in a recent TV variety series. Hesitantly, I offered the opinion that overweight couldn't be camouflaged in tight-fitting clothes, and suggested black velvet toreador pants, a stiff, stand-out jacket with a mandarin collar encrusted with jewels, and adding the comfort of flat shoes. "That means no girdles!" she said.

Several weeks later, Judy filled in for an ailing star in Las Vegas, and I felt like Dior when I saw the photos of her wearing the costume design I'd suggested.

When the manager of the Interlude Club, Gene Norman, asked me to extend my contract to twelve weeks, I accepted with pleasure. One minor problem existed for Gene, as previously he'd booked Nina Simone, a talented specialty singer, and her contract required top billing. To solve his dilemma, he suggested that he give Nina star billing on one side of the marquee, and me on the other. It was a perfectly acceptable solution, and when he asked what side of the marquee I preferred, I said, "The one that points toward Beverly Hills!"

My success at the Interlude in Hollywood led not only to other nightclub offers throughout the Southwest, but to a motion picture contract which would star me in a re-make of H. Rider Haggard's *She*. Before that, there had been many rumors of my doing a film, but none of them had produced a bona fide offer. A company was formed by a small independent producer, and with the enthusiasm of the financial backers running high, they arranged a cocktail buffet party for the press to announce the forthcoming

production. The gathering was held at Delmonico's, an elegant
Beverly Hills restaurant, and all of the Hollywood columnists had
been invited. Most all of them attended, with the notable exception
of Louella Parsons and Hedda Hopper. Their absence, however,
didn't prepare us for the comments in their respective columns
within the next few days. In general, their reaction was one of total
wrath, and, united in outrage, it may have been one of the few times
when they agreed on anything. Even the thought of my doing a film
apparently riled the ladies beyond measure, for it brought forth a
fountain of slashing invective in both columns, and the implication
was clear that my very presence in a movie would be a reflection on
the entire industry.

It was no great revelation that movies had grown into a billion-
dollar industry, partially by riding in on the bosom and bottom of the
female anatomy, and at that very moment, was producing an untidy
little offering starring a young lady whose only recommendation lay
in the fact that she was the current favorite of one of Hollywood's
most famous and most-married male stars—a gentleman
distinguished by his capacity for nocturnal recreation and alcohol.

By contrast to a few other film figures, I'd never been arrested,
never been a drug addict, never been hauled into court for
misconduct, and had made every effort to keep my public behavior
beyond reproach. It seemed to me that the public should have been
allowed to judge any film in which I appeared on the basis of its
merit or non-merit after it had been released, not before it even went
into production.

By then, of course, I was getting rather used to the idea of
being judged before being seen, but the vitriol that percolated from
the two most powerful women in Hollywood proved disastrous. The
producers already had many production plans in the works, and
were attempting to raise the balance of the money they needed,
planning out a budget, and interviewing directors and scenario
writers. One famous script writer, with several Academy Awards to his
credit, offered to write the screen treatment for a whopping salary
plus a percentage, with the stipulation that his name be withheld
from the production. A pen name might have made him immune to

censure, but I'm fairly certain he'd have gone to the bank under his true identity.

However, the damage had been done. The financial backers took one look at the combined efforts of the Parsons-Hopper wrecking company, and ran for the hills. The result was that the project fell flat and ended before it had really begun.

All in all, 1959 had been quite an active and interesting year. I'd known some successes, some failures, had made many new friends, and enjoyed new and unusual experiences.

Probably the two most important emotional influences of that period were contrasting ones—an affair of the heart and an affair of the bank account. My engagement to John Traub had taught me several things, mainly that the measure of real love is what one is willing to give up for it. In addition, the difficulties with the Internal Revenue Department had left me a little sadder, a good deal poorer and, hopefully, a trifle wiser.

CHAPTER 25

B etty Walton encouraged me to take an apartment in Hollywood as a base of operations, with the thought that it would open up new avenues in my career. Therefore, I had established a residence on the West Coast, and I flew about the country fulfilling various nightclub contracts, while Betty stayed in Hollywood.

Following the collapse of the movie project, I returned to the familiar world of nightclubs and most of the dates of the period were scattered throughout the East. Although Betty had negotiated contracts and arranged some bookings, the salaries were never to reach the heights I'd received while Charlie was alive.

Suddenly, I realized I was being somewhat lavish in my spending. Now, I was maintaining two households on opposite coasts, had bought new cars in both Hollywood and New York, and with a mortgage on the Long Island house and the kind attentions of the Bureau of Internal Revenue, there was little left over for the rainy day I'd heard so much about. Fortunately, about that time Betty arranged club dates in Honolulu and Australia, to be followed by a tour of the Orient.

In June of 1961, I flew directly from New York to Honolulu, while Betty had preceded me by one day from California. As it had been before, my visit to Hawaii was a deeply rewarding one. Several old friends were there at the time, among them, Jackie Cooper and Abby Dalton, who were filming a segment of the *Hennessey* TV series, and we all had fun at a native luau I arranged for them.

During that visit, the Kilauea Volcano erupted on the island of Hawaii. The source of the eruption was a cone at the bottom of the crater called Halemaumau (The House of Everlasting Fire), and the traditional home of Pele, the Hawaiian goddess of fire. I was very anxious to get some films of the exciting spectacle, and I remember that I quickly changed into one of the comfortable native mumus before leaving the hotel in Oahu for the flight to the outer island and the crater's rim. I was stopped immediately in the lobby by the hotel manager who said, "Miss Jorgensen, you cannot go to the crater wearing that red mumu. Red is the color of the Fire Goddess and she is very jealous of it!" I rushed back to my room and changed into a dress of another color, which greatly relieved the hotel manager. Although I didn't hold too strongly with local superstitions, on my way to a roaring volcano, I wasn't about to tempt the gods in any direction. Anyway, I thought it wouldn't hurt to take out a little insurance.

Correctly outfitted, we finally arrived at the edge of the crater and I got some spectacular photographs. It was awe-inspiring to look deep into the interior of the mountain, and watch it fill slowly with molten lava as it belched smoke and fire from every corner. The Goddess Pele was a raging inferno that day, and pre-armed with small bottles of Vodka we threw them into the volcano as a traditional sacrifice that was thought to pacify her anger.

Regretfully, Betty and I left Hawaii and flew to Sydney, Australia, in late July. If I'd been more observant I might have seen America's second astronaut overhead, as the following morning I shared the front page of the *Sydney Mirror* with the late Captain Virgil Grissom.

My visit to Australia lasted six months with personal appearances throughout the continent. I enjoyed the country immensely and made many friendships there before I decided to leave. There were two things that marred that visit, however. First was the fact that I didn't receive my last week's salary from the club in Sydney, and I'm still trying to collect. But more important, I found Betty and I were completely at odds about almost everything. Her extravagance made me increasingly uneasy, and I found her possessiveness irritating.

Little by little, bits and pieces began to fit together into a rather curious picture, though it didn't come to a definite breach until, on a rainy January day, we boarded an Australian freighter for the trip northward to Hong Kong.

The trip was fraught with tensions and irritations and the circumstances left me in a state of deep depression. It's difficult for me to understand why I allowed the situation to develop beyond the point of reason and good sense, but I suppose I can chalk it up to the fact that mine is a basically mild and accepting nature, and strange as it seems, judging from my past conflicts, I often go to great lengths to avoid controversy. It may well show a character disorder, but I'm inclined to let things flow along with irritating serenity rather than seek a confrontation at each critical moment.

My own fears and suspicions made me increasingly wary, and I finally began to make the noises of a dissatisfied client.

Arriving in Hong Kong, I fulfilled several nightclub engagements, and then moved on to Manila. Visiting in the Philippines was a delightful experience in many ways. I was greeted with great warmth and enthusiasm in the newspapers, and the Filipino people extended me every courtesy and hospitality.

Mayor Lacson of Manila gave an official luncheon for the governors and mayors of the Philippines, to which I was invited as a guest of honor. The Governor of Mindanao pleased me greatly when, during a luncheon address to his political colleagues, he said, "Miss Jorgensen is the best goodwill ambassador America has sent us in years!"

I played four weeks at the Safari Club in Manila, at which time I met many of the social and political figures of the Philippines, and many members of foreign diplomatic corps, with the exception of the United States contingent. At every turn I experienced nothing but courtesy and affection, and was invited to appear as a guest star in a Filipino film production.

Although for the most part my stay in the Philippines was delightful and rewarding, it also resulted in an altercation with the United States Armed Forces in the area. If the people of the Philippines lavished me with warmth and hospitality, the American military did not.

Within a few weeks of my arrival, I received an invitation from a Filipino booking agent in Manila to perform at the Officer's and

Noncommissioned Officer's Clubs at nearby Clark Field, the United States Air Force Base. The agent had okayed the agreement with the Special Service officer in charge of entertainment, and a public announcement was made to thousands of club members that I would appear on the third of March. Several of the base personnel later confirmed that announcement to me personally, and added that it was received with enthusiasm.

A few days before the performance, the Manila agent called Betty in great agitation, to say that the offer had been canceled for no apparent reason. Simultaneously, a Manila newspaperwoman told me of a circulating rumor that the base officials had refused my appearance because it would be "bad for American-Philippine relations." I was deeply upset by that, but asked the journalist not to print the item, and hoped that by ignoring the whole thing, it would just go away.

Since my arrival, I'd made many friends from the base, and on the day I'd been scheduled to appear, I happened to be a luncheon guest at Clark Field. Large signs were displayed at the club, reading: "Christine Jorgensen Will Not Appear Tonight."

Many times after that, I was asked by my fellow Americans why I refused to perform. "What's the matter, can't the base afford your salary? Or aren't the GIs good enough for you to entertain?" As my proposed salary would have been a fraction of what I usually received, it was an unfair accusation, but I had no recourse but to smile through it all, and drop the subject with an apology.

Although I was again branded as "unsuitable" to entertain the armed forces, it was common knowledge in the Philippines that strippers and off-color comics were flown in frequently from Tokyo, and it was no secret there were occasional lively "stag" parties at the base clubs. That, of course, was none of my business, but gossip continued to circulate that my appearance would have been detrimental to American-Philippine relations.

Angered by the undercurrent of controversy, Betty took up the cudgels and wrote a firm letter to the Wing Commander at Clark Field, asking for an explanation and requesting that he honor the offer. By then, my own irritation over the whole affair had been aroused, particularly as I was a welcome guest in a foreign country, and scarcely an anonymous one. The rejection from my own countrymen had begun to rankle the Philippine press, which did little to hide its suspicion. For a time, it had all the earmarks of a diplomatic incident.

As no answer was forthcoming, carbon copies of Betty's letter to him were sent to President Kennedy, New York's Senator Jacob Javits, the Secretary of the Air Force, the United States Air Force Chief of Staff, and the American Ambassador in the Philippines.

After a long delay, Betty received an answer to her letter. It was a long, rambling letter filled with misinformation, in which I was never referred to by name, but as "the act," and our complaint was completely dismissed.

Within a few days, we received a carbon copy of a letter sent to the Headquarters of the United States Air Force in Washington, D. C., from the office of President John F. Kennedy, asking that a full investigation and report of the incident be sent to him.

I have no idea what the results of his intercession might have been, but soon after, the Wing Commander was transferred back to the United States. Although his transfer may have had nothing to do with the incident, it seemed significant at the time.

After four months in Manila, my personal and professional association with Betty Walton terminated. In professional relationships, one reaches a point sometimes when there is too wide a divergence in ideas and goals. A complete break was the best business solution. She had her own professional interests and although I offered her a plane ticket to America, she decided to remain in the Philippines.

So I flew on alone to California

I remember that trip as one of fatigue and depression, and think I was as near a nervous breakdown as I would ever come in my life. I'd relied on Betty, both personally and in business matters, and the realization that I'd been disillusioned was a difficult thing to accept. Even a brief stopover in the paradise of Honolulu didn't seem to relieve my feelings of oppression, and the fact that I arrived in Los Angeles with five dollars in my handbag didn't help matters.

I wired to New York for some money, and then went immediately to the apartment in Hollywood.

My main thought at that point was to get back to work. I didn't want to return to New York in an emotional state I knew would be distressing to Mom and Dad, so I stayed on the West Coast until September, trying to get my nervous system back on an even keel and playing a few nightclub dates here and there.

Then, I heard the news from Mom that Aunt Augusta was seriously ill in Minneapolis, and on my way home, I stopped for the last time to see that grand old lady who had played such an important role at several crucial times in my life.

I'd given up the apartment in California, and once back home with my family, I made a resolution that the days of high living were over. There would be no more unnecessary extravagances in the form of personal managers, double residences, lavish hotel suites, or more than one automobile. The multiple obligations and soaring expenses had come to an end, and with them, the nervous tensions.

As a result of my new regime, by cutting expenses and living at home, I ended up with more money at the end of the year, although I played fewer nightclubs during that period. It was a much happier time, too, for it allowed me to be at home with my family where I'd always found the greatest pleasures and sense of belonging.

It's interesting that the most casual and routine events in life sometimes have such important results. July 16, 1963, was a day that would be a turning point in my career, when a friend invited me to the opening night of *Life With Father,* starring Dodie Goodman, and produced at a small, charming summer theater called The Red Barn in Northport, Long Island.

As my escort stood at the box office to pick up our tickets, a man behind the window kept staring at me very intently. By then a familiar circumstance, I turned away and thought no more about it.

The intense young man behind the ticket window was Bill Hunt, the producer-director of The Red Barn and another Long Island summer theater, Tinker's Pond. Later, I heard the story of that brief encounter from Bill himself. He turned to one of his assistants in the box office that evening, and said, "I don't know who she is but I'm going to find out, because there goes 'Madam Rosepettle.' " It was the name of the leading character in Arthur Kopit's play, *Oh, Dad, Poor Dad, Mama's Hung You in the Closet and I'm Feelin' So Sad.* To save breath and marquee space, the play is most often referred to simply as *Oh, Dad.* Bill was planning a future production of it, and looking around for someone to play the all-important role of the mother.

Several months later, he called me to introduce himself and ask if I would be interested in playing the role. At last, someone had asked me to do a play that required some acting ability, and in one of the most challenging parts in the contemporary theater. I don't remember my exact train of thought during our conversation, but I do know I was excited and thrilled at the prospect. Bill recalls that underneath my enthusiasm, I seemed very suspicious, and in his words, "I think she was looking for the gimmick, but there wasn't any. All I wanted her to do was play that part."

Bill sent me a script to read, we arranged a meeting a few days later, and it was the beginning of not only a wonderful friendship, but one of the most rewarding experiences of my career. In the discussions that followed we both got very excited about the project. So much so, that I forgot to discuss salary with Bill ahead of time, which is a very uncommon thing for any performer. To me, the opportunity was the important thing and I frankly didn't care what the salary was. I'd have done it for nothing.

Almost immediately, we began to work on a delineation of the play and the role of Madam Rosepettle, although it wasn't planned for production until July of the following season. That gave me almost six months to spend on analysis of the character and to plan out each detail of its demands. Bill was tireless and extremely generous with his time, and I learned more about the theater from him than from any single person I've met in the business since.

A short, squarely built man with snapping dark eyes, Bill walks closer to ten feet tall when he's challenged, and his responses are abrupt and to the point. He knew that I was a controversial personality, but he was totally unafraid of public opinion. "The only thing I owe the public is a good show," he said. Once he decided he wanted me for the role in *Oh, Dad,* nothing could change his course, even though he met resistance before we went into rehearsal.

The following is Bill's account of one of the earlier incidents: "Arthur Kopit's agent tried to cancel my right to do the play. I was alerted by a friend who worked for Samuel French, the play broker, and he told me the author had great objections to my using Chris. It was by no means an ultimatum, as Kopit had no casting distinctions in his contract with French, and they couldn't cancel my production so long as I paid the royalties. My friend merely assumed the unpleasant duty of passing on the attitude of the author, as a friendly warning. I said, 'Look, this isn't just a one-time shot for me. I've been around as a producer for twenty years, and I'm in this business for life!' "

Toward the end of the summer I'd first visited the Red Barn Theater, I made plans for a nightclub tour of Alaska. A few days before my departure for Anchorage, Mom had a medical checkup and the doctors discovered a malignancy. In a state of semi-shock, I made arrangements to cancel the Alaskan trip when the doctors decided Mom would undergo a series of radioactive treatments in the hospital.

With her usual candor, my redoubtable mother was foot-tapping with annoyance at the idea that I would cancel the tour. "There's nothing you can do here during the treatments," she said. "Dad and Dolly will be on hand and I want you to make that trip to Alaska. Besides, I've always wanted a totem pole!" There is very little one can do in the face of Mom's orders, and knowing that Dolly and Dad were standing by, I flew to Alaska in August, and returned toward the end of October. By the time I got back to New York, Mom had been home from the hospital for a week, looking wonderful and as spirited as ever.

I suppose that most every person in the United States and many throughout the world, remembers what he was doing and where on that long day of agony, November 22, 1963. There seem to have been only a few days of history in my own lifetime that I can remember with total recall. The first was December 7, 1941; the second, the death of President Roosevelt on April 12, 1945; the third was the assassination of John F. Kennedy.

I was in Omaha, preparing to rehearse for an opening night, and had arrived at the club shortly after the first horrifying news began to sweep the nation. I remember the scene of unreality as if it had happened this very morning. A group of a dozen or so performers hung limply around a television set, shocked into a state of frightening suspension, and watching the events as one horror lurched after another. Some of us wept, some watched in a mindless trance. Few could voice what they felt.

After hours of the nightmare had passed, we were instructed to finish the rehearsal and prepare for the performance. Most of us were convinced that no one would show up had that night, but we went through the motions of getting ready, anyway. On the contrary, the house was packed. People seemed to feel the need of preoccupation and the security of company, even strangers, as if they were seeking a confirmation of the truth.

We performed that evening, though we'd removed most of the comedic material, leaving little but the musical numbers. At the end of the show, I was asked to express a few words of our feelings, and the audience joined the entire company as we sang "God Bless America." It will always stay with me as a painful and touching evening.

The Christmas Holidays of 1963 were more joyful than to usual within our family circle, for we had additional cause for gratitude in Mom's successful recovery from her bout with cancer. The New Year held more promise—by then I'd met Bill Hunt, and looked forward to the production of *Oh, Dad* and the possibility of a growing career in the theater.

I must admit my pleasures of that holiday were somewhat diminished by another unwelcome visitation from the Department of Internal Revenue. By then, we'd become as close as a married couple, but what I wanted was a divorce. For several years, I'd been making payments to the national treasury, gradually whittling down my indebtedness and therefore I was caught by surprise when the tax agents helped themselves to my entire bank balance, leaving me with no funds whatever. As their little appropriation was made on December 31st, I judged it was their engaging way of wishing me a Happy New Year. At the risk of making the most gross understatement of this entire narrative, I took a dim view of their move.

Although I'd been making regular payments over the years, I couldn't help feeling that the total tax assessment had been excessive to begin with. Also, there had been the constant harassment and threat of foreclosure on the old homestead. I think if the tax agents hadn't been so maddeningly polite, I could have borne it more easily.

At long last, in April of 1964, I settled the whole affair and separated myself from the United States Department of Internal Revenue. When I left the investigators at the settlement room in the bank for the last time, one of them said, "See you again, Miss Jorgensen." I like to think that my reply carried the spirit of conviction: "Never again will I earn enough money for you boys to become interested!"

The days of working forty-eight weeks a year were over. It's true, big money had rolled in, but big money had rolled right out again. From then on, I vowed that I'd work less, make less money, and confound the tax officials forever more.

Throughout the first half of 1964, I was preparing myself for rehearsals of *Oh, Dad,* and heading for a July opening at Bill's Tinker's Pond Theater in Syosset, Long Island. My greatest desire was to step over the boundaries of notoriety, into the world of the legitimate theater, and I hoped to make the transition on the strength of a satisfying and acceptable performance; not by a constant reference to my past personal life. As I told Bill, "I've been illegitimate too long!"

I wasn't naïve enough to think I'd give a brilliant performance, but I hoped to make up in spirit and hard work what I lacked in experience. Actually, I regarded it as my first play, because I'd barely gotten my feet wet in *To Dorothy, A Son* nine years earlier. No matter how small, I wanted to make an acceptable mark in the branch of show business that was dearest to me.

Rehearsals started late in June and lasted only one week, which was enough to produce total panic in a novice like me. However, I'd been studying the role for half a year, and had been learning lines as I went along, so I felt I was as prepared as I'd ever be for rehearsals. Many actors in the theater are fast studies, but unfortunately I'm not one of them. I learn lines very slowly, though once having set a part in my mind I retain it, and think I could repeat it verbatim years later.

I doubt that anyone else in the world read Mr. Kopit's play as often as I did during that period of study. I read it through or worked on some part of it almost every night from the time I accepted Bill Hunt's offer. The advance preparation and his coaching paid off, and I felt as secure as anyone could feel, faced with an opening night.

There were a lot of things riding on the performance: the possibility of a new career in the theater, and recognition as an actress instead of an oddity. If I failed, I knew I might not get another chance. The knowledge that another theater, less than twenty miles away, was to open *Oh, Dad* starring Hermione Gingold, on the night before our opening, didn't lessen the tense excitement.

I didn't know it at the time, but other problems had arisen for Bill when my name was mentioned in connection with his production—in his usual protective way, he kept those difficulties from me until after we'd opened.

In a more recent interview, Bill recorded some of his impressions of the period:

> I remember that first day of rehearsal for *Oh, Dad.*
> The rest of the company was a little nervous about
> Chris' arrival and their first meeting. I don't know what
> people expect, but I suppose everyone has some sort of
> preconceived idea of what she's like, and you can
> almost feel that expectancy hanging in the air. Anyway,
> she walked in and was so genuinely warm and
> disarming that five minutes later the cast had accepted
> her like an old friend.

Rehearsals were a pleasure for me, Chris worked like a demon—attacked the work like a real pro. When I asked her to do something or talked out a point with her in rehearsal, she understood what I wanted immediately. I knew she was going on instinct, and almost invariably, it was right.

To the whole company personally, she was a delight. The last three days of rehearsals, the weather was brutally hot, and she asked if she could bring a portable air conditioner for her dressing room. Of course, I said yes, and when she arrived the next day, she not only had the air conditioner, but had brought six fans, one for each of the other dressing rooms.

Chris said she'd like to give a party for the company, and I told her I was sure the cast would like that. I didn't realize it, but she meant not only the cast, but everybody and his brother connected with the theater—actors, stagehands, ticket-sellers, ushers, parking lot attendants, apprentices—the works. I think she'd have invited the local garbage collector if she'd found him.

It's funny, you know, the minute I saw her that evening she came to the theater as a patron, I knew I'd found the Madam Rosepettle for *Oh, Dad,* and from then on, I never considered anyone else. Frankly, I'd have never done that particular play if she hadn't been available. It was a hunch, I guess, but I was absolutely sure of my choice. Many times people have asked me why I offered Chris the part in the first place, or why I couldn't have found someone else. That's easy— mainly, because I didn't want anyone else. I was buying an actress, and I'd been producing long enough to know Long Island audiences wouldn't buy tickets to see a freak, but they'd come to see a good performance. And that's just what they got.

Sure it was a risk, but if we got any kind of a break from the critics, I knew we'd be home free.

Opening night of June 30, 1964, will always stay with me as one of the most terrifying, wonderful, and jittery evenings of my life. I remember that the first act seemed to me to go very well, and Bill appeared at my dressing room with a few words of encouragement, while I was getting ready for the second act, and struggling into a black chiffon evening gown. "Chris," he said, "don't you think you should get ready for the next scene?"

" I am! "

"But you have another scene to go before the intermission, and that's the wrong costume," he said, quietly.

I'd completely forgotten about the second scene of the first act, and it was a moment of near disaster. Fortunately, I had a few minutes before my entrance, in which to stop puffing and regain whatever composure was left in me. Other than that, I think I acquitted myself pretty well for the rest of the evening.

Although I was happy about the glowing reviews, all was not sweetness and light surrounding the play and my appearances. Early indications of unpleasant conditions appeared in a Long Island newspaper, when an interview with Hermione Gingold was printed in one of its columns. Miss Gingold was appearing in *Oh, Dad* at a theater in nearby Mineola, concurrent with our production, and had played the role of Madam Rosepettle many times before, including on Broadway.

Miss Gingold was quoted in the interview as follows: "There are some veddy curious people playing my paht, Madam Rosepettle, in other productions." Asked by the interviewer if she referred to Christine Jorgensen, she answered: "I wish she wouldn't play Madam Rosepettle. It's completely out of her reach. You cahn't play it just because you've had an operation in Sweden, you know."

Miss Gingold's proprietary reference to the role as "my part" seemed rather excessive inasmuch as it had been created originally by a brilliant actress, Jo Van Fleet, whose success in the play was widely known. It was, therefore, no more Miss Gingold's part than it was mine or the dozens of actresses who have played it since. And though she was not the first to misplace the geographical location of my conversion from Denmark to Sweden, reference to the operations seemed irrelevant.

Knowing the talents of the press for misquoting their subjects, I was sufficiently curious to call the reporter who had written the interview, and to ask him for a confirmation or denial. "I still have my notes from that interview, Miss Jorgensen," he said. "I wasn't paraphrasing, those are direct quotes and taken verbatim."

A far more serious problem than Miss Gingold's public pronouncements, however, was the fact that the Tinker's Pond Theater advance sale of tickets prior to opening was the smallest in it's history. Bill told me later that advance reservations totaled all of twenty-seven dollars on our opening night. Theater parties of political and church organizations who ordinarily came to the theater as a habit canceled tickets when my name headed the cast list. Once the reviews were out, however, the ticket sales began to climb and we ended up with a successful run of four weeks.

Also, various other producers and agents came out to Long Island to see the production, which led to an invitation to play *Oh, Dad* the following summer at Playhouse on the Green in Columbus, Ohio. At last, I felt that a career in the theater would be at least a possibility. By then, I'd had a decade of the nightclub circuit and I was more than willing to leave it for the greater creative rewards of the theater.

After completing the original four weeks of *Oh, Dad*, Bill did another play, and I returned again to revive it for two weeks, closing the second run on September 13.

I hadn't earned as much money as I would have in nightclubs, but I'd had one of the happiest summers in ten years as a performer. More important, I had found someone who'd had the courage to take a chance on me as an actress. As a theater director and a business-man, he had run some grave risks, and the opportunities given to me by the intrepid Bill Hunt will never be forgotten.

CHAPTER 26

There is no hushing the sound of years. It seemed impossible, but Christmas of 1964 was the eleventh spent in our home in Massapequa, and the twelfth since the *New York Daily News* had lifted me into a world of notoriety and fame. I remember it as a wonderful and happy holiday, a festive time when we were all together as a family, blessed with tranquil minds and a maximum of contentment. Mom's treatment for cancer the previous year had been the only serious cause for alarm, and we seemed to be a healthy, happy lot.

I looked forward to the new year, as horizons seemed to be widening with the offer to do *Oh, Dad* in Columbus, Ohio, in July, and soon after the holidays, I returned to a more leisurely schedule of nightclub engagements.

Bill Hunt called me sometimes during the early spring, and asked if I would do a production that summer of Jean Kerr's delightful comedy, *Mary, Mary*. I couldn't imagine what I would play in it, as it required a small cast of five and I knew I wasn't right for either of the female characters. "Never mind," Bill said, "I'm changing the role of the attorney to a woman, and it will work just as well. It's the part I want you to play."

After reading the script, I was surprised to find that the reversal in the character would be an easy one, and required only a change in one line of dialogue. As I was anxious to add to my experience in the theater, particularly under Bill's direction, I accepted his offer with pleasure. At that point, I thought any new acting credit would be a benefit and, too, I liked the dry and witty character I was assigned to play. By then, my own particular preference was in character and "second business" parts, a theatrical expression which includes most anything but leading women.

After a week's rehearsal late in May, we opened *Mary, Mary* on June 1 at Bill's Red Barn Theater in Northport, Long Island. Again, the reviews were cause for rejoicing:

> ...Christine Jorgensen...might surprise you. She's good. Her part was originally written for a man, but she handles the reversal with aplomb.

> Christine Jorgensen...handled the comedy with effortless ease and veteran's timing. Miss Jorgensen is glamorous and entirely relaxed as an attorney with a dry, calm sense of humor.

Mary, Mary was scheduled to run eleven weeks, but with a previous commitment to go into rehearsals of *Oh, Dad* in Columbus, I was forced to leave the company on July 4, after the fifth week of the run.

It was interesting to note a slowly changing attitude by then. Bill came to me with the happy news that several organizations had requested theater party blocks of tickets before my departure from the cast. "You see, Chris," he said, "the very groups that canceled out last year are now insisting on tickets to see you." I know it gave him as much pleasure as it did me to see the change in attitude, for it vindicated his courageous move to hire me in the first place.

One group, however, remained a Long Island stronghold of non-acceptance: the East Norwich Democratic Club, which ordinarily was in frequent attendance at The Red Barn. As a resident of Nassau County, I'd attended several gatherings of both political parties, and found the rejection rather hard to accept. Originally, I was to play *Mary, Mary* for only four weeks, and the Democratic Club theater party bought tickets for the week after I was scheduled to leave. However my plans were changed slightly and I found I was able to play the fifth week after all, leaving the theater party stuck with my appearance, and delighting Bill Hunt beyond measure. The night they came to see the show, they appeared neither demoralized nor corrupted, and made it clear how much they'd enjoyed the evening.

Oh, Dad at Playhouse on the Green in Columbus, was to be my first production away from the security and comfort of Bill's direction. Although I wasn't afraid of the play, which by then was so familiar to me, I was concerned that another director might be less adroit at guiding me through my paces. My concern vanished at once when I met Ted Tiller, an extremely fine director and writer, and a talented actor. We immediately established a great working rapport and, for me at any rate, it was a wonderfully satisfying rehearsal week. It was fun to have the opportunity to work on the play a second time with a completely new cast, and I welcomed the chance to dig deeper into the role of Madam Rosepettle.

Again, *Oh, Dad* was a hit with the critics.

> ...Christine Jorgensen lavishes the role of the mad, mad mamma Rosepettle with attention to the creation of character as well as to detail in revealing it. Absurdly grand, she is also equally wry.

> ...Miss Jorgensen gives strikingly effective account of the role of Mme. Rosepettle, playing the monstrous matron with compelling wit and impressive acting skill. Her long, second act monologue, indeed, is genuinely a technical tour de force.

Sometime during the two-week run in Columbus, Ted Tiller handed me the script of a play he'd been commissioned to write for the closing production of the season. It was his own version of Henry Fielding's eighteenth-century novel, *Tom Jones*. I was fascinated by the script, and particularly intrigued by the character part of Miss Western, which had been created in the film by the incomparable Dame Edith Evans. When I read the manuscript, I couldn't help wishing myself into the role of that saucy, raucous eighteenth-century matron. As I'd never done anything remotely like a classic or period play, I thought the idea of trying for style would be especially challenging for me.

With a great many misgivings, I approached Ted and asked him if the part had been cast as yet. He told me it had not, and I broached the idea of my doing it. Ted was gentleman enough to show immediate enthusiasm, and presented the idea to the management. Fortunately, it met with the producer's approval too, and I eagerly agreed to play in *Tom Jones* on a straight stock contract, at considerably less salary than I was receiving for *Oh, Dad*. Therefore, closing night of *Oh, Dad* at Playhouse on the Green was not cause for as much regret as usual, for I knew I'd soon be back with the company to begin rehearsals on the new production of *Tom Jones*.

Between the two productions, I returned home to find that Dad's health had deteriorated considerably. For the past year, he'd been suffering from polycythemia, a condition in which the blood contains an abnormally high number of red cells. In addition to the indications of general debility and the aging process, he was also suffering from glaucoma, which brought on the necessity of having an eye removed surgically. I was home during the week of his operation, and once we knew that Dad was recovering with no complications, I felt free to return to Columbus for the first *Tom Jones* rehearsals in mid-August.

From the first moment, the entire company was caught up in the excitement of working on a new production. A large cast of thirty-five actors made it extremely difficult to put together with only a week to go before opening, but Ted Tiller's skillful, rapid-fire direction, and the enthusiasm of the entire company, made it all dovetail when the time came to play it in front of an audience.

Personally, I had great fun. The role of Miss Western was an energetic challenge and a lesson in style, and I was particularly interested in working out many problems of eighteenth-century mannerisms and speech. I spent almost every available moment away from rehearsals working with the period costumes and circulating the air with a good deal of vigorous fan-waving.

I remember the dressing rooms were hectic with a dozen actresses packed into a small room and sandwiched between the balloon-skirted gowns, wig blocks, and other paraphernalia of the production. Yet it was a wonderfully jovial and high-spirited group and I looked forward to the fun of each night's performance.

Rollicking through *Tom Jones* was one of the most rewarding experiences I'd had in the theater. The production was extremely well received by both critics and public, and I felt much regret on the night we had to close after a two-week run.

During the stay in Columbus, my nightclub agent called and asked if I would consider a contract to entertain at several American military bases in Germany. As I hadn't been in Europe since 1954, I accepted the offer immediately. Within a few days the contract arrived, and I was scheduled to fly to Germany on September 15, about ten days after closing *Tom Jones,* to appear in fourteen performances in a ten-day period, beginning September 17.

But even as I made plans for the trip, the wheels of controversy were beginning to grind again, and it was to be a striking repetition of the events in Manila, three years before.

Six days before my scheduled departure, my agent received the following telegram from his counterpart in Germany: CANCEL JORGENSEN DUE TO MILITARY ORDER ACCORDING TO SPECIAL SERVICE REGULATIONS. Although I'd already signed a contract with the German agency, booked my flight and made all other arrangements for the trip, I had to bring all that machinery to a halt until an explanation was forthcoming.

It came three days later, not to me personally, nor to my agency representative, but to the entire world. The United States Army released the following statement to the press:

FRANKFURT, GERMANY, SEPT 11 — THE U.S. ARMY'S 3D ARMORED DIVISION HAS REFUSED TO ALLOW A FORMER GI TO ENTERTAIN AT ITS ENLISTED MEN'S AND NONCOMMISSIONED OFFICER'S CLUBS.

THE ENTERTAINER IS FORMER PVT. GEORGE JORGENSEN, JR., 39, WHO HAS TAKEN THE NAME CHRISTINE SINCE UNDERGOING MUCH-PUBLICIZED SEX-CHANGE OPERATIONS IN DENMARK.

A DIVISION SPOKESMAN SAID YESTERDAY THAT
"WHILE THE DIVISION BELIEVES THAT MISS JORGENSEN
IS PERFECTLY FREE TO PURSUE A STAGE CAREER, IT WAS
FELT NOT IN THE BEST INTERESTS OF THE DIVISION TO
PERMIT HER TO PERFORM IN OUR CLUBS."

I am perfectly aware there is no law that says the United States Army, or anyone else for that matter, is forced to employ me as an entertainer, but I wondered why they had waited from the time the contract was first signed on July 9 to September 8, when it was finally canceled. Apparently, one of the anonymous members somewhere in the military echelons had shaken his head in outrage and dissent, or plain old-fashioned fear at making a debatable decision.

As the Associated Press release was used widely, I had an uneasy feeling that it could have future harmful effects on my career. Time proved me to be right, and for several months after the public statement, I didn't receive a single job offer, a circumstance that was unprecedented up to that point. Most theatrical contracts are signed months in advance, and as I'd anticipated playing in Europe for the balance of the year, I had closed off that period to other bookings that might have taken its place.

Although the fact that I entertained American troops in Europe was of no concern, I felt it was extremely important to have the freedom to do so, and once more, it was time to stand up and be counted. It seemed to me that I'd been relegated to the position of a second-class citizen and, as a minority of one, I decided to throw caution out the window and "make a few waves" of my own.

I promptly sent a letter to President Lyndon Johnson, outlining the difficulty and including copies of the press release and other pertinent documents. Carbon copies were sent to Vice-President Hubert Humphrey, New York Senator Jacob Javits, and the United States Army Chief of Staff.

Within a week, I received a reply from Senator Javits, acknowledging my letter, and stating the matter had his immediate attention in asking for a full report. A few days later, I received an answering letter from the Department of the Army:

Dear Miss Jorgensen:

The President has asked that I reply to your recent letter concerning the entertainment of our armed forces personnel.

Although it is regrettable that the circumstances to which you referred have caused you embarrassment, intervention into the decisions of an area commander governing the utilization of entertainers at military clubs and messes is not appropriate....

The contract to which you referred, and a copy of which you furnished in your correspondence, was in no way binding...since the contract was between you and the booking agent. Clubs and messes, by regulations, are not authorized to enter into contracts with entertainers themselves...In this regard, therefore, there was no legal, nor in fact, moral obligation on the part of the local area commanders to honor a contract between you and the agent.

I regret that the circumstances in this instance preclude a more favorable reply. However, it is not considered that your rights to entertain members of the armed forces, now or in the future, were infringed upon by the cancellation of your appearances within the area of the 3rd Armored Division in Germany.

Sincerely yours,

J. K. Woolnough

Lieutenant General, GS

Deputy Chief of Staff for Personnel

The "buck-passing," as they say in the army, had gathered momentum, and the technical loophole had been found. It was indeed true that a performer's agreement was made usually with the agent who booked the military clubs, not directly with the army itself, and they were not legally bound to honor the contract. However, the army had made the initial offer through the agent in Germany, long before it decided my appearances would "not be in the best interests of the Division."

Be that as it may, there was little I could do further, except to regret the time and money I'd lost, to say nothing of the prestige.

By the late fall of 1965, although Dad had been slowly adjusting to the loss of his eye a few months before, it was obvious to all of us that his decline was more pronounced.

My father had always been a very active man. He had a solid, strong, and weather-beaten look about him, produced by his outdoor activities as a builder and master carpenter, as well as his great love for fishing. But he'd had to give up driving and the pleasures of his beloved boat, and forced into a more sedentary life of quiet reading and watching television, both of which were limited by then, he began to age noticeably. It was clear that Dad just simply was losing interest in life, and becoming more detached and slower paced. It was a sad and hurtful thing to watch, and we found it difficult to summon our usual holiday spirit as Christmas of 1965 approached, though Mom, Dolly, and I went through all the motions.

On Christmas Eve, he began to fail alarmingly, and I thought he might die during the night. There was no change for the better the next morning and we took him to the hospital where he stayed for two weeks, during which time he had only a few lucid moments. He died on January 8 of the new year.

I think Dad looked on his life with few regrets but one. His great natural talents for mathematics and science, and particularly the technical aspects of radio, had equipped him for a professional career in that field, and essentially that's where his heart lay. But with his characteristically accepting nature, he followed the simpler demands of the building trades, and adopted the philosophy of "what was good enough for my father is good enough for me."

He was an easygoing, simple man with a gentle disposition, though there was no place in his life for the irrelevancies and minutiae of daily living. At times detached, he had a marvelous way of dropping a curtain down over trivial conversation or events.

He always had been extremely loyal to me, and deeply interested in the scientific aspects of my case, which he understood with intelligence and accepted with grace.

One thing he did find difficult to understand, however, was how I could make money and still sleep until noon, and I don't think he could ever equate the two. Always a hard worker himself, sleeping late, in Dad's book, was simply incompatible with making a living.

The world is never quite the same when death leaves its shocking vacancies, though someone has said, "Our dead are never dead to us until they are forgotten."

Throughout the first few months of 1966, I stayed close to home as much as possible, taking only those club dates that would keep me away a few days at a time. In April, however, I flew to Hawaii for a two-week engagement and, as always, enjoyed that tropical paradise of the South Pacific.

As summer approached, Bill Hunt called to say he was planning the production of an original play entitled *A Nice Place to Visit,* and he felt there was a role in it for me. Again, I accepted with delight, not only because it would add to my theatrical experience, but it meant I'd be home with Mom for the entire summer.

As usual, I enjoyed working with Bill, particularly in creating a part that had never been done before. Reviews for the production were good on the whole, and we had fun during the four week engagement.

In the summer of 1966, I received some news which had once seemed so important, but now was only tepid information. By chance, I met a childhood friend whom I hadn't seen in fifteen years, and we sat at the house enjoying our reunion and reminiscing. At one point during our visit, I said, "You know, I never did find out who sent the letter to the *Daily News* that exploded the first publicity in 1952. It's still one of the unsolved mysteries in my life."

My friend looked at me in surprise, and found it difficult to believe when, as he said, "Most everyone else of our acquaintance knew." He then proceeded to tell me the correspondent's name: a "friend" from Askov Hall, the Danish-American Beach Club, and a contemporary of my parents. It was rumored that he'd received two hundred dollars for the information.

In 1952, I'd thought of it as a Judas-like betrayal, and over the years I'd had various suspicions, but as I look back on the anxieties of the period, I wonder why I was so intent on discovering his identity. When I finally knew, I found it filled me with indifference and little else, for whatever animosity I'd felt had vanished long before. Fourteen years had passed, and the news had struck while only the irony was hot.

There is a Chinese proverb that says, "The longest journey must begin with the first step."

As yet, the term "transsexual" is not found in any dictionary. Referred to by Dr. Harry Benjamin as "a dissonance in sexuality," the nature and etiology of the phenomenon, however, have become the subjects of great interest and, finally, open acknowledgement from the American medical profession.

Three years ago, Dr. Benjamin's lectures and articles on transsexualism formed the incentive and nucleus for a Research Foundation that bears his name, and which was suggested and financed by the Erickson Foundation of Baton Rouge, Louisiana. The object of the Harry Benjamin Foundation is to support sex research, particularly in the areas of gender identity and gender role orientation; specifically, transvestism and transsexualism.

Their research is developing a greater knowledge of the biological, psychological, and social backgrounds of transsexuals who request sex reassignments, and investigating a realistic treatment for them, along with scrutiny of the legal implications.

On its staff, the foundation has a team of experts representing the allied fields of sexology, and the advisory board includes leading specialists in psychiatry, psychology, endocrinology, genetics, sex research, neurology, surgery, hypnosis, and law.

The present investigation of a transsexual subject begins with a complete personal history, and involves psychological tests and evaluations, sex history, and social interviews. Endocrinological, x-ray, electro-encephalographic, and chromosomal studies are made. Postoperative examinations follow to assess the therapeutic value of the conversion operation and hormonal treatment, and the subject's social and psychological adjustment to the new, chosen gender.

A booklet on the aims of the Harry Benjamin Foundation
states:

> So long as it is not possible to adjust the mind to the
> body in transsexual patients, however, by applying
> presently available psychiatric methods, the reverse, of
> adjusting the body to the mind through hormone
> treatments and surgery, should be tested, if the patients
> are to be given relief from their suffering. Much
> medical and public education will be needed, not only
> to overcome unfounded prejudices still widespread,
> but also to perfect operative techniques. On the
> performance of the sex reassignment operation, the
> plastic surgeon, the gynecologist, and the urologist are
> particularly concerned.
>
> Research subjects who have undergone sex
> reassignment surgically and hormonally often need
> assistance in becoming rehabilitated, psychologically
> and occupationally, in their new life pattern. Scientific
> study of the psychology and sociology of this
> readjustment is another aspect of research that the
> Foundation proposes to sponsor.

In August of 1966, the *Journal of the American Medical
Association* answered an inquiry from a doctor in Ontario, Canada,
who requested information on the medical management of a case of
transsexualism, then under his care.

Two months later, the following item appeared in a *New York
Daily News* column: "Making the rounds of Manhattan clubs these
nights is a stunning girl who admits she was a male less than one year
ago and that she underwent a sex change operation at, of all places,
Johns Hopkins Hospital in Baltimore. Surprisingly, the hospital
confirms the case, saying surgery followed psychotherapy. Such
operations, although rare in this country, are neither illegal nor
unethical, according to a Johns Hopkins spokesman. Officials at a
number of major hospitals here agreed with Johns Hopkins on the

legality and ethics of the operations but none could recall such an operation ever having been performed in New York."

Slowly, the gates of medical recognition and approval were opening wider. Heretofore, most mentions of transsexual cases had been confined to the sensational aspects by the press, and the medical profession in the United States had hesitated to enlarge on its significance, or to give its official sanction regarding ethics.

November 21, 1966, brought the most startling public statement on the subject in fourteen years, when the following article appeared on the front page of the *New York Times:*

> The Johns Hopkins Hospital has quietly begun performing sex change surgery.
>
> The Baltimore hospital, one of the most eminent teaching and research institutions in the country, has also established a "gender identity clinic," staffed by a special committee of psychiatrists, surgeons and other specialists, to screen applicants for the operation.
>
> Although the controversial surgery has been performed in many European countries in the last fifteen years and by a few surgeons in this country, Johns Hopkins is the first American hospital to give it official support.
>
> Two operations approved by the committee of specialists have already been performed, the first last September and the second last month...They are said to be recovering satisfactorily.
>
> In the male-to-female operation, which takes three-and-a-half to four hours, the external genitals are removed and a vaginal passage created.
>
> Female hormone treatments before and after surgery gradually reduce secondary male sexual characteristics such as body hair and enhance feminine appearance through breast development and the widening of hips.
>
> About ten percent of the 100 applications received by the hospital have been from women, on whom a transformation operation can also be performed.

The men and women who seek sex change surgery are called transsexuals. They are almost always physically normal, but they have a total aversion to their biological sex that dates from early childhood. They have the apparently unshakable conviction that they are either female beings trapped in a male body or males trapped in a female body.

The overriding desire in the case of men is to be accepted as women. For this reason, psychiatrists believe, they are often sexually inactive before surgery because of their distaste for homosexual relationships.

Although transsexuals frequently assume the identity of the opposite sex without surgery, they are distinguished from transvestites, who derive pleasure from wearing the clothing of the opposite sex but have no desire for a sex change.

While opinion is not unanimous, many leading psychiatrists and psychoanalysts who have examined transsexuals, believe that they cannot be helped by psychotherapy. Such persons, moreover, are regarded as prone to mental breakdown and depression, suicide and, occasionally, self mutilation.

Dr. John E. Hoopes, a plastic surgeon who is chairman of the Johns Hopkins committee, said last week:

"After exhaustively reviewing the available literature and discussing the problem with people knowledgeable in this area, I arrived at the unavoidable conclusion that these people need and deserve help."

Transsexualism is thought to be relatively rare and far more frequent in men than in women. Dr. Hoopes said transsexuals in this country probably numbered in the thousands.

About 2,000 persons have undergone sex change surgery. Of these, perhaps 500 are from the United States. The best known is probably Christine Jorgensen, formerly George Jorgensen, who was operated on in

Copenhagen, Denmark, in 1952 and has since become a nightclub performer and actress.

Virtually all the operations have been performed in Europe, Morocco, Japan, and Mexico. A few surgeons have performed the operation in this country, probably not more than a dozen times in all, but many hospital boards have refused to permit it.

Experts in the field believe that the Johns Hopkins decision that the surgery does not violate legal restrictions on mutilation or ethical and moral codes will lead to its being performed at other hospitals in the United States.

The Johns Hopkins committee was formed a year ago. After preliminary studies, it began accepting applications for surgery in July. Most of its patients have been referred to it by the Harry Benjamin Foundation here.

The foundation is headed by Dr. Harry Benjamin, an endocrinologist, who has been studying and treating transsexuals, often without charge, for the last 15 years.

Dr. Benjamin has led the fight to have these persons regarded as a distinct medical phenomenon and coined the term transsexual to describe them. Earlier this year he published a book, *The Transsexual Phenomenon*.

His work is supported by the Erickson Foundation of Baton Rouge, Louisiana, which also pays the cost of transsexual research at Johns Hopkins. The foundation, headed by Reed Erickson, also supports research in air pollution and human resources. Mr. Erickson is a consulting engineer of independent wealth.

The Johns Hopkins clinic examines only two patients a month. There already is a long waiting list. Applicants receive a thorough physical and mental examination from the committee, which costs $100. Only those who show no signs of psychosis and appear to have a degree of insight into their condition are accepted....A number of psychiatrists familiar with the subject regard the majority of transsexuals as emotionally normal except for their gender confusion, which leads to intense feelings of frustration.

"It flies in the face of everything I believed when I began," said a Los Angeles psychiatrist-psychoanalyst, who has done considerable research in the field. "They are shockingly normal except for that one area."

After surgery and about two weeks of hospital care, the overall cost of which averages about $1,500, the patient is asked to be available for further study at the hospital. Also, for a former male, for example, to retain external female characteristics, he must continue receiving female hormones.

"This program, including the surgery, is investigational," Dr. Hoopes said. "The most important result of our efforts will be to determine precisely what constitutes a transsexual and what makes him remain that way.

"Medicine needs a sound means of alleviating the problems of gender identification and of fostering public understanding of these extremely unfortunate individuals. It is too early in the program to be either optimistic or pessimistic."

The origins of transsexualism are not yet certain. No organic basis for the condition has been found, but research is continuing into the possibility that it may be at least partly due to heredity or abnormal glandular functions before birth.

Psychiatrists believe that transsexualism is caused by prolonged conditioning early in life, perhaps within the first three years. Some cases, in which a mother wanted a daughter instead of a son and raised her child accordingly, seem obvious, but the origin of others is obscure.

By means of the family histories that it takes from transsexuals, the Johns Hopkins committee, as well as the Benjamin Foundation, hopes to shed new light on the problem. Similar investigations, although without surgery, are also being carried on at the University of California at Los Angeles Medical Center.

Other newspapers and magazines throughout the country quickly followed with their own stories of the extraordinary announcements from Johns Hopkins.

In closing their summary of the events, *Newsweek* magazine stated: "Some psychiatrists object to sex-change surgery because they believe transsexuals are deeply disturbed homosexuals who wish to change gender to resolve their conflict. Says Dr. Charles Socarides, a New York psychoanalyst specializing in the treatment of homosexuality: 'Such operations are doomed to ultimate failure because they do not change the underlying conflict.' "

It was clear that the controversy still raged, and probably would continue to raise doubts, but at last the subject was discussed and examined openly and sanctioned by one of the most respected medical institutions in the world. Time had been the leveler, an old and common arbitrator.

If I proved to be a catalyst in some of these events, I had seldom been aware of it. Never at any time have I regarded myself as a crusader or a rebel fighting for a cause. Except on a few occasions, and those only when my personal freedoms were threatened, I've never been very good at carrying banners into battle. From the beginning, my only thought was to seek a way of life I felt had been my rightful destiny. In essence, it was a search for dignity and the right to live life in freedom and happiness. It was a mold that could hold true for me alone and for no other, and the fact that I solved a particular and highly personal problem, for me, was the only thing of importance.

This book, then, is not meant to be a history of transsexualism or a study of its medical management. I leave that to the experts. Within its own framework it is indeed a unique problem and one with which only a few people can identify. I have attempted to tell the story of one life, and except for a few compartments of the mind which no one, not even I, can enter without apology, it is as truthful and straightforward a statement as I know how to make.

Above all, I've tried to correct the misconceptions that have prevailed over the years, and to answer the questions most frequently asked concerning the circumstances of my transformation. I'm aware that with the great number of facts contained within these pages, and an equal exposure of emotions, I will no doubt lay myself open to further censure and criticism, and I am quite prepared for that. I had no wish to create an apologia for my life, I merely wanted to set the record straight.

Through the years, I've encountered about every attitude and response known to the human emotional spectrum. Some people thought me a courageous pioneer, others regarded me as disgusting and immoral; some of the clergy considered that I had committed an ungodly act. Why these reactions to me should be so explosively pro and con, only God or the Devil knows, and I suspect they are both puzzled.

Many times, I've been accused of living a masquerade as a female, but if I have not already made it clear I will state again that, in my view, the real masquerade would have been to continue in my former state. That, to me, would have been living the lie.

I suppose another main purpose in this narrative has been to relate the facts of how I adjusted to the world and how the world adjusted to me, now that time has allowed a more objective examination. Though, indeed, my outward appearance was changed, I think I'm basically one and the same person I was in the earlier part of my life—perhaps calmer, more accepting and certainly happier. I've found that my eagerness for living has in no way diminished.

I've often been asked if, given the chance, I would make the same decisions and seek the same goals. My answer to that is unequivocal—yes. It's possible, with the advantage of hindsight, I might have handled some of the subsequent events differently, however. Had I been more experienced, I think I would have opened up the avenues of information to all of the press immediately after the story broke in December of 1952, rather than keeping myself an exclusive property of the *American Weekly* until the article series appeared several months later. I believe the early news blackout was responsible for forcing the press to invention, producing untruths which have lingered through the years.

If I have been harsh in my treatment of the press, it is because at the time I felt it invaded the last chambers of privacy, and I particularly resented the energetic pursuit of my family. I'm also aware, however, that the press was merely doing its job to satisfy the breathless anticipation of the public. The unusual, especially in sexual anomalies, is what the public wants to read with breakfast coffee. Of course, the public has every right to a truthful presentation of the facts, but it seems to me there are still some limits to be placed on the invasion of privacy.

In an enlightening book entitled *The Press in the Jury Box,* by Howard Felsher and Michael Rosen, the authors make the following statement on the intrusions of the press:

> Any story involving a nationally known celebrity or socialite is big news—and therefore a kind of hormonal stimulant to the instincts of all reporters. Any time a celebrity or a member of the social whirl is involved in a crime, a love affair, an accident, or almost any activity less commonplace than shopping at the supermarket, it becomes news.
>
> There is no way of fighting back, though, when the press gangs up on an individual. It is in the area of individual liberties that the press most needs examination. In this area, it may be aggressive, even barbaric. Privacy, pride, dignity—anything that helps a person hold up his head can be destroyed by the press in search of a story.

In retrospect, however, I have to qualify my feelings about the press, for there has been more than one occasion when I've had cause to be grateful to the men and women in the newspaper field. I'm well aware that without their attention and the ensuing publicity, I would never have been in a position to pursue a career as a performer. Admittedly, its compensations have been enormous.

Therefore, like Janus, the press has presented two faces: one detrimental and one advantageous.

Another question that is continually asked of me is why I capitalized on my notoriety, and I'll reply again for the sake of clarification. Briefly, once skyrocketed to prominence, there was no place to go and nothing else to consider but the entertainment world. It would have been impossible to live in anonymity in some rural, uninhabited area or remote cave. No matter how much I wanted to pursue it, and I did not, life as a social recluse was eternally denied.

Fortunately, I had expert guidance that led my career into professional channels, and with a potential talent and a great deal of hard work, it blossomed into a successful way of making a living. An easily overlooked fact is that I did not make my first appearance as a nightclub performer until eight months after the first news stories. I feel no need to defend my career in show business, for I think I've proven I have as much right to function as a legitimate entertainer as anyone else.

It is also true that I am not a dedicated artist, willing to starve for my art in some dusty garret. I have not a great enough drive for recognition as an actress, but I do have the desire for growth and development in my chosen field. Only time, experience, and more varied roles in the theater can prove the point. I can only say I am willing to try.

I suppose the final question to answer is, "Has it been worth it?" I must admit, at certain moments in my life I might have hesitated to answer. I remember times when I lived in a crucible of troubled phantoms, and faltered in the long, painful struggle for identity. But for me there was always a glimmering promise that lay ahead; with the help of God, a promise that has been fulfilled. I found the oldest gift of heaven—to be myself.